Bird:

The Legend of Charlie Parker

Bird:
The Legend of Charlie Parker

by Robert George Reisner

DA CAPO PRESS

Library of Congress Cataloging in Publication Data

Reisner, Robert George.
  Bird.

  (A Da Capo paperback)
  Reprint of the 1975 ed.
  Discography: p.
  1. Parker, Charles Christopher, 1920-1955.
[ML419.P4R4 1977] 788'.66'0924 [B]   77-8877
ISBN 0-306-80069-1

10 9 8 7 6 5 4

Published by Da Capo Press, Inc.
A Member of the Perseus Books Group

Bird:
The Legend of Charlie Parker

Acknowledgments

The author wishes to thank the following individuals and firms for photographs used in this book: Hugh Bell (pages 3, 5, 9); Dial Records (page 77); Bertrand Miles (pages 78, 118, 236); Jeffrey Morton (page 140, top); Robert Parent (pages 10, 24, 30); Duncan Schiedt (page 96, bottom); Verve Records (page 127); and Ray Whitten (pages 101, 199).

Sincere thanks are due to Martin Williams for the Ross Russell interview beginning on page 196 and also for his invaluable editorial assistance on the entire manuscript.

The interview with Tutty Clarkin on page 66 is by Jean Stein vanden Heuvel and appeared originally in *Esquire*. It is used with the kind permission of the author.

Contents

I Remember Bird

by ROBERT GEORGE REISNER

who's this writer?

I first met Charlie Parker on a rainy night in 1953. I had been to a party on the East Side of New York City. It was around 12:30 P.M. when I saw a large, lumbering, lonely man, walking kind of aimlessly. I recognized him and was amazed and thrilled, but what the devil was he doing in this poor Jewish neighborhood, walking by himself in the soaking rain?

"You're Charlie Parker," I said. "I'm Bob Reisner. What are you doing by yourself?" There was absolutely no one around but him and me.

He smiled a big, warm, brown smile. He said, "My wife is having a baby, and I'm kind of walking off my nervousness and waiting to call back."

I walked around with him and remember asking him where he lived, and he said, "In the neighborhood." It was Avenue B. He could see I wondered why a guy of his tremendous reputation lived in such an out-of-the-way poor section. "I like the people around here," he said. "They don't give you no hype."

After a while I brought him back to the party I had left, and everyone was terrifically surprised and delighted with my find. And I was so exhilarated with having seen my hero that I felt I should leave him there and go home. It was just too much. I got up to go. My friend, Lex, the host, was awed. "He's an old friend," I boasted, "and I just recognized him in the street."

"Where are you going now, Bob?" Lex asked.

I told him I was going out for a while and would return shortly with Louis Armstrong.

A year and a half later I was to see him again under very different circumstances. I had started a new career. At that time, I was an art historian, and I was living in Greenwich Village and teaching a course at the New School for Social Research. But as a side interest, I was also working at the Institute of Jazz Studies; people I met in the Village shared my interest in jazz—particularly, modern, cool, progressive, or any of the terms given to the new sound. In general, they were a pretty hip bunch, but we always had to traipse uptown for any *jazz moderne*. So I decided to become a jazz promoter.

The reasons were threefold: to learn more about jazz and jazzmen than I could by just reading about it in books; to get my hands dirty; to see it as a

11

way of life; to propagate and proselytize and open up the Greenwich Village area to modern jazz; to give a fair balance to a section that just had Dixieland—Nick's, Condon's, Stuyvesant Casino, Central Plaza. Lastly, of course, I also wanted to make some money. I cased every logical place and finally settled on the largest. The place had to have enough seating capacity to pay for a band solely on admissions. It was a place called The Open Door. I liked the name too. It was reminiscent of the club called The Famous Door on 52nd Street. After a little persuasion, the owner, Sol Jaffe, gave me a crack at Sunday nights, a tough night to do business, a night when a lot of places stay closed. On April 26, 1953, I launched the first of my Sunday jazz bashes.

Dave Lambert, the bop singer and arranger, was a great help in setting the aesthetic policy of The Open Door, and he often suggested the line-ups to me. One day he staggered me by saying, "How would you like to feature Bird next Sunday? I asked him, and he said he would like to play in your place."

"I'm sorry, Dave," I said. "I've already booked Toscanini and Horowitz. Are you kidding? Why man, that's great! I'm running to the printer right now to make posters reading Bob Reisner presents Charlie Parker."

"No, Bob," Dave corrected. "Bob Reisner presents BIRD. Just Bird in large letters."

"But," I said, "will everyone know that Bird is Charlie Parker?"

He smiled. "If they don't know, they'll ask."

The guys got scale plus. Bird got a percentage of the house, and he packed them in. It was a lovely beginning to what was to be the first of many sessions. The later sessions always ended with arguments.

As I look back now they are funny, but, then, they were far from humorous. We yelled at each other but always made up the next day, and, though I swore never to let him work for me again, I knew if he just honored me by asking me to let him play, it was my duty to do so.

He was one of the most difficult individuals I have ever met. He was suave, cunning, urbane, charming, and generally fiendish—too much. He could butter me up, lull me into position, and then, bang!—a great betrayal. I have seen managers quit on him in succession like horses shot under a general. Musicians feared and loved him. Like the comedian who wants to play Hamlet, Bird fancied himself a business expert and virtually assumed command of the business end of the Sunday sessions in which he appeared. He was pretty shrewd about it. I always gave him the first numbered ticket on the roll, and he would match it against the last ticket to check the take. Something would always be wrong; he saw to that. Anything to start a fight, to accuse me of treachery, of cheating him, even though I never did—and I'm sure he never really felt I did—but, nevertheless, he went to preposterous lengths in his farcical belligerence.

One time I bought a roll of second-hand tickets and the outer layer was faded from age or sun. During the evening, he came around to check his first ticket with the one I was up to. "Bobby, you bastard, you bought another roll than the one I started with."

I looked at him amazed.

"Look at the color of my ticket and the color of these! "They're different," he said.

"You're nuts!" I said. "The first few are faded." And I looked around the audience, spotted one of the first customers who was still there, because no one ever left till the end. I asked the customer for his ticket and showed it to Bird. He beamed and said, "What's the matter with you? You don't think I meant it. Man, you're not subtle."

He picked up his alto and blew some piercing sweet sounds as if he meant to soften me. As I stood there at the curtain, watching him create his music, someone came up and peeked through the curtain. "Is that Charlie Parker playing?" he asked, as Bird's fingers were flying over the keys. "No," I said. "He's just counting the house."

The Sunday sessions were full of suspense and drama. Would he show? Was he well? Would he hang around or wander off? One night he disappeared, and I found out later that he played across the street at another place called The Savannah Club for free or, maybe, a couple of drinks. He felt he could not be bought. When he played free or for a few friends, he was at his best. His performances were uneven, but what seemed bad temper and perverseness—like falling asleep on the stand—is understandable, considering that he had advanced ulcers, dropsy, bad heart, and with it all, he could play like a dream and could melt and cow people and fell a two-hundred-pound man with a blow. Bird was the supreme hipster. He made his own laws. His arrogance was enormous, his humility profound.

After a performance, Bird, his manager (of the time), and myself were in conference, which meant that Charlie was raving and cursing at us. He also allowed the other cats to stand around a long time before we paid them. Finally, in exasperation, his manager said, "I quit! You think you're God, better than anyone else." Bird's face became sorrowful, he ceased ranting, and, with a sweet serious face and in a quiet tone, he said, "Man, I was born out of a pussy just like you."

One evening things were swinging. People were drifting in, and Parker had them glued to their seats. No one danced, just drinking in the sound. Then it was intermission. Bird was walking around smiling, shaking hands, checking with me on business details. Suddenly I heard music from the bandstand. Usually we put on the juke box for fifteen minutes till the band went back on, but now I saw two men, one with a guitar and one singing— cornball junk, tourist stuff, phoney jive, "Get your kicks on Route 66," plink, plink! I could hear slight groans from the audience. I went over to the stand.

"Gentlemen," I said, "you're excellent but not for this audience. Get out."

They glared at me. "Man, don't bug us in the middle of our number."

"I'm manager here," I said.

"Charlie Parker hired us," they countered.

"Are you sure?"

"Ask him."

I walked away. Bird would never hire those clowns. "Charlie, you didn't hire those guys on the stand."

"Yes. I did," he said.

"The audience is reacting unfavorable, and I'm throwing those idiots off."

"If they leave, I leave," he said, and I was stymied. I knew that Bird's taste in music was catholic, that he dug classical music, and he always turned on the radio in a car to listen to pop music and even hillbilly; but this stuff was really bad. I just sulked. After a few moments he came over to me, put his arm on my shoulder, and said, "You fool, you just don't understand business. We're full up. These cats are so bad that some of the audience will leave. We need a turnover."

"Bird," I said, "you're a supreme con man. Pulling a hype on this audience that loves you?"

"Bobby," he said, "bread is your only friend."

At another time he disappeared after the first set and returned at 3:00 A.M., when the band was packing up. He looked at them a little bewildered and, taking out his golden horn, he said, "Come on, let's put this show on the road."

The last session I remember at The Open Door was a thrilling experience, as always. It was an unscheduled appearance; he just dropped in and played. He seemed possessed that day—he had been playing all day long. In the afternoon, I had heard him at the Bohemia. The club was empty, except for the help, myself, and the four musicians playing with Bird—Ted Wald, bass; Bill Heine, drums; Warrick Brown, piano; and a trumpet player, a sweet little cat who is always present on every jazz scene and whom everybody calls "Face."

Those musicians may advance technically, but they will never in their lives ever play as they played that afternoon. Bird was crowding his last brief time with fierce beauty. Trumpeter Howard McGhee once said, "Whoever the musician is who plays with Bird, he feels he's playing shit next to what Bird is putting down." But the opposite was true, too. Bird drove and inspired average musicians to excellences they themselves never dreamed they could reach. A couple of other people drifted into the Bohemia, and they sat down with stoned expressions. The waiter did not even bother to ask for their orders. We were all witnessing a miracle that was happening and that happens over and over again in jazz all over the country—beauty being created on the spot, creativity lost on the air but leaving its imprint on the brains and visceras of its listeners. Usually, this miracle occurs late at night, but the time I speak of was afternoon.

The one word which is used most often by musicians in describing Bird is "soul." Bird had so much soul. They forgave him his trespasses when, at times, Bird felt evil, because they knew he poured so much soul into his art that it must have created an imbalance at times. Like a great many geniuses, he was a perfectionist. On some Dial records, they have issued the unreleased master, and you can listen to a slight sample of Bird's artistic demands. He'd start and restart until it was perfect. He was rarely satisfied with his own playing and, therefore, suspicious of praise. Howard McGhee said musicians would go up to him and tell him how great he was playing, and he would make a disgusted face and turn on his heel. So I never praised him as much as I would have liked to; it was hard to suppress it. One night he played so great it was unearthly. After the date, I said to him, "Bird, you were blowing snakes tonight."

"Yeah, I know it, man. I just couldn't get together with myself."

Charlie Parker, in the brief span of his life, crowded more living into it than any other human being. He was a man of tremendous physical appetites. He ate like a horse, drank like a fish, was as sexy as a rabbit. He was complete with the world, was interested in everything. He composed, painted; he loved machines, cars; he was a loving father. He liked to joke and laugh. He never slept, subsisting on little cat naps. Everyone was his friend—delivery boys, taxicab drivers. He died in the apartment of a Baroness. No one had such a love of life, and no one tried harder to kill himself; but try as he could, it was hard to tear down that magnificent body. "Bird has disintegrated into pure sound," I heard one musician say.

On March 12, 1955, a Saturday, at 8:45 P.M., he succeeded in his self-destruction. I met him on New Year's Day, 1955; we shook hands and spoke about forthcoming plans. "You know, Bobby, I never thought I'd live to see 1955," he said.

"Did you ever read the *Rubaiyat of Omar Khayyam*?" I asked him.

He grinned—he always knew what you meant—and quoted the lines:

> Come, fill the Cup, and in the fire of Spring
> Your Winter garment of Repentance fling;
> The Bird of Time has but a little way
> To flutter—and the Bird is on the Wing.

He never refused a challenge. If you dared him to play Russian roulette with you, he would. He was a thrill seeker. It was a delight for him when a friend of mine, Bob Benson, invited him for motorcycle rides. It was this terrible curiosity, this hunger to encompass all experience, that was to be his ultimate ruin.

I am proud to say that I featured Bird in a Town Hall concert on Saturday evening, October 30th, 1954. It was his last public concert performance, and he played magnificently, entrancing the meagre audience. The concert was poorly advertised, due to limited funds, and consequently suffered. Bird was in a happy mood and transmitted it into his horn, or rather the horn he borrowed from Gigi Gryce, who was also on the bill. Just before he went on, he and I had finished a water-drinking contest. I was thirsty and was sure I could beat him. We went to the water cooler with a little paper cup. I quit after the fifteenth cup, and the Bird continued on with a few extra, but I'm sure he could have gone on and on.

Because of union rules, the stage hands could not stay on, and the curtain had to go down. It was a pity, for Bird was really wailing, and he could have kept that audience gassed for hours. The union delegates were backstage to get the money due the musicians. They had been very kind to me. Bird was in trouble with Local 802. A few months before he had been playing at Birdland, and during his performance, he fired the entire string section that was backing him. Later that evening, despondent over the incident, he attempted suicide by swallowing iodine. He was discovered by some neighbors who found him writhing on the bathroom floor. He was rushed to the hospital and saved.

After that he started to undergo psychoanalysis at Bellevue regularly. The union fined him the cost of the wages of the musicians. I asked them to permit him to play and allocate a part of his pay against the fine. In view of his troubles, they were very understanding.

I have heard several versions of the Birdland firing incident. In an attempt to commercialize him and gain a wider audience a couple of albums were issued called *Bird With Strings*. Against a schmaltzy, smooth string section that played the melody straight, Bird would come in like a zither, swoop and glide and create delicate musical traceries. Long-time fans put these albums down, but the albums introduced him to thousands who had never heard of him. The albums were among his best sellers. Birdland was trying to capitalize on the records. The strings played "East of the Sun" and Bird came in with "Dancing in the Dark." It was the weirdest. In front of the audience, Bird said, "You guys can't play; you're fired."

Another version, and one more credible, was told to me by Tommy Potter, the bassist who was playing the gig. "The night it all happened, it was Dinah Washington's birthday, and Bird's also. Dinah had a party backstage, and Bird got juiced. During one of the intermissions, he went out in front of the club, opened the door of a cab, and sat down on the floor of the taxi sideways with his feet on the ground. The taxi driver asked him where he wanted to go, and he said he just wanted to sit there. There was a little tug of war, and Bird rolled into the cab. The driver got in and drove over to a police station and left Bird there. With Bird gone there was no need of the string section, so the Birdland management fired them.

No one messed with Bird's music. He went along his way, and his way was right. So says every modern alto sax player and the voicings of every jazz instrument; so says the Hollywood studio, big band arrangements. He went on a summer excursion boat up the Hudson one day, and he was frolicking with a group of Polish people. Out came his horn and Bird was playing polkas for them. One of his ambitions was to compose a jazz ballet. He wanted to study under Paul Hindemith at Yale. There was so much he wanted to do. How much further he would have gone in his musical explorations had he lived is impossible to say. Perhaps not too much, because the miracle of Charlie Parker is that he seemed to have sprung full grown from the earth. His style seems to have been fixed from the beginning. Hear him on early Jay McShann records such as "Hootie Blues" or "Dexter Blues" as far back as April, 1941, and, from out of the solid Kansas City jump beat, emerges the free-flowing eloquence and idea-jammed notes which he was permitted on perhaps fifteen seconds of a three-minute record. Bird said his first awareness of the sax was Rudy Vallee. Another person who Bud said taught Bird so much was Buster Smith. His first major influence was Lester "Prez" Young. Bird played everything like it was the first time. When he practiced he would play one tune continuously, then graduate the same tune in a different key. He always used to hang out with the older kids. When he started to hang around the stand at the age of fourteen or fifteen, they would throw him off.

Bill Graham says of him: "He would borrow a horn, anybody's horn, and it would always come out his sound; it didn't matter if it was a thin or thick reed—he could make a trombone sound like an alto." One night a key fell off his instrument; he broke a spoon and fastened a part of it with chewing gum and tape and blew the rest of the evening without much difference in sound.

Bird was not afraid of death. He embraced it. He was on intimate terms with it. Charlie Mingus says that once Bird came over to him and said suddenly, "Drop dead." Mingus, a little startled and taken aback, said, "Why do you that to me, Bird?"

"Because you want to," Bird said with a smile.

Mingus said that, at that time, he had been depressed, and Bird felt his mood. "Would you die for me? I'd die for you," Bird would say to Charlie Mingus.

Musicians and cliques of fans were so crazy about Bird that, at one time, that was all the records they would buy, just Parker. Some took it a step further. They would tape just the Bird portion of the records, omitting all the other parts. They would also tape dances he played.

Bird had quite a formal side to him. Sometimes, it would take the form of exaggerated politeness, but it was both charming and amusing. He was not an aloof person; he was very accessible. If he sensed that someone wanted to meet him and was shy, he made the overtures. With a warm smile, I can hear him say, "I'm Charlie Parker. People call me Bird."

Mr. and Mrs. Bill Graham and Bird.
Below:
Bird with Tommy Potter, bass; Duke Jordan, piano; Miles Davis, trumpet; and Max Roach, drums.

My mother was very impressed with his courtliness. It was a good thing that she was not present at our business conferences. Once, in the back room of the night club, we were winding up a session, and Bird was saying, "You son of a bitch! You lousy bastard!" Just then, a woman patron came in by accident. Bird turned and said, with a little bow, "We're conducting a little business. I'll be with you in a moment."

Around 1952, at Max Roach's house, Max asked Bird to write a tune for a record date. On the spot, at the table, he wrote "Chi Chi."

At a date at Chateau Gardens in New York, in 1950, Willie Jones got up on the stand to play the last number of a set. At that time, he was a beginner, and Bird knew it. Everyone was waiting for Bird to call the tune. Willie hoped it would not be too up tempo, as he had not perfected the tempos he now makes with ease. All of a sudden Bird started "52nd Street Theme," which is a very fast tune. Jones was skuffling all the way through, playing on instinct rather than ability. He was afraid to stop. He kept on going, because he was afraid of being embarrassed. At the end, he went to Bird and said, "I'm sorry for dragging it through the last number." Bird said, "I know. I did it to help you," and to Willie the message came through as: whenever you go on the stand, be ready.

Dick Katz says, "He never played to impress anybody, which means he was an artist." Charlie's sense of the surrealistic was sharp. His escapades are legion. One day he was astride a horse in the center of New York and attempted to ride into Charlie's Tavern. A few nights, he dressed in dungarees, a T-shirt, and broad canvas suspenders, looking just like a Kansas farmer, a toothpick in his mouth. He stood in front of Birdland, creating a scene of strange incongruity. Bird would approach an extremely affluently-clothed individual and say, "A jazz musician, I presume."

He was tricky; he was shifty; he could put up more defenses than anyone. He was terribly charming; he was monstrously aggressive. He had a big thing about race. He was not paranoic about it, but he never made a real adjustment to it. Bird partially solved this problem by becoming one of the greatest musicians who ever made sound. Life has a wacky set of checks and balances at times, and adversity sometimes makes for greater efforts and accomplishments.

Bird was neurotic, but the great strides in the arts are not made by happy, well-adjusted people. Art is a form of sublimation and is created by neurotics and compulsion-ridden people, not by the happy, nine-to-five, family man. Neurosis itself is not productive; rather it is burdensome. But it is the suffering that is reflected in tranquility, or that is sublimated, that produces art. It is somewhat like the thought of Wordsworth, when he said that poetry is great emotion reflected in tranquility. Neurosis cannot be of too great an intensity or the person is immobilized by it.

Bird's resentments got the upper hand at times, and he made bad impressions upon some people. It must have been one of those nights with an acquaintance of mine. In describing his first meeting with Bird, he said, "Once I sat with Bird . . . he tried his damnedest to put me on about race. He just talked, but, inside, he was shrieking. First, he tried to be clever. Then, he degenerated. I was embarrassed for him. I resented his attitudes, and I resented his bad playing that night. He was trying to perpetuate a myth that musicians are a race apart. The next time I saw him, he was walking with Bud Powell on Broadway, and they were both bumming money from people. Musically, however, they are the greatest."

Bud would say of Parker, "If you want to swing, you gotta go by Bird." Bird, who could be salty at times, and who once said to a hopeless rhythm section, "Let's play the 'Star-Spangled Banner'; I think you can play that," was usually fulsome in his praise of fellow musicians. To club owners, he would say, "You kiss their shoes; they don't kiss yours." The list of people he admired was quite long. Bird said, "Prez laughs when I tell him that I'm a fan of his and have been for years. I used to sit under a platform in Kansas City and listen for hours, because I loved the man. Prez would say, 'You're a fan of mine?'" To Ella Fitzgerald he remarked, "It's a good thing you don't play a horn. You would take a lot of jobs from us."

It was Bird who was one of the first appreciators of the late Clifford Brown. He told Art Blakey about him. He said of Brown, who was living in Philadelphia, "If you're going to Philadelphia, Art, don't take a trumpet player with you." Thelonious Monk could do no wrong. He would say of this original and creative man of music, "The Monk runs deep." Once he was playing with Bird, and, when it came time for his chorus, he seemed lost in his private world and not a sound came from the piano. Finally, after a long stretch of time, he struck one note. Bird leaned over to him and said, "Crazy! Monk." He was always enthusiastic and all out in his response to those he felt he could learn from.

He followed one of his idols, Buster Smith, to New York. Of this, he said, "I used to quit every job to go with Buster, but, when I came to New York and went to Monroe's, I began to listen to that real advanced New York style. At Monroe's, I heard sessions with a pianist named Allen Tinney. I'd listen to trumpet men like Lips Page, Roy, Dizzy, and Charlie Shavers, outblowing each other all night long. And Don Byas was there, playing everything there was to be played. I heard a trumpet man named, Vic Coulsen, playing things I never heard. Vic had the regular band at Monroe's with George Treadwell, also on trumpet, and a tenor man named, Pritchitt. That was the kind of music that caused me to leave McShann and stay in New York."

His fervor for Dan Byas was not reciprocated at that time, because the tenor man, a big strong expatriate, living in France, tells the following incident. It seems that, when he first heard Charlie's music and expressed his opinion to Parker, he said, "You ain't sayin' nothin' on your horn." Bird gave him a hard look and told him to come outside. Byas walked out with him. Bird pulled a knife. Byas calmly drew out a blade of his own. Bird looked at him, smiled, and put his weapon away with the remark, "I really think you'd cut me."

He was never envious or worried about his jazz supremacy. While listening to some records of tenor man, Sonny Rollins, whom Parker liked, someone remarked to Charlie, "Sonny's a cat whose coming up very fast, Bird. Watch out." Bird smiled and said, "There's a lot of room at the top."

Humility is sold by public relations operators as something people expect from the highly talented. Parker was no humble genius. He knew what he had and what went into it. He said, "I lit my fire, I greased my skillet, and I cooked." Almost singlehanded he saved jazz from "riffitis monotonous" or death due to oversimplicity and made it into an art form, giving it new dimensions of structure and feeling. Bird was an apt nickname. He was free, and he sang. His music soared, swooped, and glided. His fingers flew over the alto sax. He was a strange bird in that his migratory habits were not fixed. He could turn up anywhere. At a fancy dress party in Harlem, where he suddenly emerged from a room with his horn and played a long solo of extraordinary beauty. His attire was conspicuous. He was completely naked. Bill Heine told me, "If you were a friend of Bird's, you were in danger of being suddenly kidnapped off the streets by him and whisked into a cab. Bird was a man who would brook no hesitation, and who would want to hesitate anyway? It usually meant the best music—sometimes a record session of Bach's music, which Bird described as 'wild.' " Walter Williams, an artist, remarked to me, "The man was full of surprises. One night, at five o'clock in the morning, I hear my doorbell. I'm wondering who it is that calls at this hour. It can't be someone in physical distress, because there are five flights to climb. I called out, 'Who's there?' but there was no answer. I opened the door, and there was Charlie. All he said was, 'Got a match?' I gave it to him. He lit a cigarette and left without another word. I looked out my window and saw him get into a cab and drive off."

One evening he emerged from a cab, when it pulled up in front of Birdland, in pajamas. He had sneaked out of a hospital where he was taking a cure. Rushing up to Oscar Goodstein, the manager, he said, "I need a drink." His usual dress on the bandstand was a brown pin-striped suit, always unpressed from constant wear. Some of his extreme devotees used to crumple their own pressed pants so that they would be like his. They thought it was a new style. Passing by the Montmartre, a Village bistro, one evening, I saw a few of their employees eject a belligerent customer. It was Bird. The irony of the situation was that the juke box was playing, and the record was one of Parker's, and he was tossed out as his solo was pouring forth.

Bird could be cruel. He always liked to get on first (take the first shot). He was in a room with two guys he didn't like. They were too frantic. He shot

himself up first, taking his sweet time about it; he let the stuff go in very slow
—he was milking it. He extended the hypodermic to the next person, and as
the party reached for it, it slipped out of Bird's hand to the floor and smashed
to pieces. It was their stuff, and Bird showed his gratitude to them for sharing
it with him by depriving them of it.

Donna Lee (the selfsame for whom the record is named) was leaving town
one day. She was going back to Ohio. She had two children. All she had was
two dollars besides the fare for her and the kids. Bird said, "How can you
feed those kids? You need more than two dollars." She said, "That's all right.
We'll make out anyhow." She was indifferent to the situation, and he was
salty. He figured she should try to hustle up money to take care of all her
expenses. They were in a car. He went to a gas station and asked for two
dollars worth of gas. When the tank was filled, he said, "Oh. I forgot my
wallet. Pay the guy—I'll give it back before I leave." And she's still waiting
for it. This is the very attitude that Baudelaire felt in his essay entitled, "Beat
up the Poor"—an attempt to rouse dignity in a pauper by further cruelty.

Donna Lee was playing bass in a joint with Bird and some guys. It was
1945. She had just resumed playing, after a protracted absence from the
instrument. Her fingers had become soft again, and she developed big blisters
on them. Charlie told her the best way to raise calluses on her fingers right
away was to break the blisters and pour whiskey into them, which she did
right there and then. She stood around on the podium, talking, and letting her
fingers cool off, when in the middle of the set, the bass player threw his bass
at her and said, "Finish this." So she had to play bass; and they played that
one tune for about half an hour, and blood was on her fingers. The bass
player and Charlie were sitting smiling, and, when she got through, Bird said
that was how to get calluses. So she made it. This might also indicate why
there are not too many girl jazz musicians.

Bird could be kind. He was very generous with tunes. He would lend his
tunes and sometimes he would hear them later on the radio, or someplace else
—stolen. One evening Bird came up to Oscar Goodstein and asked him for
five-hundred dollars. Oscar said, "No, I'll give you five dollars." Bird said,
"Make it three hundred."

"I'll give you five," Goodstein said.

"Make it two hundred," Bird said.

Anyway, O.G. gave him twenty dollars, and Bird slipped out of Birdland
and through the kitchen. There he passed another musician, who was looking
for something to eat. This cat was beat, had nothing. Bird dropped the twenty
dollars on him, and went back to O.G. to ask him for more money. Don
Joseph, a trumpet and cornet player, tells of Christmas Eve, 1954 in Greenwich Village. "Bird said, 'Merry Christmas' in a booming voice, and we
walked down the street. We saw an old Negro bum, who asked for a quarter.
I had no money, and neither did Bird. Bird looked around with tears in his

eyes. 'If that guy is broke, that's a drag, ain't it?' I asked him if he believed in Jesus Christ, and he said, 'No, I don't.' Then we saw Bob Reisner tacking up a sign about a forthcoming concert of Bird at The Open Door, and Parker said, 'Doesn't Reisner look like a Dickens character?' "

Kansas City, Missouri, was a town that Bird loved and hated. He said he didn't want to be buried there, but he is. It was a wonderful place to learn music. Jazz could be heard around the clock. Some joints never closed. There were over fifty night spots and plenty of masters to learn from; Bennie Moten, Walter Page, Count Basie, and dozens more. There were and still are two musicians' unions, white and Negro. There is a strong tradition of brotherhood among the Negro musicians. They teach each other. The Kansas City Negro jazzman does not seem as aggressively tough as the eastern musician or as servile as the deep southern Negro. Parker was loath to speak of his early life. A few statements were squeezed out of him.

"As for my beginnings," he said, "I came up in Kansas City when the joints were runing full blast from 9 P.M. to 5 A.M. Usual pay was $1.25 a night, although somebody special like Count Basie could command $1.50. There were about fifteen bands in town, with Pete Johnson's crew at the Sunset Cafe one of the most popular. Harlan Leonard was in town then, along with George Lee's, and Bus Moten's little bands. Lester Young, Herschel Evans, and Eddie Barefield were playing around. Top local pianists were Roselle Claxton, Mary Lou Williams, Edith Williams, and Basie.

"I remember the time I tried jamming the first time, when I was just starting to learn. It was at the High Hat, at 22nd and Vine, in K.C. I knew a little of "Lazy River" and "Honeysuckle Rose," and played what I could. It wasn't hard to hear the changes, because the numbers were easy and the reed men set a riff only for the brass, never behind the reed men. No two horns jammed at the same time.

"I was doing all right until I tried doing double tempo on "Body and Soul." Everybody fell out laughing. I went home and cried and didn't play again for three months. Even before that time, I tried playing a job at the Orchid Room with my friend Robert Simpson, and they threw us out. My friend Simpson played me a bad trick subsequently—he died."

Parker left a deep and exciting impression on Kansas City. Three years after his death, standing on 12th Street and Vine, I spoke to a random group of guys who flattered me by judging me hip and asking me if I wanted to buy some "gangster cigarettes." I congratulated them on an interesting term for pot. Then I asked, "Did you know Charlie Parker?" "Oh, Charlie Parker," they replied. The way they said his name was a beautiful thing. The intonation was crowded with many things. It was synonymous with getting high on life.

"Yeah! Yardbird," they said, "We'd catch him whenever he'd come to town, either at Tootsie's Mayfair or El Capitano or the Orchid Room. One night

Bird had a job playing in a small K.C. roadhouse with a seven-piece band. There was only one hang-up, his horn was in hock. In order not to enter the joint saxeless, he had the other alto man enter first and go to the men's room, which faced the back of the establishment. He then passed the horn out the window to Parker. Luckily, they were seated in a dimly-lit room in back of some other musicians. During the night, they surreptitiously kept passing the horn back and forth between them."

He always got a horn somewhere. After his death, there were a lot of people who wanted an alto he had played. Where was one? It was like the search for the Holy Grail. One was found in a grocery store near his house. He had borrowed ten dollars and left the instrument there as security. Chan has one. Amid the maze of figuring out who was to get what of the Parker estate comes the humble request of wife number two, Geraldine, who says, "When I married him, all he had was a horn and a habit. He gave me the habit, so I might as well have the horn."

His attitude toward the law was one of amused cynicism. It was another institution of society you played with. It only became unfunny when they took away your cabaret card so you could not play night clubs. At a time when he was having ID card trouble and was prevented from working, he took his family, deposited them at the Welfare Board, and told the Board, "Here! You feed them."

He drove fast, just for the hell of it. He saw a police car, but that didn't make him slow down. The police car gave pursuit and finally made him stop. Bird got out, didn't say a word. He walked over to the car, peeled off a five-dollar bill for each officer, got back to the car, and drove off.

To the hipster, Bird was a living justification of their philosophy. The hipster is an underground man. He is to the second World War what the Dadaist was to the first. He is amoral, anarchistic, gentle, and overcivilized to the point of decadence. He is always ten steps ahead of the game because of his awareness, an example of which would be meeting a girl and rejecting

At the Open Door: Charlie Mingus, Roy Haynes, Thelonious Monk, and Bird.

her, because he knows they will date, hold hands, kiss, neck, pet, fornicate, perhaps marry, divorce—so why start the whole thing? He knows the hypocrisy of bureaucracy, the hatred implicit in religions—so what values are left for him?—except to go through life avoiding pain, keep his emotions in check, and after that, "be cool" and look for kicks. He is looking for something that transcends all this bullshit and finds it in jazz. The ads I ran in connection with my night club ventures read, "Bob Reisner says: the three great life experiences are sex, psychoanalysis, and cool jazz." As for religion, Parker described himself as a "devout musician." As for society, he said, "Civilization is a damned good thing, if somebody would try it." He lived for pleasure intensely; luckily, one of his pleasures was music. Parker transcended the cliche's of life by the force of his art.

His death was felt powerfully in these circles. For days and weeks afterwards, on sidewalks and fences I saw the crude legend written in chalk or crayon, BIRD LIVES. To the hipster Bird was their private possession. They did not want to talk much about him; they treasured their little brushes with him; and, once in a while, I could extract a sentence or two, which always had some uniqueness.

One said, "Just like Keats and Shelley, he died after making his most exquisite statement." Another said, "In an oriental tradition, Charlie Parker committed suicide on the doorstep of a society that rejected him." Lucky Thompson said, "Bird was trying to break through the sound barrier of music." And still another remarked bitterly, "Everyone treated him like a bum, so he obliged by acting like it." Charlie Parker suddenly became a major deity of the Beat Generation, along with Dylan Thomas and James Dean.

But his influence stretched a lot farther than the beats and the hipsters. The United States Army newspaper *Stars and Stripes* had an item that a dead Communist soldier in the Korean conflict had in his gear a record of Parker's entitled "Bird of Paradise."

No matter how low a state he reached, he was always the cheerful cherub. Without a cent in his pocket, he once turned to me and said, "Look at all the food in the stores and the money all around you. How can you feel insecure?" Not long before his death, he was standing on a corner, reminiscing and optimistically planning, "I'll get my old group together, Max and Miles, Duke and Tommy." And then he, who created so much of the music, said with a laugh, "If I don't know the tunes, I can learn them."

And as to the music he created, the speed of his playing was the first thing that got to people. Slow down these records to 16 r.p.m. and you hear perfect little structures. His authority, direct attack, and lyric fierceness have never been surpassed. Perhaps the greatest tragedy of his life was that he sounded better in person most of the time than on records. When asked his best on wax, he replied sadly to a *Down Beat* reporter in June, 1951, "I'm sorry, but my best on wax has yet to be made. . . . If you want to know my worst on wax, that's easy. I'd take "Lover Man," a horrible thing that should never have been released—it was made the day before I had a nervous breakdown. No, I think I'd choose "Be-Bop," made at the same session or "The Gypsy." They were all awful."

He is too harsh with himself. His incredible melodic lines, the complex rhythms, the light tone with almost no vibrato are remarkable. His shadings, rococo embellishments, and phrasing are breathtaking. André Hodeir writes perceptively of his style in a chapter of his book, *Jazz: Its Evolution and Essence:* "Parker definitely seems to have been the first to bring off the feat of introducing into jazz a certain melodic discontinuity that yet avoids incoherence." He goes on to give examples of the implacable logic of certain solos. Bird's sense of time is incredible. I quote Hodeir: "Parker's idea of rhythm involves breaking time up. It might be said it is based on half beats. No other soloist attaches so much importance to short notes (eighth notes in quick tempos, sixteenths in slow). . . . Bird's accentuation comes alternately on the beat and between beats. The astonishingly rich rhythm of his music comes from this alternation, from these continual oppositions."

Bird rarely spoke of his music. He created his advanced harmonies and progressions, both stated and implied. Perhaps his most quoted statement was: "Music is your own experience, your thoughts, your wisdom. If you don't live it, it won't come out of your horn. They teach you there's a boundary line to music. But, man, there's no boundary line to art."

In the pages that follow are talks between the author and other people who knew and loved Charlie Parker and his art.

They too remember Bird...

Bird with Oscar Peterson and Flip Phillips.

Overleaf:
Thelonious Monk and Charlie Parker.

Angelo Ascagni

Angelo Ascagni describes himself as a jazz fan and a painter. He was tremendously impressed by the good fellowship he found among musicians. Ascagni was concerned that I write something about his late friend Dean Benedetti, who died of pneumonia a few years ago. Dean, an alto sax player, born in Susanville, California, introduced Ascagni to Parker. Benedetti was fanatic in his devotion to Bird and his art. He had a tape recorder, and he followed Parker all over and just took down his solos. He would find out where Bird was going to play and board a bus for the destination two days before. He recorded in the basement of the Onyx Club. He recorded off the air, anywhere he could. He would sneak into Birdland with the apparatus under his coat and creep around looking for an electrical outlet. The solos have never been found as yet.

Bird was above all things an honest man. I was in his home—used to mind his kids. He lived simply and comfortably and without ostentation. He always tried to stay clear of artificialities. He tells people what he thinks and what he feels. A lot of people are not used to such candor and think that Bird is strange. Bird just did not fit into the pattern that people expected and wanted to put him in. I remember being in France with him. The French jazz critic and famous discographer, Charles Delaunay, was annoyed with Bird because he failed to fill an engagement which he arranged. "You know," he said to me, "Charlie Parker has complexes." I guess this was the understatement of that year, 1950. Bird, contrary to all the glowing pieces we read about, which tell how the Negro jazz musicians are feted and worshipped as heroes in Europe, whereas in America, they are treated as minstrel buffoons, did not enjoy the full treatment, the royal welcome, the feting which is generally accorded the jazz musician from America. Bird wanted to be treated as a human being. He saw in this European attitude a sort of subtle prejudice working. He refused to fit himself into the mold of an African genius, an uninhibited primitive spirit, or any of the idolizations which the European apposes to the American abuse of the Negro.

Being an ex-impresario, I felt a twinge of sympathy for Delauney, and I said to Ascagni, "Surely you can see that Bird wasn't very considerate in not showing up for an engagement." Ascagni said, "People who love Bird and his music—when they came to a place where he was supposed to be and didn't show— said to themselves, 'Bird just doesn't feel like playing today.' If you want to go and hear some music you can go to a hotel lounge where there is a trio that plays every day, day in and day out; they always come on time; they'll always be there, but you'll never hear great music. It is one of the fallacies of middle-class society to think they can turn artists on and off to fit ticket sales. They want them to play the way they do and to behave the way they think a musician should behave. If they know the guy has some spirit, they shouldn't have these guys if they care about behavior." Delauney must have understood this for he was not too angry. Ascagni and I went into a little by-road discussion of jazz in general and the best places for it to flourish, and Ascagni felt that the permissive atmosphere of night clubs was the best condition rather than programmed concerts in concert halls and college auditoriums. Actually jazz history has proven him correct.

One of the nicest things I recall is that I always felt safe with Bird. You got a kind of well-being because he was sure of himself. He always knew where he was going and why he was there. I guess his charm was a big factor in this. He could make the biggest drag in the place like him. One day we were having a beer at the Short Stop, which is across the street from Bohemia where has was playing—musicians always go to other bars during their breaks, either for cheaper beer or a change of scene. A guy was looking very indignantly at Bird, because Bird was the only Negro in the bar at the time, and the guy must have been sore at the world. He kept throwing sullen looks. I don't know if Bird noticed it, but suddenly Bird flashed one of his warm smiles in the man's direction and the guy spoke, but his words were now friendly. Bird had disarmed him with a smile. "Don't you play across the street?" Bird nodded. "I bet you play good saxophone." "I play okay," Bird came back.

He one time took me to Birdland. They wanted me to pay, but Bird put up an argument, "This place was named after me."

> *Ascagni said he felt Birdland was annoyed at Charlie because they never met a musician who thought he was so important.*

Sometimes when you met Bird, he'd have a roll on him that could choke a horse or he'd be twirling the keys to a brand new car, and other times, not too much later, he'd be scuffling and ask you for a half dollar. But he never panicked. Bird never worried about money or food or anything. "In a place like New York, how can you worry about money." There's always a place to make out. He feels that the whole thing is a racket. There is such a quantity of things, you don't have to worry about it.

The only way you could please Bird was by being yourself and not worrying about him. You could relax with him. Towards the end of his life, everybody was worried, but he wasn't. He was in very bad health, but he didn't speak of it. He was always optimistic and had big plans. He spoke to me of a prolonged engagement at a club and he said to me, "When I stop playing, we'll be laughing in each other's faces."

The best relation with Bird is a simple one. He felt that the moment was the important thing. He could be very generous or you could be very generous. But he didn't like this middle-class business of paying back exactly whatever favor has been given. Bird doesn't like a guy who extends so many favors and then wants them back. Any famous person gets played up to as a hero by strangers. Bird used to take half of these people. It's like in every field where a guy is a figure. They forget about their own living—really a bug (guys who latch themselves to great ones). Bird asked them for money. It's natural for him to act that way. But if you say no to him, it's the same thing.

He used to have a good time with intellectual things. He was good at pricking intellectual balloons. Someone would ask him, "What is civilization?" "I think civilization is a wonderful thing." Bird enjoyed these questions. I would bust laughing. He'd talk in bravado style.

He was a funny master of ceremonies. When he finished his numbers and he introduced the next performer, he would say, "The management has gone to enormous expense to bring you. . . ." This kidding escaped the management who would be beaming.

He did not like whistling or stamping or any distasteful show of enthusiasm after a selection. "Mild applause will suffice," he would say.

Harold Baker

Harold Baker was a lead trumpet man with Duke Ellington's band for twelve years and four months. In the early thirties he played in the bands of Erskine Tate, Fate Marable, and Eddie Johnson—later on with Don Redman and Teddy Wilson. He is affectionately called "Shorty."

Naw, he was no thirty-four when he died. I was born May 26, 1913, and Charlie was older than me. Bird would always call me Brother Baker. It might be years but he would come over to me, take my hand, and say, "Brother Baker," and I would say, "My Man." I took a liking to Charlie the first time I met him. Nobody disliked Charlie in Kansas City. You could go in front of the Booker T. Washington Hotel, and they would be talking about Charlie. Bird started out on C melody sax. He was playing with Jap Allen's band around 1931. I tell you some of the guys that was in the band. There was Jap Allen on tuba; Thamon Hayes, trombone; Eddie Durham, trombone; Booker T. Washington, trumpet; Ed Lewis, trumpet; the Douglas brothers on alto and clarinet; Clyde Hart was on piano. Clyde later played on a lot of famous Bird records. In the early days, Bird was a very passive person; only till he got to know you real well would he let his hair down. In later years, the only time you catch Bird extra quiet was when he was broke. If he had $100, he would spend it; he was very generous. He would set a whole bar up for drinks. He was very generous with his musical knowledge and would always take time out to explain something to a musician. He could explain it to him on the musician's own instrument, he was so remarkably musical.

All Bird wanted to do was to live to play that horn. The horn comes before a woman. After the horn then maybe he would talk to someone. If you saw Bird go into a club, you could trace a definite pattern to what he would do, and I'm talking about a place where he wasn't playing. He would go to the bar and slowly but surely start edging to the bandstand, retreat a few steps, and then edge closer till he was next to the man with the alto and till he eventually ended up with the alto. He always carried his mouthpiece with him, except for a time when he was suffering from a great deal of mouthpiece loss from admirers and souvenir hunters, but a little while later he was back carrying it around again.

There were a lot of people in the world who wanted to try out these new things. Charlie proved he could do it. He was liable to start with the eleventh or thirteenth note of the key he was in. He always built the opposite of the average musician. He might play something I like, but I would never start on the same note. I would turn it around. He would run through sixteenths and thirty-second notes like a tornado and then he'd come right back to loafing. The clarinet and the alto are two of your fastest instruments. He was playing about three times as fast on the alto as is usually played, but he would never lose his patterns. He knew what he was going to play before he moved a finger. You have to have a chart in your mind. A lot of guys forget their changes. Bird would ramble, but he always got back to the key. When I first heard him, he seemed to be playing something different all the time. I knew he was right. The rhythm section was always with Charlie. I never heard anybody play so fast. It was so fast the drummer was playing two beats. But fast as it was, it was clean, just like he was explaining to you while he was talking to somebody else.

He did his finest things with small combos, but he loved big bands. Listen to how he sounds (we were listening to Bird with a Norman Granz big band); he's just like a kid at a Christmas tree. The band plays the tune straight and they're giving Charlie ideas. They keep feeding him and he's chalkin' all the time. When I'd see him, it was mostly music talk: "What do you run in here? What do you run when you get to the bridge?" Because he is not running the correct changes. We used to carry a little slip of paper like many musicians do with the names of tunes and the substitute changes that we liked whenever we were in a session.

Harold "Shorty" Baker said that the radio is the greatest source of inspiration and education to the musician. "I used to fall asleep and wake up in the morning with it on. You hear so many different kinds of things. You'd be surprised at the riffs you can discover in hearing a church service."

In line with Bird's love of big bands, I asked Brother Baker if the

Duke ever asked Parker to join the band. He said that Ellington approached both Charlie and Fats Navarro, a fabulous bop trumpeter who died of a combination of t.b. and narcotic addiction. Fats was very flattered at the offer but not at the salary. He replied in a kind of sweet, soft way that he had, "Yes, Baby, the sound would knock me out, but I have to have the bread. I could make it for $350." Bird laid an even bigger price on the Duke. Ellington's reply was, "I'd work for you, Bird, if you paid me that kind of money."

When Bird died, Ellington said, "Charlie Parker made a tremendous contribution to the fabric of modern-day sounds. There are countless records and performances by innumerable artists in which you hear a certain phrase, and you immediately see Charlie's picture in your mind's eye."

Ahmed Basheer

In the last four months of his life, Charlie Parker was almost daily in the company of Ahmed Basheer. There is something serene and comfortable about this man. Born in St. Louis on July 10, 1928, he became a Muslim in 1949. He came to New York with $1.25 and no profession or trade. He is presently working toward an engineer degree at City College and attends to his religious interests at "The Ahmediyya Movement in Islam," the headquarters for the faithful. Under a rather loose

Bird with George Duvivier.

financial arrangement, he worked for Bird. He was part manager, part valet, and part lay analyst. Bird's association with Basheer may also have been a last attempt at getting away from bad habits. The religion of Islam forbids drinking, cursing, and promiscuity.

Bird offered to buy me a drink. He said, "What are you drinking, man?" I was starry-eyed with awe. I said, "Anything that you're drinking, man." He quickly noticed my worshipful mien and proceeded to avoid it. "What are you drinking?" he said again, to bring out my individuality, to keep me from idolizing him. I finally said, "Well, a soda." This was before I had become a Muslim. I was then known as Thomas Henderson. I accepted Islam in my twenty-first year in July, 1949.

The next time I saw Bird, I was coming out of the Montmartre, a Village bistro. I saw Bird coming across the street and greeted him with the Muslim salutation, "Assalamu Alaikum." (Peace be unto you.) Bird returned the greeting with "Wa Alaikum Salam." (And unto you peace.) He called me aside and said, "Speak to me." I said, "What do you mean?" He said, "Speak to me." I thought for a moment, and then it occurred to me that he wanted me to show him proof of my right to say the Muslim salutation. He figured that, if I didn't know what I was doing, I should stop faking. I recited to him in Arabic the first Surah (chapter) of the holy Quran (Koran). As I was finishing the recitation, he grabbed me ecstatically, shaking with pleasure. Just then we saw a young alto player, a particularly close friend and protege of Bird's, who was so ill he needed help getting home. Charlie felt worried about him not feeling well. I volunteered to see him home, and then Bird agreed.

Charlie Parker was interested in the Moslem religion. His Mohammedan name was Saluda Hakim. He knew a little Huranic Arabic.

One afternoon as I got back to the Village from school, a friend from my St. Louis days came over to me and said, "Bird's around the corner lying in the street." I said, "What's the matter with him?" He said, "I don't know, but he fell out, and some of the fellows are trying to help him up and bring him to." I told him that I would see him later and ran around the corner and found that Charlie had fallen right in front of 4 Barrow Street, where I lived. I asked one of the fellows who was holding him up, Harvey Cropper—a very talented painter who was giving Bird art lessons—if I could help him. Harvey said, "Everything is under control; Bird just needs to be taken some place where he can lay down." I said, "I live right here; let's take him inside." They all agreed.

It was quite a job getting him upstairs. He was big-boned, and he had put on a lot of weight in the last years. Bird was so relaxed and yet he wasn't out. It took four of us to maneuver him up the stairs. I led the way. We laid him in my bed and pulled off his shoes, and he began to twist and turn, and he asked in a kind of stupor, "Who is Muslim? Where is that fellow who is a Muslim? I want to hear some of the Quran." I took my Quran and began to read to him in Arabic. He seemed quite affected by it. He would put both hands over his heart and then at his sides but after I read about three verses, he asked me to stop.—"It's too beautiful." As I was reading, the others left because he told them to get out. And when I finished reading, he told me to get out. Before I left him, my friend who told me about Bird's accident came in the room to see how he was. Charlie said, "I know you fellows are trying to keep an eye on me because you don't want me to kill myself, but regardless of what you say or do, I'll have to die, and that's all there is to it. It won't be anything to it; it will be very easy. I'll just simply maybe jump off a bridge or something some night, and you fellows will hear about it." He was very sick. "Nothing you two can say can save me. I have made up my mind to it. It's going to happen." My friend said, "Bird, don't say that. I have admired you for years. I can't think of your dying. Look what you'll be doing to all of the people who love your music! You'll really be taking something away from them." I said, "Don't talk like that. You can best serve the world by remaining alive. Many people would listen to what you have to say; all you have to do is talk." Charlie said, "Shut up, get out, and leave me alone. You don't know what you're talking about. I'm telling you, it's best that I die."

We left him alone, not hurt because of his blunt words, because he said them with a touch of love behind them, but we knew like all artists the world's failure to receive the love that he was trying to give and receive was weighing him down, and he believed that his death would solve his problems.

He stayed on as a guest in my one room for the rest of his life. He slept for four hours after his attack which is two hours longer than he usually slept at a stretch. His eyes opened and he said, "Listen, I want to tell you something. About every month or so I have pains that are so severe until I have to get in touch with a doctor. I'm going to give you the names of two doctors that you can call. All you have to do is to tell them my name, and they will know what to do." I copied down the names that he gave me and also the addresses and telephone numbers. He further said, "I would like for you to call my mother out in Kansas City and tell her what's going on. Tell her to send me some money and give her this address." I went to call his mother, but I was a stranger, and I couldn't get the proper response. I told her Charlie wanted some money, and she said, "I just sent Charles some money the other day. I haven't got any money." I said, "Okay, I will tell him."

I told him the results of the call, and he said, "That cute little thing. She sure is hard to handle sometimes. I had better go and talk to her myself;

I know how to handle her."

He dressed, and we walked out together to a telephone booth in a subway. It was so early in the morning that it was the only one open. He didn't have any success either. He came out of the booth smiling and said, "She's all right. She just thinks I'm a little mischievous at times."

We went and sat in a little park in Sheridan Square. Because of his indifference in financial matters, he let himself get caught without my cash and no change of clothing, but he seemed to be rather content, and he talked to me in a philosophical way. He said, "Look how beautiful it is early in the morning. Do you want me to show you something? Do you want to see Allah? Look East, way down there by Broadway. See the sun ready to come up? That's God. Everything that you can see and everything that you can't see is Allah." He was beginning to get tired, sitting there, so he said, "It would be nice if we could go somewhere and cool out." We went and woke up a friend who got up happy and sleepy-eyed and played records for us. Bird made himself comfortable and cooled out.

The next day I was talking to a friend in my room when a knock was heard at my door. I asked who it was—no answer. A knock was heard again, and a powerful voice roared out, "The police." I opened the door to discover Charlie standing there. Chips Bayen and I became Bird's managers. We worked it out so that while one was at school or at work, the other would always be with Bird. We forced him into a cab uptown, to his mother-in-law's to pick up his clothes (he was then separated from his wife—nothing serious). I waited for him at a bar on Sixth Avenue and 52nd Street. Charles Parker came walking down 52nd Street with a contemplative air, like he was passing through a ghost town. He looked at The Deuces, The Onyx, all the clubs he used to play, and they were all strip joints. Just a ghost town.

Bird loved movies, good and bad. We saw *Carmen Jones* four times. He must have enjoyed that movie because Max Roach had a part in it. "They sure cooked that picture," he said. His phrases and the way he expressed himself was a joy, it was so original, pithy, humorous. He sort of was like a father to me. "I'm gonna take you to one of the best places to eat, real kosher." It turned out to be Toffenetti's, and they walked in looking very raggedy—Parker wrapped in his parka coat with attached hood which he never took off. He ordered with dignity but never rudely, because he had a special affection for waiters and waitresses, for all people who do the honest, common, necessary jobs.

Bird ate very well but not every day. His eating habits were odd. He ate every two or three days and slept about the same way. After the meal Bird said that they should go over to the Gale Booking Agency. "I've got to go over and see my judges." He called his bookers his "judges," because he felt they had the power over him and controlled his working. He got this term "judges" from a foreign movie he saw, some sort of fantasy film where three heavenly judges decided the fate of some of the characters. Since he deeply resented the bookers and felt they were robbers, he sarcastically referred to them as his "judges."

We went down to Baltimore where Charlie played at a place called the Comedy Club for a week, and I saw that his shoes were shined, that he was on time, and looked neat on the job. We stayed at the home of the hat check girl. She was a very hospitable woman and thrilled to have such a boarder. Bird could be very generous at times and before they left, besides paying for their keep, he left a five-dollar bill in the coffee cup after breakfast.

One night Red Prysock, the tenor sax player, and Charlie were playing a bowling machine game in the club, and when Red took his turn and did not make a particular brilliant shot, Parker exclaimed, "Give it here. Let me show you how to play. I'm going to show you how to play this game! I can beat you at anything you want to play!" "Anything, Charlie?" Red asked. "Anything!" Bird replied. Red asked, "Music too?" "No," replied Bird, "that's something else. That's art," as if to say that each man had his place and stature, that you could not say that one was better than another.

The Baltimore engagement was a huge success despite lateness, docking of pay, hassles. Bird fired the musicians hired by management and replaced them with Wade Legge, piano, Will Bradley, Jr., drums, and Earl May, bass. When we started back for New York after the gig, Bird turned to me in the car and said, "Basheer, I don't let anyone get too close to me, even you." I said, "Why?" He said, "Once in Kansas City I had a friend who I liked very much, and a sorrowful thing happened." Basheer said, "What?" figuring the guy must have cheated or betrayed him. Bird said, "He died."

"You know, Charlie," I said to him once, "you seem to function best when we only have our bare necessities." He said, "You're right. What more do we need?"

Bellevue Hospital, N.Y.

Charlie Parker was admitted to Bellevue Hospital, Psychiatric Division, September 1, 1954. He was discharged September 10, 1954. His age, given on admission, was 34. His wife's name was Chan. The patient was admitted following suicidal attempt by ingestion of iodine. The diagnosis was acute and chronic alcoholism and narcotic addiction.

Past history—eight months in Camarillo State Hospital, California in 1945 for nervous breakdown. The history from his wife was that, when drinking, the patient threatened his wife and children and exhibited suicidal tendencies. There had been one previous suicidal attempt by ingestion of sulfuric acid. The wife related the suicidal attempt to the fact that the patient's father was killed—details unknown. This suicidal attempt was precipitated by an argument with his wife.

While on Ward PQ 3, which is the semi-agitative ward, the patient exhibited passive dependency and proved ingratiating and friendly to all physicians. Psychometric testing indicated a high average intelligence with paranoid tendencies. Evaluation by psychiatrists indicate a hostile, evasive personality with manifestations of primitive and sexual fantasies associated with hostility and gross evidence of paranoid thinking. Psychoanalytic diagnosis: "latent schizophrenia." Patient was discharged on September 10 to the care of Dr. ——.

The second admission to Bellevue Hospital was September 28, 1954—discharged October 15, 1954. The patient committed himself to the Psychiatric Pavilion, stating that he had been severely depressed since his previous discharge, that he was drinking again, and feared for his own safety. Admitting diagnosis: acute alcoholism and undifferentiated schizophrenia. The doctor interviewed the patient and thought that ECT might be necessary. A spinal tap was performed: colloidal gold curve was negative; and blood Wassermann was 2+ positive.

Nurses' notes indicate that the patient on ward was lazy and kept bothering nurses for doses of paraldehyde. Apparently, there was no true adjustment while on ward. There was a history given that the patient was treated in 1945, in Los Angeles, for lues with penicillin, bismuth, and arsenic. The neurological examination was negative during this Bellevue admission. On October 15, 1954, the patient was discharged in his own custody.

Walter Bishop, Jr.

Walter Bishop, Jr. can be heard with Charlie Parker on a Verve LP. His father is the noted ASCAP song writer. Walter, Jr. served in the Air Force from 1945 to 1947. After that he enlisted in the Art Blakey Messengers. He toured with Parker and was musically associated with Andy Kirk, Terry Gibbs, Kai Winding, and Miles Davis. He was out of music for two years but returned in 1955. He was a familiar figure at Birdland on Monday nights during the spring and summer of 1959, when he was the leader of various groups that play when the regular groups are off. Bish plays in the tradition of Bud Powell.

Bird and I got along so well, because he knew I would not take any shit from him. Bird's personality was such that at times he was very overbearing and overpowering. If there was one flaw in your make-up, you didn't stand a chance with Bird. If you were in the least bit uncertain of yourself when there was an issue or any type of difference between you and him, if you were the least bit shaky, you didn't stand a chance with Bird. The only way to stand up to him was to be as resolute in your way of thinking as he was in his. Before I ever worked with Bird, I heard countless stories of how he messed around with the guys, wouldn't pay them their loot. How he owed this one so much money and didn't give this one what he was supposed to get. In my whole association with Bird there was only one time that I can say he did me out of any money, and the sum was so small, seven dollars, that I chose to overlook it in view of future work that he had for me. But I let him know that I was wise to what was happening, not to think that he was pulling the wool over my eyes.

I'll give you an example of his overbearing ways. We worked a gig in Boston, and we were about to get paid. There was a discrepancy between him and Kenny Dorham. Kenny said he had $100 coming to him, and Bird said that he had drawn $60 so that he only had $40 due him. Were you an outsider or a bystander listening to the conversation and what later became an argument, you would have sided with Bird, because the man was so strong he actually had Dorham believing that he drew $60 more than he had. He had such an overpowering personality, just like his horn. He didn't get away with not paying Kenny, but he came very close. If it was an oversight on Bird's

44

part or if he was actually aware of what was going on, I don't know, but if you were listening you couldn't help but think Kenny was trying to take advantage of Bird. In his expansive way, Bird would say, "Kenny, you're my boy. You're my children. We're one big family. I'd lay down my life for you," and I think he would.

But he was never overbearing on the stand. He always did his best to make you feel relaxed. I remember it was in the St. Nicholas Arena where I first had a chance to get acquainted with him. It was around 1944. I was a young kid with more courage than knowledge. I was going all around, sitting and jamming. I had such a strong desire to learn and become part of the scene. I suffered all sorts of indignities. I was chased off a set or somebody would call a tune I didn't know or I could be sitting up there at the piano and a horn man would call down to a friend, "Hey Joe, come up and play piano with us." As if I was not sitting there at all. These things were perhaps good in a way. They made me vengeful and competitive. I would go home, lock myself in my room, and practice for hours on end. If there was a certain tune that caught me on, they would never catch me on that tune again.

That night at St. Nick's, I had a chance to sit in on a number with Bird. I was both anxious and nervous, and with good reason. It was an all-star night, and musicians like Ben Webster, Oscar Pettiford, Erroll Garner, and Buck Clayton were there. The tune called was "Savoy." During the piece, my hand slipped and struck a wrong chord. Bird turned around and said, "What was that?" It was said in admiration, for with his deep musical feeling, what sounded wrong may have contained something weird, exciting, and beautiful for him. "Damn," he said, "who is this cat?" Then he asked me to call off the name of that change. I could never remember what wrong chord I hit.

In the next six years, I really strove. As I said before, I felt I was ready for Bird several years previous to the time he hired me. There was only one pianist who surpassed me, who came between me and Bird, and that was my idol who I patterned my playing and style after, Bud Powell. I was a demon. At one time, I was gobbling up piano players. I mean cutting them. It was Bird or bust. Bud, well, he was the best, but Bird and Bud's personalities clashed. Bud was leader status himself. Bird probably said to himself, "This kid is a bitch, but I'm not going to fire Al Haig for him." I had come so far up the ladder, then come up against a brick wall. I came on a period of bitterness, and then I started to relax my grip. Frustration at getting so far and getting no further. I said the hell with it. I stopped striving there for a period. All for nothing. All that survival of the fittest stuff. That's the way I learned as fast as I did. From night to night, I would get hung on tunes and then go home and practice them. I never got hung on the same tune twice. The next time I would go down there, and that would be the first tune I would ask to play, the one I got hung on the night before. I would sit down at the piano, and they would call out "All The Things You Are."

"Sorry, man, I don't know that."

" 'The Way You Look Tonight.' "

"Don't know that either."

"Hey, what the hell do you know?"

"Man, do you know 'Cherokee?' "

Truth is, I knew the outside, but I didn't know the channel. I didn't have the heart to say another tune, so when it came to the middle I played very, very soft. Nobody could hear me but myself—though they tried to listen, they cracked their ears. And after the middle I came in loud and strong, twenty-four bars loud and strong. The middle soft, very, very soft. Things like that came up in later years once in a while, but, with Bird, if you didn't know a tune, he would take the time to acquaint you with it. Sometimes we got to a record session without any rehearsal. Bird would have some little bits of marks on scraps of paper. "Here, Miles, this is how it goes." We did a number, "Star Eyes." I didn't know how the tune went, but Bird knew I had big ears. He just ran it down once or twice, and I got it.

From 1951 on I had achieved my life's ambition, to be playing with Bird. It had come a little too late to bring the tremendous elation I would have felt if it had come several years earlier, but, nevertheless, it was a wonderful experience going out on the road with Charlie and the string section. Bird conducted himself beautifully on the tour. He was never late. He fronted the band impressively and with dignity. All in all, he was everything a leader should be. I guess that is why I felt so bad about an experience we had in a town called East Liberty, a suburb of Pittsburgh. We were booked in a big lavish spot called Johnny Brown's for a week, and, in that week, we played to the poorest business imaginable, considering that Bird had some fine and popular records going, "Laura" and "April in Paris." The first night there were three parties in the place. I felt sorry for the owner, and I felt sorry for Bird and the guys in tuxedos and bow ties. It couldn't have been poor advertising, because it was a small town, and everybody knows what's happening in a small town. We had a similar experience, but not quite as bad, in St. Louis at a place called The Riviera. I attribute this unhappy booking to the home office's bad packaging. They had us with Ivory Joe Hunter and his band and Butterbeans and Susie. These people are good performers, but it just did not gibe with our music or the people who came to see us. Even the strings, beautiful as they were, proved confining at times, and we would have them lay out every once in a while so that Bird, Roy Haynes, Teddy Kotick, and myself could wail a set or two. It was very refreshing to get to play 16 bars of consecutive piano.

I remember one time we were in St. Paul, Minnesota, and looking for marijuana. Bird and I got in a cab. We couldn't find any in St. Paul; nothing was happening in St. Paul. We went all the way to Minneapolis. We got out of the cab, walked a few blocks, and Bird stopped. He looked around and I said, "What's the matter, Bird?"

"God damn, Bish, you know one thing. I stood on this very same corner thirteen years ago, looking for the same thing. I guess a man never learns." Sure enough he found some old cronies, old numbers men, pimps, hustlers, old-time racketeers who were still on the scene since the time thirteen years ago when he came through with Jay McShann. These guys came through with what we were looking for. He'd go to a town and try to find a familiar landmark, or something, some semblance of the past that said "You're on the right track." Two blocks this way, a particular corner. He was looking for places or people. He always found it.

His philosophy of life, in a sense, belied his life. He often said to me, "Bish, the greatest thing man can do is to find self-satisfaction. If it makes you happy to eat that glass, well, eat it." But the greatest thing he did was not the way he lived his life but the way he affected others, what he left behind for posterity. The man was so influential in his field that he gave happiness to thousands. Thousands live and breathe Bird. Another thing he said to me about getting high, using heroin. I asked him why he was using it, or something. I forget how it came about, but anyway he said to me, "Bish, you know there's quite a number of things wrong with me. I go to this heart specialist, you know, give him a hundred dollars for the relief of my heart. He treats me, don't do no good; my heart is still messed up. I go to this ulcer man, give him seventy-five dollars to cool my ulcers out; it don't do no good. There's a little cat in a dark alley around the corner. I give him five dollars for a bag of shit; my ulcer's gone, my heart trouble gone, everything gone, all my ailments gone."

Dig this. Bird, he was something. One time we were in St. Louis, Missouri, and Bird gave this little trombone player some money to get some stuff for him, about thirty dollars. The kid left us waiting in the jitney. He didn't come back, and the meter kept going up. We were real upset about that, so we went around town inquiring about the kid, and we found out where he lived. The next morning (incidentally Bird carried a pistol around with him) we got to the kid's house. The kid's mother thought we were police. If you didn't know Bird and he put on his authoritative air, you might very well believe him. "Madam," he said, "is your son at home?"

"No," she said, "he isn't."

Bird said, "Madam, I'd like to have a few words with you."

"All right," she said.

"Madam," he says, "your son did me a grave injustice. It involved a sum of money. Thirty dollars, to be exact."

The lady said, "How did it come about?"

Before he went into that, he got up and said, "Who lives here with you?"

So the lady said, "Oh, my husband—he's out to work—and my daughter Ellie May."

He says, "Who lives in that room there?"

"Oh, that's my boy's room."

"Do you mind if I inspect it?"

"No," she says, "you can look at it," and Bird goes in and searches it like an officer to see whether the boy was hiding.

"What's up there, Madam?"

She tells him it's an attic. He goes up there and doesn't find anything. By this time the woman is thoroughly scared and puzzled. She doesn't know what to make of it. Bird said, "I trusted your son with thirty dollars. We're in town on business. We'll be in St. Louis until such and such a date, and so, Madam, I give you fair warning. If your son doesn't make restitution to me by such and such a time, I wouldn't venture to say what will happen to him. I assume you feel for your son's welfare as all mothers do." By this time the woman was all shook up.

"Okay," she said, "you come by tomorrow at this time, and, if Bone is home, he'll see you." The kid was called Bone, because he played trombone. Well, the next day we came back, and the boy wasn't there, but the woman told us to come back again, because she was getting something from her son-in-law, who had a bank account.

"Is that satisfactory to you, Mr. Bishop?" Bird asks me.

"Yes, Mr. Parker, that's perfectly satisfactory," I replied.

We got the money back. We never saw the kid again. Word got to us that he was waylaid and robbed, and I'm inclined to believe it, because Charlie Parker is the idol of all musicians, and I don't think that for thirty dollars the boy would have done what he did. It would have been worth fifty dollars to the kid to get high with Bird and be in his company. I ventured an opinion that I thought it was cruel of Bird to do what he did, but I was told that it was the third or fourth time in the past few days that he had given money to people and they disappeared, and he was determined not to let it happen again.

Again in St. Louis on the same gig, we were riding around in a cab when this guy pops up from somewhere and says, "Bird, your trumpet player got hit on the head with a steel pipe, and some cats robbed him, and they took him to a hospital." Bird did not seem too perturbed. He calmly said, "Bish, come with me." And we went back to our hotel and Charlie's room, where he opened his suitcase and took out a pistol. "Little Benny" Harris was the unfortunate trumpet player, and we did not know his assailants, but we did know the section of town where Benny hung out. When we got there, we discovered the whole thing had been exaggerated. Harris was not in a hospital but just walking around with a little bandage, quite capable of playing that night. What had happened was, he had entrusted his money to an acquaintance and waited at the person's home for his return. When the guy was a little late in getting back, Benny proceeded to walk out of the cat's house with some of his clothes. The fellow returned at that moment and that's when the trouble started.

Bird with Walter Bishop, Sr., famous songwriter.

Art Blakey

Born in Pittsburgh, October 11, 1919, by 1936 Art had his own band and played piano. "I worked for some gangsters in a place called The Democratic Club," says Art. "I played so well till Erroll Garner came in—he took my job. I had eight pieces in my band. The gangsters liked Erroll better. He really did outplay everyone. They said to me, " 'Okay, kid, he's gonna play piano and you play drums.' And that's how I became a drummer."

In 1939, Art joined Fletcher Henderson's band. In 1940, he was with Mary Lou Williams' first group at Kelly's Stables. He then had his own band at the Tic Toc in Boston. From 1944 to 1947 he was with the Billy Eckstine band. When the Eckstine band folded, Art went traveling. He went to Africa for two years. He roamed over Nigeria, Gold Coast, and even got to India. He went there to study Islam. He also brought back lots of ideas about drumming. His Mohammedan name is Abdullah Ibn Buhaina. Since 1953 he has led his own group called The Jazz Messengers.

There was a guy in Fletcher Henderson's band who said, "Man, you ought to hear this guy Charlie Parker."

"Man, he can't outplay Willie Smith?"

"He can."

I got mad at this guy.

A little while later we met Parker. I turned to my friend and said, "Is this the bum you mean?" He wasn't dapper like a musician. He was wearing a pair of slacks, a sweater and a beret. He looked too relaxed.

After that we'd meet in train stations while we were going in different directions. He's so great, he was easy to meet.

I left Fletcher Henderson's band in Boston and I formed my own group that became the house band at The Tic Toc Club.

Billy Eckstine was forming his band and Dizzy said to him, "There's a guy in Boston; this guy can play." Billy said he knew me and that I was from his home town, but he had not heard me play. But he sent for me, and I came down to St. Louis, and there I met Bird, Billy, Sarah, Dizzy, the rest. We were playing in a prejudiced club; Billie Holiday, Billy Eckstine, Bird, Dizzy. The man told us all to come in through the back door that night, and these damn fools, they got together and they came in the front door. The guy is wigged. They all come in the front door havin' a ball. He said, "I don't want you to fraternize with the customers." When Charlie got to the intermission, they all sat at the tables and the guy was about to wig. He told someone, "You gotta get this band the hell outta here." The guys were carrying on something fierce despite the fact that gangsters were walking around with big guns up on their hips. They didn't scare Bird or anyone. Tadd Dameron was drinking a glass of water. Out of one of the beautiful glasses they had to serve the customers. Bird walked over to him saying, "Did you drink out of this, Tadd?" Tadd says "Yeah." Bam! He smashes it, "It's contaminated. Did you drink out of this one?" "Yeah," Tadd says. Bam. "It's contaminated." He broke about two dozen glasses. A guy was glaring at Bird; he just looked back coolly. "What do you want? Am I bothering you?" Bird asks him. "Are you crazy?" the guy asks. "Well, if you want to call me crazy," Bird replies. Then once again he turns to Tadd, "Did you drink out of this glass?" Bam. "It's contaminated." They put us out. They put Jeeter-Pillows in our place at the Plantation and they sent us to the Riviera, which was a colored club. There the band got started, and we went from there to Chicago and that's when I realized how great the man was.

The Man stopped the show in Chicago. It was on a Saturday night in 1944. Sarah was singing "You Are My First Love." That man came out and took sixteen bars and stopped the show. The house was packed. People applauded so loud we couldn't go on. We had to do it all over again.

He always was one for fun. The fellows were always up to pranks. They'd ride up and down the hotel halls on broomsticks or have mock fights with swords—him and Dizzy loved to do that. It's lonely in some towns, especially down South. Nobody understands you. So we get together and have fun ourselves—spill water on each other, anything that boys (for that's what we were) would do just to keep things interesting. He was a good guy. He gave a lot. In 1950-51 I was on relief. In 1951 after my wife died, Bird, who had come in from the Coast, lent me $2000 just to help me out. He was distressed by some of the idiots in the music business. You build all your life, and then you see it destroyed by fakers.

A symbol to the Negro people? No. They don't even know him. They never heard of him and care less. A symbol to the musicians, yes.

There was no rivalry between the Baroness, Bird, and myself. Nica is just a wonderful woman. A woman first and a Baroness second. She wants to be witty. Poor thing, she ain't so witty. We are very good friends, but I stopped seeing her when stories got back to my daughters, and they sounded on me.

Bird died trying to kick his habit. He tried to kick it the wrong way, by drinking whiskey. The whiskey is the thing that killed him. The heroin was preserving him—the heroin did not kill him. He tried to do what people asked him to do, that's why he's not here today. After a man shoots dope for four-teen years, how you gonna stop him? His system cries for it. If he uses it, the heroin will preserve him, it won't destroy him. I know he died trying to do what society asked him to do, which is impossible. Our society has to find out that the people who are using dope are not crazy or criminal, they are sick people. This man had been sick for fourteen years and nobody would help him because they didn't know. They didn't know he was sick. They don't understand heroin.

You do not play better with heroin but you do hear better. Bird said that he wanted to kick the habit so that he could tell people what he heard. It is something like a neurotic. While he is suffering, he cannot produce; but reflecting about his pain, he can create. Musicians who have been junkies and then rid themselves of the habit, have sometimes really then come into their own musically.

Rudi Blesh

Noted jazz historian, lecturer, author and art authority, Rudolph Pickett Blesh has written Shining Trumpets, They All Played Ragtime *(with Harriet Janis), and* Modern Art USA. *His latest works are a series of monographs on significant modern artists. He had a record company (Circle Records), and he is presently on the Faculty of Queens College. He has made great contributions to the study of early jazz, but he resents anything that represents him as allied to any musical camp. He is appreciative and knowledgeable about honest creative effort of any period.*

Every year the New York *Herald Tribune* sponsors a youth forum where world issues are discussed and prominent personalities are invited to speak.

Young people from different lands attend. Virgil Thomson was in charge of the morning session on March 5, 1949, when he presented some artists from the Metropolitan Opera, and I presented a jazz concert featuring a Dixieland group and a Bop group.

I had assembled the two best bands that I could, led by saxes instead of trumpets. In the traditional contingent there were: Sidney Bechet, soprano sax; Buster Bailey, clarinet; Sidney De Paris, trombone; Ralph Sutton, piano; Walter Page, bass; and George Wettling, drums. The modern men were: Charlie Parker, alto; Kenny Dorham, trumpet; Al Haig, piano; Tommy Potter, bass; and Max Roach, drums.

There has always been a lot of partisanship in jazz. This program was a completely impartial presentation for people to hear and judge what they preferred, or better still, to hear the fine qualities in both types of jazz. We let the bands alternate on numbers of their own choosing. Bird's group led off with "How High The Moon." Bechet followed with "I Know That You Know." At the bell, Bird came out with "Barbados." Bechet followed swinging with an ad lib "Blues." Bird dug in close with "Anthropology." Sidney traded punches with "Dear Old Southland." It was declared a tie. Nobody won, and everybody won. The audience cheered.

The musicians were extremely friendly. Sidney Bechet, who never gave praise to anybody, said to Bird, "Man, those phrases you make." Parker's off-the-air comment was: "That is as it should be. There's an awful lot of bullshit, this music is good or bad. It is good or bad, but not because of the kind of music—but because of the quality of the musician."

The success of this clambake prompted WOR to put on another similar "battle." The program was called "Bands for Bonds." I thought it should be presented in a more controversial way for this show. I represented "Ye olde moulde fygges" and Bop had its champion in the person of Barry Ulanov. We had a script of good-natured razzing. Each band had three numbers to play, but the switch was that the second number each group played was to be a tune called by the opposition. The Bop men called for "Sunny Side of the Street" and that was no problem for the Dixielanders, who then called for "Tiger Rag." There's nothing a Bopper can do with "Tiger Rag." But it is to their credit that they struggled with it. Everything about the session was fun, especially the rehearsal where Wild Bill Davison yelled "I can play Bop," and he proceeded to blow some crazy riffs. At that moment Dizzy walked in and said, "Man, you are with us." They hugged each other and played a duet together.

> *Note: The next day the* Herald Tribune *reported that "Classic Jazz had won a complete and undisputed victory!" See Barry Ulanov's account of the same incident.*

At Birdland: Clockwise at table, Ahmet Ertegun, Rudi Blesh, Dizzy, Mr. and Mrs. Jorge Guinle, and Bird. Standing in rear is Sahib Shihab.

August Blume

August Blume first heard Parker at a place called Billy Berg's in Los Angeles around Christmas of 1945. He was told about this place by two Negro fellows who worked in the Navy with him. Negroes were not allowed in this night club at that time, so out of principle, August did not sit out in front, but dug Parker from the kitchen where a bunch of Negro fans were copping sound. Attendance out front was very poor. Blume kept a scrap book, collected all the original Guild, Savoy, and Dial records, and haunted back-stage from the Comedy Club in Baltimore (Blume's home) to the Apollo Theatre in New York. August is presently a Radio and TV relations representative for RCA Victor.

There was this musician's girl who had a bad case for Bird's music. She left her fiancé to follow Charlie. But the story had a funny ending. The musician went out looking for the girl and found her registered in the same hotel as Parker. She had asked for and managed to get a room right next door to Bird. She had put a chair against the wall, and she would sit there, her ear glued to the plaster, listening to Bird's incessant practicing. Her boy friend took another chair and joined her, the both of them holding hands and listening through the wall.

And about careful listening: the dearth of dancing has been attributed to the undanceable quality of modern jazz—rather, it is the attention-drawing brilliance of the music that precludes dancing. Some 1,500 Negro Shriners in Baltimore decided to run a dance. They hired two groups: one led by Lester "Pres" Young, containing such powerful side men as Jessie Drakes and Roy Haynes; and the other led by Yardbird, aided and abetted by a "Murderer's Row" consisting of Al Haig, Kenny Dorham, Tommy Potter, and Max Roach. After ten minutes of music, I looked over the floor and out of 1,500 people only six couples were dancing; the others stood rooted to the floor. The dance had turned into a concert. As for exercise—why, I lost fifteen pounds that night from the sheer excitement.

I was struck by the presentation at the Apollo Theater in 1947. There was a big banner proclaiming Buddy Johnson and his Band, and, in little letters,

Charlie Parker's Quintet. The Apollo Theatre in Harlem really gave you your money's worth. I saw two African movies, with people running around in headdresses, and then came the live show. On a rolling stage, the resplendent Buddy Johnson Band emerged. When they finished, the curtain came down, and you could hear the clatter and noise of backstage changing. I was eagerly awaiting Bird and his group. The curtain rose, but the stage was bare. Then the guys came out pushing their instruments before them like prop men. Duke Jordan rolling out the piano, Max Roach with his drums on a little platform with wheels, Tommy Potter dragging his bass, Miles Davis shuffling out, and then Bird with his horn. Yard simply walked over to the microphone, announced the number, tapped his foot three times, and detonated a musical powder keg.

Did you know that Bird once sang vocals in the Club Tia Juana in Baltimore? He was good; his voice was not the greatest, but he swung. I worshipped the guy, because a man like him comes along once in ten lifetimes. Sure he did crazy things, like once in Chicago he got himself and his men fired by the manager and consequently stranded without loot, because he defecated in the night club's telephone booth. I guess the only thing he never did was invent an A-bomb.

Teddy Blume

I say there are only two people who were ever in Bird, really close to him. That was Walter Bishop, the pianist, and myself. My four years as Parker's manager were four of the most tumultuous years a human being ever spent. Parker was like a disease with me. He nearly drove me nuts, scared my wife half to death with calls at all hours of the night. Once he threatened me with a gun, and then a minute later, he was shaking his head in a sweat and daze saying, "My best friend. What am I doing?"

We did so many things together. I used to play the violin for him late at night. It soothed him. He loved the violin. I loved Charlie Parker, I'd forgive him anything. The only way I got free was, he died.

If I had time, I would show you. I would write a book. The story has to take place in Kansas City. The corruption—open speak-easies, open whorehouses. I would show how he tried to fight it. I would show how he tried to fight dope. How he longed with all his heart and soul to kick his own habit. He used to do a lot of broadcasting. He would discuss "the rage" [drug habit], how it was affecting youth:

"Any musician who says he is playing better either on tea, the needle, or when he is juiced is a plain, straight liar. When I get too much to drink, I can't even finger well, let alone play decent ideas. And in the days when I was on the stuff, I may have *thought* I was playing better, but listening to some of the records now, I know I wasn't. Some of these smart kids who think you have to be completely knocked out to make a good horn man are just plain crazy. It isn't true, I know, believe me. Because the time came when I didn't know what hit me—I was a victim of circumstances. High school kids don't know any better. That way you can miss the most important years of your life, the years of possible creation."

Nobody is cured. All our muscles have a natural elasticity. When you take in some kind of sedative, it relaxes all the nerves. It is so relaxed, it is unnaturally relaxed. Now when that wears off, everything tenses unnaturally. I think Bird was worse with drink than with dope. He'd say, whenever I'd catch him breaking a resolve, he knew was physically impossible, "Man, I don't have to tell you; you know what's happening." Sometimes you hear of prison and hospital guards making money selling narcotics to prisoners, and you feel hate for them. But there is another side which is the sight of a fellow human being in terrible agony and wanting to relieve him. People without drugs when they need it are people in hell. They want relief or they want to die. They will beg you to kill them. Bird tried to break the habit, but he would fall apart when he did. He said of the pushers, "They're the lowest scum." The pushers would take whatever Bird had in his pocket, eight or eight hundred dollars.

In Europe, it was even worse. He had more hashish and all the heroin he wanted. The pushers were everywhere. I tried to shoo them away, tried to get them to leave him alone. Bird loved movies, so I'd stick him in a movie. The minute he walked out of the theatre, they would spot him.

A couple of times the cops picked him up on suspicion of carrying the stuff on him. He knew all the cops personally—the detectives, too—by name. They let me be present at a search. They strip Bird clean, two guys holds his arms. They check him over with a magnifying glass. They put some instrument up his rectum. They look between his toes for the stuff. One cop showed me his arm through the glass. It was dotted with needle marks. They let him go. The law says you have to catch a man with the goods.

I sweated it out with him when he took cures, and I also gave him needles in the morning when his pain became unbearable. As I said before, I'd put him in the movies. His life seemed to revolve around four things: music, junk, sex, and movies. He'd come out, be spotted, a call would be made, and he got a supply. One big gangster who liked him very much tried to talk him out of the habit. Night club managers used to be worried about hiring him. Wherever Bird went there was a bad element, unless it was at a place where you needed money to get in, like Birdland; and even Birdland had its share of annoyance.

Bird was about fifteen or sixteen when he was put on this bad kick by some older musicians who told him if he wanted to play better, this was the stuff to take. Poor young kid, how was he to know the consequences! Bird's mind was of such a keenness that anything he did he did creatively. He was inventive about drugs. He devised all sorts of ways of taking drugs. He'd sniff up little pellets through a straw into his nostrils or, if he didn't have a straw, he used a crisp dollar bill. Some say he invented the bent spoon routine.

His speech always contained strong imagery and directness of thought. He was too bright for his own good. Bird was very angry when he saw that piece in *Confidential* about himself and his tie-up with narcotics. He wrote the author a letter, and he wanted to institute a lawsuit, but I advised him against it, because it was all true.

Kansas City is something like New Orleans. Kansas City is the home of jazz as New Orleans is of Dixieland. When he was a kid, fourteen years old, he used to go to speak-easies. He'd never play, just listen. He used to play with the band in the alley—that is the band would be inside and Bird, who was not allowed in because of age, would be outside with his ear to the wall fingering his instrument and playing. This is the way he would practice. That's how he got his name—they always found him in the yard, and so they called him Yardbird. Sometimes they would find him asleep in the alley, he was so tired. Jay McShann picked him up when he was sixteen or seventeen.

I first met Bird when he played a job with him. I was the leader of the string section when the Bird with Strings bit was dreamed up in 1950. Shortly after that I became his manager. I went on tour with Bird all over the country. I got to know Bird's drawing strength in various cities by checking record sales. He'd set up disc jockey interviews and make the best percentage deals with ballroom owners. I used to take care of all of his money. I always made sure I paid off most of his debts. I paid all his bills. I gave him reports of all his expenditures. He never looked at them.

One night Billy Shaw called me up with an offer of $1,250 to play in a town in Wisconsin. I asked Bird to decline in order to play Oakland, which he did. We made $8,800—the largest take any musician has ever made for one evening. I did this by renting a hall and advertising it myself, instead of taking an engagement.

Before one record date, Norman Granz says to me, "You are the only guy that can make sure he is here." He would be balling with a chick here at my place. I called him up and told him the buys were waiting. We had Miles, Diz, *et al.* "Make sure to bring the music."

He says, "You're always worrying. Be cool."

When he finally got there and I asked, "Where's the music?" he said, "Shucks, I forgot it." He handed out pencils and papers. He calls out the chords. So we sit there and wait. Then comes the greatest music I ever heard.

Sometimes later we were in one town and Bird does not show up for a D. J. interview. It was an important one. You know me. All of a sudden I am associated with Charlie Parker. I'm an expert on Bop. So this guy calls me up, and I bull my way through the interview. So he puts on records. "You recall this record?" he asks. I recognized the music, but as for the name of the tune I drew a blank. "For your information," he said, "that is called 'Bloomdido.'" I flipped. Bird had named the record he had made that afternoon after me.

Bird made thousands of records for anyone and everyone—anyone who would pay him. He didn't care. They knew he was a gold mine. The companies stole from one another. They taped dances, concerts, anything.

I'll never forget one of my first experiences with Bird. It was up at the Apollo Theatre in Harlem. I conducted the show, I was the first violinist, I was the personnel manager, I had all the contracts, I was the guy paying them. Saturday night the show closes, and I am in a little room in the back of the theatre. I gotta take out all the taxes. I got the debts to take care of. The guys in the band are banging on the door and yelling to get in. "Open up there, man! Give us our loot. Man, we can't wait! Come on, Teddy." I was tired from the job, and besides that, I was there two and one-half hours extra working on this payroll. Finally, they forced the door open. Bird was no help. He was out completely, sleeping through the whole riot. I took all the money and threw it on the floor in a rage. "Anybody wants to steal it—fight among yourselves." They came to their senses, backed out, and let me finish in peace. Later on Bird comes around. "Man where's the money?" "Bird, you have no money. Man, I am tired, Bird. Look, get lost." Bird would invariably draw on his salary during the week to the extent that he never had anything on pay day. One night I am walking home from the show and I'm carrying a zipper valise with my music in it and in my pockets is the entire payroll. I am walking down the street nonchalantly. Two kids come up to me and say, "Give us your money." They have a knife against me. "What money?"

"Look, man, we ain't fooling. What's in that brief case?"

"That's my music."

All of a sudden one of the kids says, "Ain't you Charlie Parker's manager?" I nodded. "Can we have your autograph?" I gave it to them, and they left. I could hardly talk.

I got a cab to take me all the way home to Brooklyn. My wife took one look at me and got scared. She ran for the liquor. When I told her what had happened, she must have recalled what Bird had said to her when I was about to embark on my career as business manager to the great man. He had said, "We are going to meet all kinds of people, but nothing is going to happen to Teddy."

She didn't know of the time a couple of hoods gave me my fare and told me to leave town, because I was becoming too much of a pest in interfering with their narcotic business. I had put in a complaint, and one of their men was searched. I took that plane. Bird did everything he could to protect me. And, if he knew of any threat to my person, he took steps. Several weeks after the near-mugging incident we were playing a dance spot in Harlem when who should saunter in but the kids who threatened me. They were all dressed up, and when they saw me, they acted like we were old friends. "You remember us," they said. "Sure," I replied, and we exchanged a few words.

"Do you think we can meet Bird?" they said. I told them that he was too busy but, perhaps, some other time. Bird came over to me and asked who I was talking to. I told him that it was the kids who accosted me on the street with a knife. Bird walked over to a phone booth, made a call. Those kids left the place, were met, and got their heads smacked around.

In Detroit, we were playing for one of the most powerful gangsters. The deal was that we were to get our money before the intermission for our protection. I walked in and asked for it. They said it wasn't ready yet. I said, "No money, no music." Someone put their hands on me. I said, "Don't use hoodlum tactics on me." I walked out. Now Bird and I had a signal. Whenever he saw me, he would play a passage from "The Hot Canary" (his personal theme song for me, because I was a violinist). If I smiled, he'd go on playing, knowing that everything was all right. If he saw me walk out, he'd put the horn down, stop playing, and follow me out. This time he went into the back room and said, "Well, Gentlemen, what seems to be holding up the works?"

"Sure, Bird, we were just counting the money."

Bird told them, "These people came here to see me; this gentleman is my representative. Don't make me have to come out here personally to collect."

This all happened at the Greystone Ballroom. The guy in charge later handed me ten dollars for being a nice guy and not telling Bird about his tactics. I put the ten dollars with the other money.

Once in St. Louis, a guy hired Bird just so that he could get out of the red. Bird solved his financial difficulties. He also laid his wife. On another engagement, the management was not so fortunate. A bonehead agent sold us to a club that wasn't a mixed place. It was in Liberty, a suburb of Pittsburgh. Nobody showed up all week. The owner became pretty nasty, and who could blame him. I didn't have the heart to ask him for all the money. The guy showed me the books. He was crying. I called that agent and gave him a piece of my mind. You are hurting this man, and you are hurting us. Bird was probably annoyed with the whole business. He made the guy put up the money. He didn't have to threaten the man. He just had to pick up the phone. I don't have to tell you what a feeling I had.

Bird never seemed to be able to hold on to money. He had been dreaming about a Cadillac, but he never could get the money together for it. "Let's make a checking account," I suggested. "You can't cash something without my name; I can't take it without your name."

He agreed. Within a short while, he had a big ten dollars in his account. All of a sudden, he got himself mixed up in a shooting in some town, and I got him on a plane heading for New York. He started drinking and, all of a sudden, began cursing me out.

"You dirty thief Jew bastard!" I am not getting upset, but the people around us are aghast at the language. I keep shushing him. "You can't throw me off the plane," he yells.

Finally, the plane lands. He is still yapping, "Where is my money? You stole my money!"

"I stole it," I admitted. "What are you going to do, put me in jail?" I used to play psychology with him. "I'll tell you what. I'll meet you at Billy Shaw's, and I'll show you a guy that can prove I stole it."

He was puzzled.

After leaving Shaw's, he said, "Where was the guy?"

I walked into a garage with him to see a friend who was standing next to a Cadillac. I was chatting with the guy, and Bird was looking at the car like a little boy at a shiny toy. The garage man said to him, "You can take it for a ride of you want. This is your car. This man," he said, pointing at me, "bought it for you." In the middle of the place, Bird picked me up and kissed me. I knew he would never have put the money together without my doing it. A couple of weeks later, he hocked it.

Very few people have been with Bird like I have. I was with him when he had a heart attack. He was put into a hospital and walked out of it and came back to my hotel room. He depended on me and trusted me. I always slept in an adjoining room to be close by. I always put his saxophone next to his bed when he slept. When he saw his horn by his bed, he knew I was there.

Let me tell you something very frankly. Here's how he lived. He never knew night from day. He ate only spasmodically. He had sex three or four times a day with three or four different women. He had more white women than you will ever have. He was a man who abused his body terribly. What the women saw in him, I don't know. He treated them like dirt. The girls chased after him. Sometimes one would follow him from state to state. I'd go to him and say, "There are a couple of chicks who want your autograph." He'd reply, "You pick the nicest one and let her meet me." They would call me in order to get a date with Parker. Usually the excuse was an interview for a school paper. It took me a long time to catch on. He always entertained them in my room, because it was dangerous for a white girl to be noticed going into a Negro man's room. So they would come to mine, and Charlie would come to my room. One girl came to him and said she was pregnant. He had to pay off this girl. I told him, "Can't you ever pick a girl over 18?" (This was an exaggeration by which I meant that his frequency of picking young girls brought him to the brink of trouble many times.) What underlies the whole thing was that Bird hated white people. He believed in the human race. After he'd had these women, he'd spit on them. He'd get as much as he could. To him, Chan, his wife, was not a white girl. Chan was different. The only person he cared about was Chan. He worshipped her, but it did not prevent him from dalliances with other women. I used to talk to him about women. "What do you gain carrying on like this?" He replied, "It's my way of showing the world that there's no such thing as white and black." And he'd make them suffer. There would be lines and droves of them. He did have a fatherly instinct. He drew a line.

I don't hold his sexual activities against him. I marvelled at the extent of his sexual powers. He's the kind of man women dreamed about sexually. Bird never stopped, never, never. I would look at him sleeping, and once I noticed him having an orgasm in his sleep. This guy was doing it in his sleep. One night we walk into a bar and there, seated on a stool and spilling over on all sides, is the biggest chick we ever saw. Bird says, "I wonder how many folds this gal has?" A guy comes over to us and says that he can fix it up if Charlie would like to meet her. He then went over to the woman and asked her, "How would you like to ball it up with the Bird?" The answer was yes. Bird said to me, "Man, I am going to have that tonight."

Later that evening she is in his room, and he makes me stay and watch. When she stripped, she revealed the biggest breasts you ever saw. After Bird got through with her, and she turned out to be the hottest thing, she said, "Bird, I will never forget you." And I said, "Bird, I will pay you for this education." His remark afterwards was, "How the hell did I ever do it?"

How the hell did he do a lot of things? How the hell did he create such magnificent music?

He never thought of himself as a genius. Ravel wrote to him, and Prokofieff wrote to him. They wanted to get some idea of how the hell he did it. Most people didn't understand him musically; they liked his speed.

His mother appreciated him from the first. She bought a two-family house just so he would have enough room to practice. I thought of so many things when I was there at the funeral services. Of a lot of the guys in the back, familiar faces who were his worst enemies. Of the man who got up and made a speech that had nothing to do with Parker. Of the undertaker who was going crazy with Charlie Parker's body—first move him there, then move him here. Of the television cameras taking pictures across the street.

I sat there by myself, tears coming out of my eyes, feeling holy, thinking of the last time I was together with him. It was on 10th Street. We both got stripped naked, and he took the saxophone out—he was so far gone I thought he was going to drop dead. He didn't know how sick he was—so hot if you could have taken his skin off he would have been happy. We were playing together naked. He would have killed me if I didn't go along with him in his whim.

I thought of the many other times I would play the violin for him or how we would both listen to Heifetz records. He liked Heifetz so much. He used to say of him, "He's the only man that screams. He's got the greatest beat." I thought of how many bills I had to pay in hotels for quilts and rugs that he burned, because he'd fall asleep with a cigarette in his fingers. I thought of the near escapes with the police and how he once had the nerve to toss me a syringe and tell me to get rid of it. I thought of all the I.O.U.'s that I had of his, enough to paper my house with. I thought of all these things, and if he were alive, I'd work with him again if he asked me.

Vince Bottari

Vince Bottari says, "My brother brought home a 78 rpm record entitled 'Hot House.' There was a solo by Parker on that disc that decided me on the alto. In 1954 I used to listen to him at the Open Door or hear him jam at the Montmartre (two Greenwich Village places that are no more)." Bottari was born in Brooklyn, New York, on March 29, 1934. For the past five years, he has studied with Lennie Tristano.

It started at the Open Door. I was walking around looking for a session. Nothing was happening in most of the places. So I decided to stop at the Door. When I got there, I saw a few friends of mine, and one friend told me that Bird was back from a stay in Bellevue after the death of his daughter Pree. As I was talking, Bird came out front and saw that I had my horn. So he asked me if he might play on it, and I very willingly said yes. They had some music going on there at the moment, and we decided to go to Arthur's, a little place across the street from the Nut Club on Seventh Avenue where musicians played for free. Arthur's great dream was to have musicians, who had a following, play for nothing. At the time, there was a piano player whose name was Jinx Jingles and a drummer on the scene named Al Levitt. So Bird started right in playing on my horn. Bird started playing the blues and must have played fifty choruses, each one thrilling to hear, especially coming out of my alto. He played for a good while afterwards, and then Jackie McLean who was also there played next. And then with Bird sitting right under the stand, I very nervously attempted to follow up what had just went before. I played a few tunes, and when I finished coming off the stand, I looked at Bird and he smiled and nodded, which made me feel pretty good. That ended our little session at that spot.

Having no place to go, five of us wound up uptown where a friend lived.

We were sort of clinging to Bird. But my friend wasn't at home, so we decided to go up to my drummer friend, Tom Wayburn's pad, up around 72nd Street and Riverside. We were in a bar having a few drinks when we decided this. Bird had been drinking and wasn't feeling too great. We thought about getting a cab and one of the fellows had been talking to a merchant mariner at the bar and invited him to join the crowd. This guy was willing to pay for the cab, so we were off. When we got there, Bird had fallen asleep in the cab, so we very gently tried to awaken him, and as we were doing this, the cab driver began nudging and pulling on Bird's leg trying to get him up. He got Bird awake but angry. So Bird jumped out of the cab and cursed out the driver, who seemed to be afraid to retaliate so Bird let it go at that. So we went down to this friend's pad which was a basement studio. He had a piano there and Jinx, being with us, thought we would play some. When we all got down there, Bird was still pretty groggy and sat down on the bed and started to fall asleep again. Now this sailor, who probably had drunk a lot, started annoying Bird, asking him to act a little lively. Bird told the cat to leave him alone, but this guy kept bothering Charlie. He kept poking him on the shoulder constantly. When Bird couldn't stand it anymore, he stood up to the guy who was a tremendously built fellow, much bigger than Bird, and then he spat off to the side of this bruiser, almost like a Westerner sending off a warning shot. With this, this big cat stepped back and took a swing at Bird, sending him backwards up against the window. Bird caught himself on the window sill, still holding on to his cigarette, with his lower lip slightly cracked and bleeding. The big guy then started motioning with his fists. The room was very small, so the rest of us sort of creeped out into the hallway. Before this cat could take another swing at Bird, Charlie lunged forward, pushed him out of the room, and slammed the door in his face. That left us all out in the hall with this belligerent son of a bitch. Wayburn started pleading with the cat not to start anything, because it was his pad and he didn't want to get thrown out, but this guy wouldn't listen. He started shouting to Bird who was on the other side of the door holding it closed. He was still waving his fists like a fighter and yelling, and calling Bird a phony, to come out and fight. He called Bird a "dirty black bastard." There was a few seconds of silence, and then like a bolt from the blue, the door swung open and Bird came out charging. He hit this fellow smack on the jaw with such ferocity that it sent him flying backwards through the door of the john in the hall, where he landed on his ass. This cat's eyes start to roll, and he passed out. At the start of the fight, one of the fellows had gone to call the cops, and they arrived just about then and broke it up. This guy had gotten up and was backing away, and Bird was still swinging at him. Charlie was cursing him out, calling him "you no-colored son of a bitch." The two cops sent this big cat on his way, and we all started going up the street, seeing that we probably wouldn't play there. When we got outside, one of the officers who was pretty hip asked Bird what had happened.

Charlie told him what the guy had called him. The cop just smiled at Bird and said, "So what?" as if to say that there are always those kind around, and Bird smiled back and looked pleased. With the whole thing over with, we walked down the street and stopped in at a Nedick's for coffee. Bird kept repeating that he was sorry it happened and felt bad about the whole incident.

Pietro Carbone

Pietro Carbone is the proprietor of one of the most unusual and anachronistic shops in Greenwich Village. Carbone is a master out of the Renaissance. He repairs and builds stringed instruments. In his shop, Charlie found a haven in hectic times.

Bird was extremely founded in the past. He had an instinctive sense of tradition, and he loved to hear some of the ancient music that was sometimes played in the shop. He realized that there were worlds beyond his music.

He felt that in 1946 he had gotten to the limit of expression on his instrument. He once said, cradling his horn in his arms, "There's too much in my head for this horn."

I knew him some fifteen years. In the early 1940's he played at a place in the Village called The Swing Rendezvous. I will never forget the rapt interest he took in the lutes, citterns, gourds, zithers, recorders and ancient drums which are strewn around the place or how quietly he'd sit in a corner of the shop with provolone cheese, olives, and wine, eating with great relish. Varese was his God. They finally met in my shop one day.

From the accounts that I've read of Paganini, of his stormy life, of his musical wizardry, how he was the hero of the balcony—I always felt that Bird was very much like him.

Teddy Charles

Born Theodore Charles Cohen, Teddy Charles plays vibes and composes. He hails from Massachusetts where he was born in 1928. He studied at Juilliard and has gigged with Benny Goodman, Chubby Jackson, Oscar Pettiford, and many other big-name musicians. Extremely active, he leads his own combo at night and is an A. and R. man for a record company by day.

We were up at the Prescott Hotel one night; Bird, myself, and another musician were sitting around gabbing. Bird was doing most of the talking, and he was on a metaphysical kick. Charlie, on certain occasions, could talk up a storm. This night, however, he was being a little tedious, "I always sit facing the East," he said. "The East is the source of all inspiration, and I get my inspiration from Mecca; therefore, I always sit facing the East." At this point the other fellow added his conversational gambit, "Stop bullshitting us, Bird." At the time Bird was sitting facing due southwest.

At another time we went down to a "wild" [swank] bar in Rockefeller Plaza. Bird sauntered in wearing his Bermuda shorts. He was not wearing a monocle, but he was affecting a British accent that had a ring of authenticity to it. He struck up a conversation with one of the patrons, telling tall stories in this accent, and ordering drinks. When the time comes to settle up, Bird says, "This chap here will take care of it." The fellow, slightly dazed, started to make some feeble objection, and a crease appeared in the bartender's forehead. Bird suddenly drops his accent completely and says, "I thought this m—— f—— was going to spring for the drinks," and damned if he doesn't carry it off by stalking out without paying.

Tutty Clarkin

One of the famous clubs around Kansas City in those days was Tutty's Mayfair, run by Tutty Clarkin. Tutty is recognized among the jazz musicians as a guy who's in the know about everybody and as the friend Bird could always count on. Tutty has retired from the night-club business and is now "custodian" of every

*stray animal and bird in the area
around his home at Lake Latowana.
I found him in his back yard bind-
ing the leg of a crippled duck. He
rapidly told me the following in a
sharp Midwestern twang:*

Charlie first worked at Tutty's Mayfair in 1937 for $2 a night when he
showed. He was one-half to two hours late every night. But you could tell he
was feeling/thinking. "Why are those cats playing when I haven't arrived
yet?" He always wore an old black slicker and an old black suede hat propped
low on his head, and he carried the sax under his arm.

He had an old sax, made in Paris in 1898, that was like nothing. It had
rubber bands and cellophane paper all over it, and the valves were always
sticking and the pads always leaking. The reeds didn't make any difference.
They were usually broken or chipped. He had to hold it sideways to make it
blow. He'd hold up the band hammering away at it in the kitchen with the
help of the cook. No food would appear, and I'd scream at Charlie to leave
the cook alone. He wore the cook out fixing that horn.

I figured if Bird was great with a broken-down horn, he'd be sensational
with a new one, so I threw his old sax into the snow and told him to meet me
in front of the music store the next day. He was there on time, and I bought
him a sax for $190. Bird cried and said, "Man, I'll never be late again." He
didn't show for two days. Then I went looking for him. I found him where
those cats hung out around 18th and Vine, but his new sax was in hock. I
always took him back. You could tell: if the sax wasn't under Charlie's arm,
it was in the pawn shop. He hocked it every week.

When I first knew Charlie, he was getting high on nutmeg. One day I ran
into the grocer who said, "Tutty, you sure must be making a lot of pies over
there with all the nutmeg your club is ordering." I knew something was wrong
and rushed back to the club to check up on the cats. I searched around, but
couldn't find any trace of the spice. Finally, I looked under the bandstand and
found the floor littered with empty cans of nutmeg. Later Charlie told me,
"Another sax player and I would chew spices and laugh at each other and
our heads would enlarge and shrink. And if we didn't play, there'd be no more
reed section."

From nutmeg Bird went to Benzedrine inhalers. He'd break them open and
soak them in wine. Then he smoked tea and finally got hooked on heroin. He
was the only man I knew who could drink with heroin. He'd come back late
from a fix for the second show and say to my wife, "Miss Leanor, I'm all put
out." A drummer called Little Phil was his dope connection. He's now in the
insane asylum in St. Jo. Dope infected his mind. Little Phil lived on the Paseo,
and after the fix Bird usually went into the Park with some friend, and they'd

blow and blow and blow through the night.

Bird slept many a time on a table in the club. He'd wake up at night. Once after three days of living this way I looked out the window and thought the ground was covered with snow. In fact the ground was covered by empty white Benzedrine inhalers.

The only way I could keep Charlie straight was to tell him his mother and half-brother were coming out. His mother watched him like a hawk. When Bird was sixteen he looked thirty-eight. He had the oldest-looking face I ever saw.

In the later days he would work for me for $30 a night. In 1953 he came out to the club one night in an open convertible with some white girl he'd picked up in town. We got word somehow that she was trying to frame him on a narcotics charge for the government. He only had time to play eight bars of "How High the Moon" when we motioned him off the bandstand and helped him to skip town. I got up and said, "The Bird goofed," and the audience understood (later the girl framed two other musicians).

If Bird ever got into trouble he'd call me from wherever he was. Every time he phoned he'd say at the end, "Tell Mama I'm all right."

Earl Coleman

Singer Earl Coleman recorded with Charlie Parker in 1946 for Ross Russell's Dial label. Russell had arranged to record Erroll Garner that day, and Parker arrived, with Coleman, as they were leaving for the studio. A three-way session was the result—Garner trios, Parker Quartets, and Coleman vocals with quartet accompaniment. Coleman is now back working in and around New York.

I first heard Bird in 1943 at the Chez Paree in Kansas City. He heard me sing sometime later and when Billy Eckstine left Earl Hines, Charlie suggested that I get in touch with Fatha Hines. I worked with the Jay McShann band and one night I met Earl Hines and subsequently did a stint with the band. I got a lot of assistance from Billy Eckstine; in fact I might say that in the music profession, Bird and B raised me.

It was over the objections of Ross Russell (owner and supervisor of Dial Records) that Charlie saw to it that I sang "Dark Shadows" and "This Is Always." I'll never forget how Charlie smiled when he heard the playback, and he said, "That's it." The record made in 1947 sold well and is still selling. He had made a promise to help me some months before when Howard McGhee and I visited him in Camarillo State Hospital some months before that record session.

Around that time, 1946-47 there was a place in Los Angeles on 27th and Central Ave. called Bird In The Basket. It was an eating place where Bird and the guys used to go to jam from twelve at night until. It was the spawning spot of a lot of great musical ideas. "Dark Shadows" and "The Chase" were conceived there.

"The Chase" is a bop classic by two tenor men: Dexter Gordon and the late Wardell Gray. Dexter and Wardell used to wash away Teddy Edwards then, cook on him every night. As for Bird, he would be playing there with a cigarette between his fingers while fingering just like his idol Prez Young did it. Well, no one could ever come near him musically. He loved Prez. "In K.C., Prez used to hand the 'charge' to me as he got off the stand," Charlie would reminisce. Bird was the greatest conversationalist I ever heard. He could discuss anything with anybody. It was frightening.

Junior Collins

Junior Collins was born in Pine Bluff, Arkansas, in 1922, but grew up in Shreveport. He started playing by ear and didn't know it was jazz. The first time he heard the word, he says, was when "a slattern in the park offered me some jazz for twenty-five cents." He came to New York in 1943 with the Glenn Miller band. He played with Benny Goodman in 1946. In 1947 he met Miles Davis and at his insistence Junior's French horn is heard on the now historic Davis date for Capitol Records called "Classics in Jazz."

My home was a kind of free and easy open house. This particular day in the winter of 1950, some fellow had come over with dirty movies, a screen, and a projector. It was amusing at first, but at the third showing, I got sort of drug with the whole business, and the guy left. Word had gotten around about the screening, and who should turn up fresh from his European tour but Bird, beret in hand. He had assumed a lot of French mannerisms in the spirit of fun. He asked for the hostess of the place, and when my wife appeared, he bowed and kissed her hand. He then inquired about the movies. I told him the man had taken his toys and left. He was put out and cut out.

It has always puzzled me how all of Bird's money dribbled away. People would be laying free fixes on him all the time so the drugs couldn't have kept him broke. He once, however, rolled up his sleeves and showed me his needle-marked arms, pointing first to one and saying, "This is my Cadillac," and then pointing to the other, "This is my home."

He would play certain tunes that no one would touch jazz-wise, and he gave them the solidity that seemed impossible, judging from the juke box renditions. Songs like "Slow Boat to China" and "Hey There."

How could we have let him walk the streets in 1954 and '55 without doing anything for him?

Al Cotton

I first used to hear a lot about Bird from Babs Gonsales. He always used to rave about Bird's sincerity as a man and artist. Once, around 1949, Bird was looking for a place to sleep; he had temporarily come upon bad times. Babs offered his pad, and Bird took him up on it. He also took Babs's clothes and put them in pawn. Babs searched for Charlie for three months, but Bird was evidently out of town or had found a good hiding place. Then, one day, they spotted each other down a street, but Bird must have seen him first, because he ran toward him waving the pawn ticket. They retrieved the clothes, and Bird gave Babs fifteen extra dollars for his trouble, and because he did not press charges.

I first met him when he played in Newark with a bunch of us. It was at a place called The Silver Saddle. They used to have Monday night all-star affairs. This was around 1950. That night was an inspiration I'll never forget. He was very kind to us all that night. Come to think of it, he was always almost exaggeratedly courteous to fans, except when they complimented him on his playing and he felt doubts about it. One evening, in the bar next to Birdland, a young fellow walks up and says, "Mr. Parker, you sounded wonderful tonight." "What?" Charlie answers. "This isn't my horn. The B sharp key isn't working; the reed is all chewed; how can you say that?" The kid is a little stung at this, but he bravely faced up to Bird and said, "What has a guy got to do to pay you a compliment?" This touched Parker, and he smiled and said, "Okay, man, okay, but this still isn't my horn; the B sharp key doesn't work; and the reed is all chewed up. But thanks."

Charlie had this to say about his attempted suicide with iodine after the Birdland firing incident: "I had to go to some extreme to get out of this financial mess I was in. They would fine me out of business; they could hang me legally. I could never pay all I owed, but, if I was judged insane at the time, I couldn't be held responsible. So I daubed a few drops of iodine on my lips and tongue, a little soap suds in my mouth, did a lot of play-acting, and I was committed as a mentally unadjusted person who could not be held responsible legally."

One of the things I remember him saying was, "Baby, don't never get on the bandstand with no differences on your mind. Keep the bandstand like it was a pulpit—clean. If you got any differences among you cats, leave them in the audience. When you come down, you can resume your differences."

Harvey Cropper

Harvey Cropper is a talented artist who now lives with his wife and son in Sweden. He studied at the Art Students League and also with a Buddhist priest for ten months in Japan. He was a close friend of Parker's and gave him art lessons.

Bird liked to play chess. He was a rather weak player, a little too impatient and restless for the concentration a good game requires. But he wouldn't play with weak opponents, so he always lost.

I asked him once about the way he disappointed people by not playing when he was scheduled. His reply was, "You're an artist; paint a picture for me right now." He never felt right about playing unless he was giving his best. His was not the role of an actor but rather of a playwright. The jazzman is more than a musician who plays someone's music; he is a composer. Someone showed Bird the picture of Dave Brubeck on the cover of *Time* and said, "You should have been on the cover instead, Bird." Charlie replied, "My watch doesn't work that well. I don't show up to all my gigs." He was and he liked everyone around him to be as honest with their art as possible.

He didn't like Norman Granz. He said of him, "He's made one million dollars, and he's on his way to two, yet he's the most frightened man in the world. He takes jazz musicians, and he removes them from others. He puts them in a box."

When he was fifteen, he came home once and found another man in his mother's bed. His parents had been separated for some time, but this did not prevent Charlie from bitterness at what he felt was gravely wrong. He cursed

his mother, threatened to run away from home, and, for a short while, mani-
fested hostility. One day his mother explained that, even though he saw her
just as a mother, she was still a woman, still a female, lonesome and desirous
of love and the feeling of being desired and wanted by a man. Charlie understood.

In art he liked Picasso and Rembrandt very much. Toulouse-Lautrec delighted him, and he was going to make a musical album of his impressions of
them.

He once became annoyed at someone who asked him what rhythm section
he was going to use on a certain engagement. (He probably didn't know; he
usually chose whoever was available at the last possible moment.) His reply
was, "What's the difference? The only reason I use a rhythm section is so
that *you* can hear me." Once I came to the door and he was standing there
horn in hand and he asked me to listen to something. He played without putting his mouth to the instrument, just fingering, the rhythm of the pads making
the music. He once said, "You and me might break up. I might lose all my
friends. But I always have this; this is mine," and he hugged and kissed his
horn.

At his first Paris concert, someone gave Bird a big red rose, and during the
performance, Charlie waved the flower, kissed it, and ate it, petals, stem, and
thorns.

Bird wanted musicians to have more power in the music industry. He
wanted them to have more control over records, personnel, radio, and other
areas.

At his daughter Pree's funeral, he had them play some music of Bartok.
He would say if you mentioned Bartok or Beethoven, "You mean *Mr.* Bartok
or you mean *Mr.* Beethoven." If you said that you heard a certain musician
he would say, "You heard a horn player."

I've never seen him really belligerent except once when he almost started a
fight in a pizza place because they were deliberately being rude to us. Why
they were nasty is odd, because Charlie ordered the biggest pizza imaginable.
It cost seven dollars and was enormous with slices of meat on it and slews
of mushrooms. Nothing happened except that Charlie had to eat the whole
thing himself, because it was nearly time to go to work for most of us and it
wasn't our idea of breakfast food.

He was extremely popular in the East Side neighborhood where he lived.
His credit was good everywhere around there. One of his friends was a blind
Polish man whose business was taking numbers. The numbers game was ideal
for him, because he could carry all the figures in his head and not be subject
to the professional hazard of writing them on slips of paper and being caught
with physical evidence. Charlie admired this fellow very much, and it was
understandable because all numbers men have good memories, but this guy

could take fifteen two-cent bets from a housewife and store it away with his others like Bird read a music score.

Bird wandered into Small's Paradise one night and went up front to talk to one of the musicians. Some of the people said, "Play, Bird," but Charlie didn't have his instrument with him so he just turned around and smiled to us, and then someone did what we all did spiritually at that moment. The fellow said, "Here, Bird," and he slid his alto across the floor like a beer across a bar. Bird picked it up and played long and clear.

Bird's personality was powerful, but he always wanted you to be you. He wanted the pressure of your appetites on him. Very few people did that. Maybe they were overawed.

Bird wanted you to be real. He was tired of being patronized. In a cab an idolatrous white musician was going on about what a shame it was that Bird did not get all the glory, money, credit, and gigs he should have because he was Negro. Bird answered him by saying, "I was in this European concentration camp, and there was this terrible smell of people, and the bodies were stacked high," and he went on a while about the horrors he witnessed which were perpetrated on the poor, helpless Jews. This particular musician was Jewish and Bird made up this fantasy in order to dish out some patronization to him. He, in fact, wanted to provoke him, to bring him out, to draw out fire.

Poverty and want angered him. He came into my room one night, and saw a fellow sleeping on the floor. He went over to him and slapped him hard in the face. The guy awoke surprised. Bird thrust a five-dollar bill in his hand and told him to go to a hotel.

One night he asked me how much money I had. I said five dollars. He told me that we didn't need any money. "Give me the cash, and I'll pool my money with yours." I gave it to him. He put down thirty-five cents and then picked it all up. We went over to the Bowery. Bird went over to the first derelict, pretending he was a detective. He suddenly punched the guy in the stomach, and, when the man clutched at his middle, Charlie thrust the $5.35 in his hands, and we left, completely broke. Bird stopped at a corner, turned to me, and said, "We've got a project—we're gonna get drunk and we're going to Brooklyn." We began at twelve o'clock at night. We panhandled from tramps, who are quite generous among their own. Bird won a considerable number of drinking bets at bars. We accomplished the first half of the project, but we never got to Brooklyn.

He was a charming recounter of fanciful stories that he would weave on occasion. This occasion was a hot summer's day, and he said how nice it would be to go swimming. I did not know how, and he said he would teach me. Then he said how we would go to Coney Island. "The place is very crowded with people so you have to swim out about ten miles. There you will find a school of dolphins who are sporting in the waves and who are very friendly. You just get on their backs and ride around. There is one who rolls on his other side and likes to be tickled under the chin. If you are tired, you just ask them to ride you into shore, and they will gladly deposit you on some isolated part of the beach so that no one will see that you were too weak to make it by yourself."

"There's such a thing as a dope fiend, a drug addict, and a user. A person who takes aspirin is a user. But there's such a thing as a dope fiend, and they should be killed, eliminated, done away with." A dope fiend was a fanatic without control; an addict was one whose body has been physically mastered by drugs—an unfortunate who is trapped medically; a user, and he considered himself a user, is one who, consciously and in full control, takes drugs from time to time.

With people that he was not particularly interested in, he would be very pleasant and say exactly what they wanted to hear. He'd go along with you on anything. The people he liked and cared about, he wrangled with and hurled thunderbolts at; he pecked and pecked at them to make them interact with him. But with the others—once someone asked him what he thought of Guy Lombardo, and he told them he was very good. I asked him later why he said that when I know what he thought of the music. He said, "What's the use of starting anything with people like that?" Those folks hearing their own tastes seconded by Charlie Parker were more than ever reinforced in their bad taste.

Bird took cabs everywhere, and he had a special thing going each time he entered one. He was very imperious but generous and would often take the cabman in to eat with him, letting the meter run. If the taximen were in any way hostile, Bird would figure out some way to beat them out of their fare.

I recalled an incident in a cab where Charlie had grabbed some money of mine earlier in the evening, during a jazz concert I was running. It was a bald swindle, and Harvey had witnessed it all, and I asked him how he accounted for Bird's high-handed manner that night. He said that I had said something to Charlie about taking care of his affairs better. I had cautioned him against being taken. He felt that I was the one who was more likely to be shorn, and he proved his point by gypping me that night.

Years ago I was speaking to Baby Lawrence, the phenomenal dancer, who said he was looking for a new form in music to dance to. The first time he heard Bird play, he came back and announced, "I found the form."

His middle name was Christopher, and he was a traveling saint but he did not care for the name and would never tell it to anyone.

He had favorite expressions. He would look at you intently, head jutting out and in a seriocomic way saying, "You know one thing?" or "Let me tell you one thing."

He was disappointed in his son Leon. He used to worry about him. He wanted to teach him to play, but Leon had found himself a lot of goof-off companions. There was a young boy of seventeen, an orphan that Bird took under his wing. He was called Junior Parker. He used to sing at Birdland.

This lad took to unsavory habits, and so he, too, failed Bird.

Once, between sets at the Open Door, a girl came up to him and said she would like to sleep with him. He gave her a sad little smile and said, "It can't rub off." Perfect strangers came up to him and offered him dope, but they did not do it out of any love for him. They were trying to get into a relationship, they wanted to brag, to say they got high with Bird. They thought it might rub off. Charlie usually would fluff them. With one particular disreputable-looking junkie, Charlie made like the fellow was a cop. "You see," Charlie said, "this fellow is trying to get me raided."

He loved women to shower him with affection, to hug him, and give him little kisses.

I gave him painting lessons, and he was an apt pupil. He never wanted me to use slang. I guess he felt it did not suit my personality. I loved him and I'm sure he felt warmly about me. He offered me $500 one night, if I would spend it all for fun and not a cent for paints and canvas. I refused. He argued, saying that we should go to the Stork Club. At the time, the way he was dressed, he'd have had difficulty getting into the Automat. Bird was my teacher.

Ernest Daniels

Ernest Daniels, who lives down the street from Mrs. Parker, is a drummer and vibraphonist who played with Parker during the early days in Kansas City.

I was some years older than Charlie but that doesn't make any difference with musicians. We became good friends and played together in Lawrence Keyes' band for a year and a half. When we first got to know each other he used to come by my window at twelve or one in the morning, throw a pebble against the window, and we'd go to jam sessions and play. I'm not positive about the years, but I'd say it was around 1934-35 that we were with Keyes. They were tough depression days.

The band was not union but managed because it was very popular and filled halls at a quarter per person, of which the band got a percentage. Local bands had much more support in those days. All of those men of Kansas City could have made it in other places around the United States, but most of them stayed because they could make livings on their local reputations. Today, with so few big Negro bands, what can a musician look forward to?

It was on a Thanksgiving day in 1936. There was three of us in a car; myself and George Wilkerson, a bass player, and Charlie sitting in the back with the drums and bass. I was driving and we were going one hundred and fifty miles into the Ozarks. We were eight miles from our destination when it happened. We were in a Chevrolet following this Buick driven by our boss Mr. Musser. Our speed was seventy or seventy-five miles an hour when we came to a sheet of ice in the road, the car swerved and turned over several times. I was thrown sixty feet from the car, hospitalized for thirty days for multiple bruises and a punctured lung. Bird broke a couple of ribs but was doctored at the spot and didn't need hospitalization. George Wilkerson died that night. The instruments were all tore up. Mr. Musser paid all the bills, bought me a new set of drums and an overcoat. I consider it a turning point in Bird's life because he got a little money out of a law suit we had against Mr. Musser, who made no objection to this suit, feeling his liability coverage would help us (he was a big man, reputed to practically own the town of Eldon, Missouri). With this money Charlie bought a new Selmer, whose action I hear is a little faster than the other kinds of altos—It gave him a lift.

One Halloween night, George E. Lee fronted Lawrence Keyes' band; Lee was a singer. This was at Paseo Hall on 15th and Paseo Street. Lee paid the down payment on our initiation fees and we went union. When you were making ten or twelve dollars a night, that was big money and that was non-union, but we were drawing big crowds. After we went union we didn't make that much.

Charlie had a very nice disposition, kind of happy-go-lucky. During the time they had the comic strip Popeye, Charlie used to imitate Popeye's deep toned voice, and he used to make that deep tone on his horn. They used to have jam sessions every night. Professor Buster Smith was one of his great inspirations.

In Earl Hines's band I hear Charlie walked off with that job. In two weeks he was playing the whole repertory and taking solos.

Some people get recognition, and they buy clothes and put on airs, get a big head, but, he was still Charlie. It didn't change him at all. Some people think, "I am fast now. I travel by plane; everything is fast now." He was just the opposite. He was a guy that never did grow up.

Playing music, there are always temptations. You meet a lot of people. There is always women that follow musicians. Musicians are friendly people. I have never used any type of dope. I haven't been around too many dope addicts. I wouldn't want to be around anyone who was. There are always exceptional people in the world. You don't know why they are. He was happy-go-lucky.

Curly Russell, bass; Bird; Arthur Taylor, drums; and Miles Davis.

Miles Davis

Born in Alton, Illinois, in 1926, Miles Davis was playing in an East St. Louis band at sixteen. His is the trumpet heard 'round the world. Parker saw the promise in him and always kept sending for him. The most recalcitrant, jazz-resistant person will be softened by the lyricism of Miles's horn.

I knew about Charlie Parker in St. Louis. I even played with him there, while I was still in high school. We always used to play like Diz and Charlie Parker. When we heard they were coming to town, my friend and I were the first people in the hall, me with a trumpet under my arm. Diz walked up to me and said, "Kid, do you have a union card?" I said, "Sure." So I sat in with the band that night. I couldn't read a thing from listening to Diz and Bird. Then the third trumpet man got sick. I knew the book, because I loved the music so much. I knew the third part by heart. I had to go to New York then.

In September, I was in New York City. A friend of mine was studying at Juilliard, so I decided to go there too. I spent my first week in New York and my first month's allowance looking for Charlie Parker.

I roomed with Charlie Parker for a year. I used to follow him around, down to 52nd Street, where he used to play. Then he used to get me to play. "Don't be afraid," he used to tell me. "Go ahead and play." Every night I'd write down chords I heard, on matchbook covers. Everybody helped me. Next day I'd play those chords all day in the practice room at Juilliard, instead of going to classes.

I used to play under him all the time. When Bird would play a melody, I'd play just under him and let him lead the note, swing the note. The only thing that I'd add would be a larger sound. I used to quit every night when I was playing with that guy. I'd say, "What do you need me for?" That man could swing a whole band. One of the record companies should have recorded him with a good, big band. Then you would have heard something!

Kenny Dorham

McKinley Howard Dorham played with Bird steadily from 1948 to 1950. He was always on tap for the next five years, and Parker called on him frequently. Once in a while, Kenny had to take jobs outside

music to support his family. He used
to be a prize fighter. Born in Fair-
field, Texas, in 1924, he was playing
piano at seven and trumpet in high
school. He sometimes switches to
tenor sax. He played in the Paris
Jazz Festival of 1949. A pioneer in
the Bop movement, he debuted on
Savoy Records in 1946 with a group
called the Bebop Boys.

I first joined Bird's group at the Royal Roost on Christmas Eve of 1948. I took Miles Davis' place. He recommended me for the spot. I'm from Texas, and I used to hear Bird playing down there with McShann. Bird was great about everything, except money sometimes. He had to have a lot of everything, and money was one of the things. I had drawn $20 in advance, and when the time came for me to receive the balance, he said, "You drew $100."

"What!" I said in amazement.

"What proof do you have that you didn't draw $100?"

It looked like we were going to fight all night. In this instance, I circumvented a long fight against Charlie's persuasiveness and strong debating technique. I picked up a blade and I said, "I am going to cut you with this razor blade, Bird." He paid me unbegrudgingly, turning the whole thing around with the statement: "I wanted to see where you was."

In 1949 Bird had all Paris at his feet. He was playing a concert and there is this part in "Night In Tunisia" where the break comes and Bird has to fill it in—well, he does, and the whole place cracks up. Bird, in all his life, never witnessed such enthusiasm. He just stood there with an expression of exuberance on his face. I said to him "Gone, Bird." (Kenny creates two words by saying "Gone" as "Go on"—"G'on, Bird.")

He was all music. He needed to have everything. When he played, he couldn't play long enough, and nothing stopped his playing. The more drugs he took, the more he went on playing. Bird was a high-starred person. Early in his career, he had a Cadillac and a chauffeur. He always had a crowd of people around him, and he gave different jobs to each one. "You go get my horn. You get me some pot. You do this. You do that." And they would jump. Some years later, he came to my house, and the picture was different. He was scuffling, and he wasn't liking it. "Here I am, Charlie Parker, and everybody is raving, and nothing is happening," he said. He had this big agent hassle. He wasn't getting the benefit of his tunes. He was disgusted with his agents. He had gotten to the point where he really was something, but he didn't have anything. He got a razor and started cutting himself across the arm. I was just walking around the room, and then I saw the blood. I guess he was just being dramatic, because the cuts weren't very deep.

The last gig I worked with Bird was the now historic Birdland engagement. It was a drag. Bird came in a little late, and trouble started right away. He had words with Oscar Goodstein, and when Oscar said go and and play, Bird, indicating Bud Powell who was in no fit mental condition to, answered, "What am I going to play when you give me this to play with?" Then Bud and Bird started to feud. Bud said, "What do you want to play, Daddy?" Bird said, "Let's play some 'Out of Nowhere.' "

Then Bud—that giant who was a shade below the caliber of Parker—asked Bird, who could play in any key and any time, "What key you want it, Daddy?" Bird snarled back, "S, Mother."

Very little playing went on that night. Mingus was fuming. He went up to the mike and said, "Ladies and Gentlemen, I am not responsible for what happens on the bandstand. This is not jazz." Bird kept telling Bud to stroll (just play mild accompaniment). Art Blakey had a strange look on his face. He acted like nothing was happening; he tried to cover up by being as show-manly as possible. Art and I did most of the playing.

Poor Bud, when he got his publicity, he was on his way down. In 1950 he started to deteriorate fast, and with all that, he can still play more than any-body else. He is still the protector of the faith, but in the 1940's, he was really taking care of business in the jazz department.

Ralph Douglas

Ralph Douglas was Charlie Parker's favorite cab driver. Douglas is a devoted fan and follower of modern jazz and has an especial fondness for modern musicians. Bird was crazy about taking cabs. He would get into a taxi and merely say, "Take me out of this neighbor-hood." He liked to drive himself, and owned cars on and off, but he took the sensible attitude that it was cheaper to ride in cabs. He was a well-known figure to cab drivers.

I dug him ever since I heard a record of his called "Cool Blues." After that I bought every record of his that came out. I used to park my cab in front of any place he'd be playing and, sure enough, he'd see me and he'd say, "Don't move, Baby, just wait." Bird used to call everybody "Baby." Sometimes he shortened it to "B." He'd say, "Don't move, B," and I just stayed there and waited even if it was three hours. I didn't take any fares, I'd just wait. He always straightened me. He was a very generous guy when he had it. Once I picked him up after he finished a gig at Birdland, and he said to me, "Let's just take a ride around town," and we rode around till 7:30 in the morning through the park, around midtown, up to Harlem, dropping in at all the spots. I remember we stopped at Minton's, and Bird bought me a taste.

When he was short he'd ask me for a couple of beans, and he always paid me back. Once, when I took him home, he said, "Come on in, man. I want you to dig my crib." He was living over on Avenue B at that time, and the neighborhood was poor but Bird's pad was decked out very nice. He excused himself for a minute, and the minute turned into a half hour. When I went to investigate I found he had fallen asleep on the toilet seat. I helped him to a couch. He had played hard that night, and he was very tired. I cut out.

One time I picked up Bird and Bob Garrity, the disc jockey who was broadcasting from Birdland at night and taught flying by day. Bird was juiced, and he wanted me to drive him to some stables at 65th Street between Columbus Avenue and Central Park West. These stables are open to public view. Bird got out of the cab, leaned over the partition, and talked to the horses. He told us to go home. We did, leaving him there talking to the animals.

One night I walked into the Downbeat Club. Bird was there just visiting. He got up and sat in for a few numbers. He was blowing at a terrific tempo. The drummer, who was not too experienced, could not keep up with it. Suddenly Bird stopped cold, turned to the musician, and said, "Man, get up." He espied Max Roach sitting there, signaled to him, and finished the set with Max.

Tommy Douglas

About clarinetist and alto saxophonist Tommy Douglas, Jo Jones said, "He was and still is one of the most proficient sax players alive today. Several jazz musicians came up around him, and I think Parker brushed with him somewhere along the line. Like Benny Carter or Don Redman were regarded in the East, Douglas was in Kansas City."

Charlie Parker was playing with me when I cut the band down to seven pieces. He was on alto. He was about fifteen then, and he was high then. I told him he was in for trouble, and I used to have to go and give a taxi driver ten and fifteen dollars to get his horn out of hock because he was high on that stuff. Finally he lost the horn and I got mad and wouldn't get it for him. The taxi driver soaked his horn and wouldn't tell him where he had it.

When I was blowing, he'd be sitting there smiling and tapping his foot, and I figured he was just high off that jive, but he was digging. I took a Boehm-system clarinet (I played both Boehm and Albert) over to him one day and he came back the next and played all the parts, he was that brilliant. It wasn't any time before he was playing all the execution, and it was that clarinet that started him soloing. (I started on Boehm because I was originally a classic musician and it took me nine years to learn the Albert system, the one all the New Orleans guys used. I had to learn because the other didn't swing—too much execution.)

I was playing almost the same way, way out. What caused me to do that was studying theory and harmony. I made all passing tones and added chords, what we call intricate chords today. I was doing all that then in 1935, and in order to get all that in, it called for a whole lot of execution. Naturally I couldn't just run notes and, I had to figure out a style, but nobody understood it.

One night I was working with three of my guys at a little place run by the guy who runs the American Cab Company now, and an old drunk asked if we could play "Stardust." Well that was one of my pet tunes, and I had a whole lot of chords I could work on. The piano player made the four bar introduction, and I made all kinds of intricate chords, parallels, everything. When I got through the old drunk guy comes up and says, "Here's a dollar. Now play "Stardust." That woke me up. Maybe I should play the melodies. So when somebody asks me to play "Stardust," although maybe I bend it a little, I always let them know what I'm playing.

This has always been a blues town, in fact the territory has always been a blues territory.

Parker gave up tone for execution. I try to keep as much tone as possible, but you have to cheat a little if you want to make it swing.

Billy Eckstine

Billy Eckstine was born William Clarence Eckstein in Pittsburgh on July 8, 1914. He billed himself "Xstine" until he finally came to be called "Mr. B." Eckstine formed his historic band in 1944; in 1947 the band broke up owing to lack of engagements and the recording ban. In 1951 he went out as a single and has been very successful since.

Let me tell you about Bird and how I first heard him play. The vogue before the war was to have a breakfast dance on one day of the week. Every club in Chicago, at some time or another, would have a breakfast dance, with the show going on at six-thirty in the morning.

One spot there, the 65 Club, had a breakfast dance one morning; and they had a little combo with King Kolax on trumpet; a kid named Goon Gardner, who would swing like mad, on alto; John Simmons on bass; and Kansas Fields, drums. It was more or less a jam show, for, after the show, all the musicians would blow in there. We were standing around one morning when a guy comes up that looks like he just got off a freight car, the raggedest guy you'd want to see at this moment. And he asks Goon, "Say, man, can I come up and blow your horn?"

Now Goon was always a kind of lazy cat. Anybody that wanted to get on the stand and blow, just as long as Goon could go to the bar and talk with the chicks, it was all right with him. So he said, "Yes, man, go ahead."

And this cat gets up there, and I'm telling you he blew the hell off that thing! It was Charlie Parker, just come in from Kansas City on a freight train. I guess Bird was no more than about eighteen then, but playing like you never heard—wailing alto then. And that was before he joined Jay McShann.

He blew so much until he upset everybody in the joint, and Goon took him home, gave him some clothes to put on, and got him a few gigs. Bird didn't have a horn, naturally, so Goon lent him a clarinet to go and make gigs on. According to what Goon told me, one day he looked for Bird, and Bird, the clarinet, and all was gone—back somewheres. After that, I didn't see Charlie for, I suppose three years, not until he came to New York with the McShann orchestra.

There used to be a joint in New York, a late spot up on 138th, called Clarke Monroe's Uptown House, where the guys all jammed. I had learned trumpet—fool around with it, you know—and used to go out and jam at Monroe's. Bird used to go down there and blow every night while he was with McShann at the Savoy, and he just played gorgeous. Now, by this time I was with Earl Hines. The war was on, and a lot of guys had to leave to go in the

Army. So we sold Earl the idea to go up and hear Charlie Parker. Charlie was playing alto, but Earl bought him a tenor, and we got Bird in the band then.

We had about three weeks off to shape this band up, and we were rehearsing every day at Nola's Studios and going up to Minton's at night to jam. Bird couldn't get used to this tenor and used to say, "Man, this thing is too big." He couldn't feel it.

One night Ben Webster walks in Minton's, and Charlie's up on the stand, and he's wailing the tenor. Ben had never heard Bird, you know, and says, "What the hell is that up there? Man, is that cat crazy?" And he goes up and snatches the horn out of Bird's hands, saying, "That horn ain't s'posed to sound that fast."

But that night Ben walked all over town telling everyone, "Man, I heard a guy—I swear he's going to make everybody crazy on tenor." The fact is, Bird never felt tenor, never liked it. But he was playing like mad on the damn thing.

Now I'll tell you a funny thing about Bird when we were with Earl Hines. He used to miss as many shows as he would make. Half the time we couldn't find Bird. He'd be sitting up somewhere sleeping. So often he missed the first shows, and Earl used to fine him blind. You know, fine him every time he looked at him. Bird would miss the show; Earl would fine him.

We got on him, too, because we were more or less a clique. We told him, "When you don't show, man, it's a drag because the band don't sound right. You know, four reeds up there, and everything written for five." We kind of shamed him.

So one time we were working the Paradise Theatre in Detroit, and Bird says, "I ain't gonna miss no more. I'm going to stay in the theatre all night to make sure I'm here."

We answered, "Okay. That's your business. Just make the show, huh?"

Sure enough, we come to work the next morning; we get on the stand—no Bird. As usual, we think. So, he said he was going to make the show, and he didn't make it!

This is the gospel truth. We played the whole show, the curtains closed, and we're coming off the band cart, when all of a sudden we hear a noise. We look under the stand, and here comes Bird out from underneath. He had been under there asleep through the entire show!

Another thing happened at the Paradise. You see, Bird often used to take his shoes off while he was up on the stand and put his feet on top of his shoes. He wore those dark glasses all the time he was playing, and, sometimes, while the acts were on, he would nod and go off to sleep. This particular time, the act was over, and it was a band specialty now. So Bird was sitting there with his horn still in his mouth, doing the best of faking in the world for Earl's benefit. Earl used to swear he was awake. He was the only man I knew who could sleep with his jaws poke out to look like he was playing, see? So this day he sat up there, sound asleep, and it came time for his solo.

Scoops Carey, who sat next to him in the reed section, nudged him and said, "Hey, Bird. Wake up. You're on." And Bird ran right out to the mike in stockinged feet; just jumped up and forgot his shoes and ran out front and started wailing.

That first band I had—that was a pretty fabulous bunch of guys. About nine of them came over from the Hines band. First I got Diz for MD [musical director], then tried to get most of the other guys that left Earl. Bird, meanwhile, had been working with Andy Kirk and Noble Sissle, but by that time was back in Chicago. I called Bird from New York and asked if he wanted to come in with me. And Bird had all the eyes in the world to come in the band.

We came back into New York to rehearse, and we were all buddies—like I told you before—we were the clique. We knew the style of the music we wished to play. We wanted another alto player, and it was Bird's idea to send for a kid called Robert Williams—Junior Williams out of Kansas City, who had played alongside Parker with Jay McShann. So, when we got him, we needed a baritone player, Leo Parker (no relation to Bird), who had been playing alto up to this moment; but I went downtown and signed for a baritone, for Leo, and put him on it. At that time Art Blakey was with Fletcher Henderson. Art left Fletcher and joined me at the Club Plantation in St. Louis.

That is where we really whipped the band together—in St. Louis. We used to rehearse all day, every day, then work at night.

Art Farmer

Art Farmer has become known to a wider public during the last five years, but young musicians from the West Coast are likely to say, "The first modern jazz we heard was from Dizzy's group, Howard McGhee, Charlie Parker, and Art Farmer." Farmer moved to Los Angeles from Phoenix when he was in his last year of high school, and he often went to Billy Berg's, where Gillespie and Parker were playing, before the management discovered that he was under age. Before forming the Jazztet in 1959 with Benny Golson, he worked with Gerry Mulligan, Horace Silver, Lionel Hampton, Wardell Grey, Teddy Edwards, Benny Carter, Jay McShann, and Gerald Wilson, among others, and during his years in New York, he got almost never-ending phone calls from a&r men and contractors who wanted a trumpeter who could sight-read tough scores, play first rate jazz solos, and make time.

In 1946 I was in California. Bird had left Dizzy or vice versa. Bird used to go to a place on Central Avenue in Los Angeles called Lovejoy's to play, an after hours place. One night him and me walk into the place, and there's no one there to play with except a guy who is playing piano. This fellow is not very good. He plays like the guys who played in the silent movie days. I figured Bird would be drug and wouldn't want to play with anyone like this guy, but Charlie took out his horn and played like everything was normal. Walking home I asked Bird if he was terribly put out by what had happened and he said, "Well when you're trying to do something, you try at every opportunity to get with whoever it is, and you never let yourself be drug by your surroundings."

That same year Bird had a group consisting of Miles Davis on trumpet; my brother Addison on bass; Joe Albany, piano; and Chuck Thompson, drums. They played at a place called the Finale Club in a section of L.A. called Little Tokyo. Some chick who was writing for a Negro newspaper came down one night to review the group. She was escorted by Dootsie Williams, a trumpet player who acted as a sort of musical consultant. It was their considered opinion that Bird was saying nothing. What's more, his manner was arrogant and he was not too approachable. He had with him, she wrote, a little black, wispy trumpeter who had better technique than Bird. The bass player, she graciously said, had an indefatigable arm. But Bird just played flurries of notes without any content.

I showed the paper to Bird not knowing what to expect, perhaps great indignation. He just gave a bitter little grin and said, "She's probably all right, but the wrong people got to her first."

And then he said of Gillespie, who had left the West Coast, a musical battleground where bop was coming in for censure, "Diz got away while the getting was good, and I'm catching everything."

Warren Fitzgerald

Warren Fitzgerald was born in Philadelphia, April 3, 1927. He started playing at the age of seventeen. Warren gained recognition on Philadelphia's Columbia Avenue, comparable to New York's 52nd Street. He played with Bird a couple of times at the 421 Club in Philadelphia.

Bird was a most generous person. I called for him once to go on a benefit date at a Naval hospital in Philly. I was driving a Nash Rambler and Bird, who loved cars, asked me if I'd let him take the wheel. I said yes, but felt a little embarrassed because the gas was low, in fact almost nil. Bird drove it a bit, pulled into a station, and bought the fuel. He had the tank filled to capacity. It's the kind of thing he'd do, nothing halfway. He played the benefit, and some guy taped it, which is *verboten*. Bird confiscated the tape but in a peaceful way. He asked to loan it to dub a copy. He just never returned the original.

Lon Flanigan, Jr.

Lon Flanigan lives in Geneva, New York. He is an amateur musician and is in the sauerkraut business. He is the kind of fan that drives a hundred miles in an evening to hear a couple of sets. Back from overseas, Lon first heard Bird at Billy Berg's in Hollywood in 1945. He was kind enough to answer a request I had put in the pages of Down Beat *in 1955, asking for info on Parker.*

I never knew Bird personally until 1952. Early that year, the Times Square Hotel in Rochester began a policy of importing well-known jazz musicians as singles, using a house rhythm section. Bird was brought in for a week in May. I arrived in the place shortly after nine the first night of Bird's engagement, and as I walked in the door, I heard a piano player playing the melody of "Honeysuckle Rose" in a style that could not be classified as jazz of any type by any stretch of the imagination. I thought for an instant it was a novelty record on the juke box, but I saw a disconsolate looking Bird on the band-

stand, and, after the piano had finished his chorus, Bird went into the riff
"Scrapple from the Apple." The drummer was about equal to the pianist.
They were probably two high officials of the Rochester local.

I was sitting at a table with a couple of musician friends, and, when the
painful first set was over, Bird came to the table. My friends knew Bird and
introduced me. We began to sympathize with his predicament. Bird's comment was, "I need a rhythm section like old people need soft shoes."

Luckily, this happened on a Tuesday night when most of the good local
musicians were not working. Enough of them were in the house to provide
Bird with a decent beat for the rest of the night. Bird took the manager of
the place aside, and, with some help from us, convinced him that his house
band did not play an appropriate style for a bebop musician. The next day,
Art Taylor and Walter Bishop arrived by plane to salvage the rest of the week.

I spent six consecutive nights in Rochester. Bird played the best jazz that
week I ever heard. Several of us musicians got to know him pretty well. I think
we were all a little surprised to discover what a "swell guy" he was. I always
had the notion that he was probably pretty weird and withdrawn. Nothing of
the sort. He impressed me as being a very warm and friendly person. I think
he enjoyed his week in Rochester. It must have been a relief to him to get away
from the characters who attached themselves to him in New York.

Bird made no secret of the fact that someone had put him on a bad kick
when he was fourteen years old. I got the impression that he wanted desperately to quit dope, but that he had resigned himself to the fact that he
couldn't do it. He spoke of developing a sound mind in a sound body, of
playing only a few more years and then going to Europe to study composition,
of settling down and becoming a good family man. But there was something
about the way he spoke of all this that made me think he knew damn well it
was all a dream. He just wasn't the self-denying type, and he knew it. One
night he invited me to have dinner with him at the hotel. We ordered roast
beef with mashed potatoes. Bird looked at me over a mountain of mashed
potatoes and said a doctor had warned him he had to take off weight, so he
was eschewing bread and butter. After we had finished the meal, Bird called
the waitress' attention to the fact that he had skipped the bread and butter.
"Fattening, you know." But, while she was right there, he might just as well
order another dinner, complete with potatoes. But no bread.

On Friday night he heard a Rochester bass player and me making plans
to play golf the following day. He asked if he could go along. Of course we
were overjoyed at the prospect. So the next day we went to a Rochester muni-
cipal course and played nine holes. Bird brought along a fifth of scotch and
some soda and ice, which he somehow managed to get into our caddy carts.
The bass man had a small bag of marijuana and a peculiar looking curved
pipe with a lid on it. This would probably pass as the strangest round of golf
on record. Despite some annoyance at finding it so difficult to hit that goddam

little ball straight, I think Bird enjoyed the afternoon in the air. This was apparently a relatively wholesome experience.

Bird had evidently just completed making a batch of records with strings. He was enthusiastic about the quality and quantity of the musicians who backed him on this date. I asked him where the musicians came from on such occasions. He said, "They're mostly cats off Koussevitzky's band."

I have often thought, since hearing him talk about his records, that maybe a genius fails to understand his own work. He seemed to think that his "strings" records were his best, when practically all his admirers, myself included, prefer nearly all his combo records to any heavily orchestrated stuff. He also mentioned meeting in Paris a world-renowned concert saxophone player whose name I can't remember. Bird was enormously impressed with this man's tone, attack, and intonation. Bird said he wished he could duplicate it. I guess it's presumptuous on my part to question his judgment on these matters, but I can't quite imagine Bird's jazz being expressed through a concert tone.

I saw Bird two or three more times after that. The circumstances were usually sad. The last time was in Charlie's Tavern in New York, where I had stopped off while waiting for Basin Street Club to open. I had come to New York to hear Parker and there Parker was, in the tavern, in no condition to make that gig. He recognized me and seemed a little ashamed. He offered to get his horn, go some place, and blow.

In the foreground, Bird and John Brown; in the background, Dave Burns.

Jimmy Forrest

This tenor man was born in St. Louis on January 24, 1920. He left high school and joined the band of Don Albert out of New Orleans. He played on the river boats in the bands of Fate Marable and Dewey Jackson. He met Bird when they were both on the McShann band. He lived with him on and off for four years from 1939 to 1943. During the interview, he explained that musicians and show people live opposite lives from other people, because they have to live out of a suitcase. He then casually mentioned that he has five kids and a wife back in St. Louis. How did he do it, being on the road so much, I asked. He replied with a smile "I write home often." He is presently with the Harry "Sweets" Edison Quintet.

The Jay McShann band was delighted with Bird and his sound. Bird was so advanced for his times that it was a source of frustration to him. There was no one he could listen to. I never heard him practice; he just played. I had just bought four new shirts, and they were lying on my dresser. Bird comes in and looks at them and says, "These are sure nice shirts." I smiled, pleased that he approved of my taste. Then he says, "Which two are mine?" and he picks up two and leaves.

We used to broadcast from the Savoy Ballroom on Sunday afternoons. There was an arrangement by Skippy Hall on the tune "Cherokee," which featured Bird. . . . Bird was not on the bandstand, but nothing seemed to perturb Jay. He went on with the number anyway. Just before Bird's solo came, the band would interpolate "Clap Hands Here Comes Charlie," and, as we were playing this, in runs Parker. The radio announcer leans the microphone down to him, and Bird takes his solo from the floor.

He always used to say that if he died before the blind singer Al Hibbler, he wanted his eyes willed to him. When we played an engagement at the Howard Theatre in Washington D.C., the whole band was invited after the show to be guests of a night club called the Crystal Cavern. They also invited the show girls. Bird got the prettiest one. He didn't say a word to her, just looked at her.

Ten years later he went out as a single. When he played St. Louis at a place called The Glass Bar, he asked to have my group back him. I wrote a tune called "Night Train." "Play your song," he said. We went into it, and Charlie played the hell out of it. When it came my turn to do a solo, I didn't. I said, "What is there left to play after you're through?" He said, "That's one of the nicest things that's been said to me."

The Glass Bar gave him so much money and so much to his management office. He was overdrawn but wanted money. In the office of the place was a beautiful large desk with an ornate glass top. The manager and he were on opposite sides of the desk. Bird had put through a call to New York. He was saying, "Tell this nitwit to give me some money." He moved to hand the receiver to the man but dropped it on the glass top just before the manager could grasp it. The glass top shattered.

Dizzy Gillespie

John Birks (Dizzy) Gillespie, whom Charlie Parker once called "the other half of my heart beat," was one of the pioneers of modern jazz. From 1942 to 1946, he and Parker worked together in close collaboration, first in big bands led by Earl Hines and Billy Eckstine and later in small groups which they co-led. After 1946, Dizzy went on to lead the first big band in modern jazz; more recently, he has been working with a small group built around his trumpet playing, his vocals, and his talents as a comedian and showman.

In 1945, Dizzy Gillespie was booked into Billy Berg's club in Hollywood, and he went to the Coast with a sextet—Parker, Milt Jackson and Al Haig were with him. The audience reaction varied from apathy to hostility, and Parker became upset and unstable. He failed to get to work so often that Gillespie was asked to hire Lucky Thompson as a standby. When the job was over, Gillespie returned to New York while Parker stayed in California. Gillespie tells about their parting here.

We were always friends. Sometimes I would beat his brains out in chess, but there was never any real ill feeling between us. Whenever we met we used to kiss on the mouth. People want to believe there was animosity. The press likes it; it makes good copy.

They wanted to know why I left him in California. I didn't. I gave him his fare and he spent it and stayed on. People would say to me, "Bird invented bebop," and I would answer, "He did." Then they would say "Where do you come in?" Even my wife Lorraine always says, "Bird plays more coherently than you do."

During the war years when apartments were scarce, as they still are, my wife and I found a place which was comfortable. In order to avoid any complaints about noise, I did all my practicing in a studio and refrained from any trumpet cadenzas in the evening. Three in the morning the doorbell rang, and I opened it as far as the latch chain permitted. There was Bird, horn in hand, and he says, "Let me in, Diz, I've got it; you must hear this thing I've worked out." I had been putting down Bird's solos on paper, which is something Bird never had the patience for himself. "Not now," I said. "Later, man, tomorrow." "No," Bird cried. "I won't remember it tomorrow; it's in my head now; let me in please." From the other room, my wife yelled, "Throw him out," and I obediently slammed the door in Bird's face. Parker then took his horn to his mouth and played the tune in the hallway. I grabbed pencil and paper and took it down from the other side of the door.

The last time I saw him was shortly before I left for Europe. We were sitting in Basin Street. He spoke about us getting together again. He said it in a way that implied ". . . before it's too late." Unfortunately, it was already too late. If it had happened, it would have been the greatest.

Left to right: Buddy Rich, drums; Ray Brown, bass; Bird; Mitch Miller, oboe; Max Hollander and Milton Lomask, violins. The occasion is a "Bird With Strings" recording date.

Tony Graye

In 1952 and '53 I had a few encounters with Charlie. In Charlie's tavern I asked him if I could buy him a beer. He said, "No, but I'll have a whiskey," and, before I could plead poverty, he went and ordered a Seven and Seven. I slunk away to a table. The owner said to Bird, "Are you going to pay for this?" Charlie came over to me and said, "Gee, can you get me out of this?" I paid the tab. I then suggested an inexpensive cultural activity. "Let's go to the Museum of Modern Art." Bird took it under consideration a moment and replied, "No, I'd rather get high."

I guess it was pretty nervy on my part, but I'd always go around with my tenor sax and ask to sit in with the big boys. A powerful rhythm section thrilled me. Bird was the kindest of the Titans. Believe me, I took a lot of guff at times. Jazz is the survival of the fittest, and it's one profession where being white is not an advantage. The number of ways I've been "put on" is numerous. A leader would consent, ask me the key and tempo that I'd prefer, and then call another set of conditions to rattle me or he would ask me a tune I know and then he'd play a different one with a special arrangement. One time one of Bird's all-stars said a flat no. When I told him that it was okay with Yardbird, he said all right, but would I just wait till they played a few tunes first. I was pleased with this, but I didn't know they played one tune for twenty minutes, and a set consisted of two tunes. He pulled this thing on me the second set. The third time around, I went to Charlie, and, at his insistence, I blew a few choruses.

I was always a devoted follower. Bird was featured in the stage show at the Loew's Valencia. I met him backstage after he executed one of his breathlessly fast solos, and I said to him, "I don't know what they're paying you, but I hope it's a dollar a note." He invited me once to be his guest at the Band Box, where he was doing a spot with the Duke Ellington band—and spot it was!— because, as he complained, he only did one number in a two-hour show. He was ready to give more for the $150 a weekend he was receiving. He took out his frustration on a big plate of spare ribs, and between mouthfuls he said, "After this, we'll go out and eat a good meal."

He was listed as being on the faculty of the Hartnett Music School. I went there numerous times but never found his class. I was told he was seen there on occasions, but I guess it was just to pick up his professorial pay.

Above:
Parker with Tony Graye.
Below:
Bird and Diz.

Elliot Grennard

Elliot Grennard, an author, was present on July 29, 1946 at a recording date that Parker was doing for Ross Russell of Dial Records. He wrote a short story based on the incidents around this session. It was entitled "Sparrow's Last Jump," and it appeared in Harper's Magazine, *May 1947. The story was reprinted several times. It can also be found in Ralph Gleason's anthology* Jam Session.

He couldn't get started on anything. They did two tunes, "Bebop" and "Lover Man." He couldn't tune up. He could just fit the mouthpiece. "Oh Christ," Russell said, "I've just lost a thousand bucks tonight." He kept recording the three other guys without Parker in the hopes of salvaging something out of the session. Parker curled up and took a nap. The two tunes he got out of him "Bebop" and "Lover Man" seemed like a complete waste. He was staring into space. He had a tic. After the issuance of the story, "Sparrow's Last Jump," Ross Russell decided to issue the side. Parker never spoke to him after that, except about money.

Right after the record date, Bird went to his hotel and set fire to his room. He was then sent to Camarillo. His condition must have been brought on by lack of drugs rather than any derangement, because when the doctor gave him a shot of morphine to quiet him he was his old self again.

Gigi Gryce

Alto saxophonist and composer-arranger Gigi Gryce currently seems to contribute arrangements to almost half of those New York jazz record dates which use any arrangements. He has studied music both at the Boston Conservatory and with Arthur Honeggar in Paris on a Fulbright scholarship. He wrote lines for the books of various jazz groups for several years, but it was only after a European tour with Lionel Hampton in 1953 (Art Farmer was also in that band) that he became known to the jazz club circuit as an instrumentalist as well as a composer.

I first heard about Bird in 1944. There was a guy from Chicago in the Earl Hines band who played alto. His name was Andrew Gardner but he had a nickname—Goon. He told me about Bird; he used to rave about him. Bird was playing tenor at the time. Goon and Bird played in identical styles. They traded ideas and had tremendous admiration for each other. They had played together in Chicago several years previous. The incident is related in *Hear Me Talkin' to Ya* of the time that Bird wandered into town and into this place dressed like a tramp, unknown, just off a train he had ridden hobo style, and asked Goon if he could borrow his horn and blow a few tunes. Gardner let him, and every one was gassed. Goon used to call him Yardbird, because he was such a relaxed cat. Charlie would play with his shoes off (his feet always troubled him). He was always a very carefree person. Guys in the bands always gave people nicknames which corresponded to looks, habits, or idiosyncrasies. I don't know if Goon hung that handle on Parker, but I do know that he could have, because Gardner was a quick and creative person with a facile mind. He dubbed me Bumblebee, because I used to wear shades over my eyeglasses, and the combination of my large eyes and the shades brought this picture to his mind.

When I met Bird personally in 1946 and mentioned Goon as a reference, we became good friends. He was a frequent visitor to my place in Boston, where I was studying at the Boston Conservatory of Music. I knew him as a gentleman, a scholar, a person aware of everything around him. He was generous to an extreme. I wasn't eating too steady in those days, and, whenever Charlie came around, I knew I could stoke up and be ahead a little. Not only me, but he would treat large parties of friends, paying checks up to a hundred dollars.

I was puzzled by some of the not too kind stories circulated about him. If I was as great as he was and had to put up with what he did (such as only getting to play engagements infrequently) I probably would do twice the evil things it was rumored that he did.

We all have bad habits. Bird liked whiskey. I eat ice cream excessively. I can't do without ice cream. I could name musicians who are fifty times worse than Bird, but because they were not in the limelight, nobody cared what they did. This was a part of Charlie's tragedy, that he wanted to be left alone and have a private life of his own. He was also surprised at the fact that he was copied and imitated so much. He was not angered by it; he was just perplexed that everyone wanted to play his way. However, he was angered, hurt, and at times terribly conscious-stricken when people emulated his bad habits.

I heard that, in his home town, Bird used to go to a music store and never have to buy sheet music. He had a photographic mind. He would merely look the piece over awhile and memorize it. He was a born genius. As time goes on, I find myself thinking him greater than before; you continually come across problems, and you realize how originally Bird solved them. He had his own way of fingering. He looked for the shortest way rather than the traditional method. The person with a mind closest to Parker's is perhaps Thelonious Monk.

Bird used to borrow my horn. I always got it back. After a job, he would slip me some money, saying, "Here's a taste, man. I'm sorry it's not more." I never heard him say a bad thing about a musician, that is, critically or professionally. We could be passing by a rock and roll place, and he would stop and listen, and maybe it would be something the piano player was doing which he liked. He'd say, "Man, do you hear that? It would be a gas to play with that guy." If the musician referred to had heard that, he would have passed out. Charlie always listened for the good; the trash he let just pass his ear.

I've still not gotten over his death. I want to do the best I can for the art that such a man dedicated his life to.

Sadik Hakim

Sadik Hakim's former name was Argonne Thornton, which he legally changed in 1947. Sadik was born in Duluth, Minnesota, in 1921. He left home in 1940 and worked around Peoria, Illinois. He was one of the first bop pianists. For two years he lived in the same house as Parker in New York. He played in the orchestras of James Moody from 1951 to 1954 and Buddy Tate from 1956 to 1958. Sadik says that he played the famous Savoy MG-12079 "KoKo" date. The liner notes of this album read: ". . . to confuse matters even more Bud was constantly disappearing with Miles, and finally Dizzy showed up to add to the melee. . . ." As a final irony, a pianist, by the name of Argonne Thornton, claims he played the date or at least part of it, although this is denied by Herman Lubinsky, who conducted the session."

They called me Dents at one time. Some people used to call me Dense; they were not friends. Bird would say, "Dents, do you like my music? Maybe it's not right. Do you really think that's it?" He used to practice in the bathroom. He would lock himself in there. He never played entire tunes, perhaps the first four bars. He just played scales and intervals or he would hold one note for a long time.

I lived with him for about two years in New York in 1945 and '46. I was a boarder in Doris' pad up at 411 Manhattan Avenue. He could do anything he put his mind to. He looked at my prayer book, and, in the next few days, he was able to recite some stanzas in Arabic. One night we were listening to a mystery program before we went on our respective gigs. The theme of the program must have caught his fancy, because, when I dropped over in between sets to hear him awhile, he saw me, and he interspersed the music of the mystery program into the fast verison of "I Got Rhythm" which they were doing.

Me and Bud Powell went to see him the first day he was in New York after his stay in Camarillo. He had gotten very fat out there, being off juice and drugs. Bird had a tune he had in his head and wanted us to hear. He started to hum it. He had a funny way of humming the rhythm of the time instead of the melody. Bud was concentrating hard. All of a sudden, he slapped Bird in the face, out of frustration I guess. Charlie took him by the shoulders, held him for a moment, and laughed it off. He did become a little impatient when Doris told him to stop humming. He gave her a little playful push which sent her through a door, taking a part of it with her, and into the hall on her rump.

In Chicago, in 1942, a thing happened to him which was sort of inevitable. He couldn't get jobs because he was too good. Guys didn't like him; they were scared. He went almost a year without work. He had difficulty in even sitting in on jam sessions.

> *In this February, 1959, piece in* Jazz Review, *Sadik Hakim fills us in with some more about recording with Bird:*

The only piano on the "mystery" recording date that produced "Billie's Bounce," "KoKo," "Now's The Time" and "Thriving From A Riff" was played by myself and Dizzy Gillespie. Bud Powell was not in the studio— or even in the city, but in Philadelphia—and Miles Davis did not play any piano.

Furthermore, all of the trumpet on the records was played by Miles except for the introduction and coda to "KoKo."

All anybody had to do to find this out was to ask me. I was living in the same apartment with Charlie Parker at that time (it was November, 1945). He got a telegram from Savoy in the morning telling him to get a group together and make a recording date. By 10:30 A.M., he had written the two new blues, "Now's The Time" and "Billie's Bounce" (actually it should be Billy's, it was dedicated to Billy Shaw), and for the other two numbers he planned to use a "head" of his those fellows were playing then which was called "Thriving From a Riff" on the record and later called "Anthropology," and finally "KoKo"—which is based on the chords of "Cherokee," of course.

He asked me if I wanted to play on the date. Naturally I was quite thrilled and honored to be working with him.

When we got to the studio, the men were Bird, Miles Davis, Curley Russell, Max Roach, and myself. I wasn't in the local union and neither was Bird then, and a record date needed at least four union men. Savoy said they couldn't use my name. I didn't argue about that or about being payed either—I was thrilled to be working with Bird.

Dizzy came in after we had been there for a bit, and he wanted to play piano on the two blues so we had it set.

When the whole date was recently collected on an L.P., there were a lot of takes and some warm-up tunes that we didn't even know were being re-corded. But I will say that it's all there in the order we played in it.

After three tries on "Billie's Bounce," with Dizzy on piano, Bird left to get a better horn and reed. When he came back, "Warmin' Up A Riff" (based on what we later did as "KoKo") was just that, a warm-up we didn't know was being taken down. Dizzy was on piano.

I played "Thriving From a Riff." "Meandering" which came out on the L.P. is another warm-up we didn't know was being recorded, and Dizzy was on piano. I don't know why it got cut off that way, except that it wasn't sup-posed to be part of the date in the first place.

"KoKo" presented a couple of snags. Miles didn't know the intro or ending so Dizzy took it. (It was the only trumpet he played on the date.) He and I, therefore, shared the piano, I was there when he was on trumpet, then he quickly sat down beside me and took over.

(By the way, when "KoKo" was released, the pianist was listed on the label as "Hen Gates." But later, Jimmy Foreman of Philadelphia, whose profes-sional name really was Hen Gates, played piano with Dizzy's band.)

I made records under my old name—some with Ben Webster on Hub and with "Lockjaw" Davis on Haven, Dexter Gordon on Savoy, and Lester Young on Aladdin. Before I came to New York, I worked in Chicago with Jessie Miller and an excellent drummer named Ike Day who died quite young. Ask Max Roach and Art Blakey about him sometime—I think they were in-fluenced by his work.

I can also tell you this. Miles Davis definitely thought a lot of Freddy Webster and wanted his tone and was influenced by his style. And by Lester Young.

Charlie Parker worked with Ben Webster's group—the one I was in—on the street for a while. He never could seem to get to work on time. He came in one night with his horn hidden under his overcoat and started blowing the minute he hit the front door and made it up to the stand before we knew where the sounds were coming from. Then there was the time when he played on Ben's tenor—and you know Ben uses such a hard, tough reed that most guys can't even get a sound out of it. Bird played it with ease.

Ben Webster and Parker.

Benny Harris

"Little Benny" Harris was born in New York City, in 1919. He started playing trumpet under Dizzy Gillespie's guidance in 1937, and Benny, in turn, was the first to persuade Dizzy to listen to Charlie Parker, by playing him a Parker solo on one of Jay McShann's records. Harris played in the Earl Hines band that included both Bird and Diz, composed several classic bop lines, including "Crazeology" and "Ornithology," and later played with Charlie Parker's small groups in the fifties.

When I was twelve, I joined the Daily Mirror News band. I started on French horn and the E flat mellophone. We were once Paul Whiteman's guests. I took up the trumpet when I was thirteen. I used to practice before school, after school, after the boys club, everyday for two years straight. I liked Earl Hines; but, as far as the trumpet, there was nobody I was really excited about. When I was fifteen, I joined a band that played through Pennsylvania. During the four bar rests, I would lean on my horn and watch the dancers, especially the girls: sometimes I'd forget to come in. I got sent home. The job was no great loss because this cat was hyping us.

Bobby Moore was the first trumpeter who impressed me. He must have impressed John Hammond, for he put him in the union and, then, in the Basie band. He got wound up with fast company, couldn't unwind, and finally was institutionalized.

One of my early friends was Monk. He took me on one of my first gigs. Some rich people gave an afternoon party, good food, and $16 apiece. Thelonious was always a most fabulous pianist and so sharp. Changed suits every day. He got part of his training, traveling with an Evangelist troupe when he was quite young. He was always great, and now he is coming somewhat into his own. Sometimes it is that way; everybody might be asleep on you except the ones that know but can't help you business-wise.

About the old-time jazz. I went down to New Orleans to all the places to hear. So this is the shit I've been reading about; well, someone's been bullshitting someone. Still a little skeptical of myself, I took one of the fine guys in our outfit, and I said to him, "I'm gonna take you to some historical spots." And his reaction was the same. I've read about the funeral marches, and I've seen them, and all I can say is that those cats were so putrid that if I had to be buried that way, I'd rather be cremated.

Charlie Parker first came to New York when he was about seventeen. He worked as a dishwasher because he didn't have a horn and couldn't get any work. He worked for John Williams, Mary Lou's husband, who owned a barbecue shack. I met him then, and again when he came to New York the second time.

I pulled on Dizzy's coat tails about this guy. I was always preaching Yard. I brought Scoops Carry to hear him and he was amazed. Dizzy at that time was always preaching Benny Carter till I got him to hear Bird.

I would say that I was very tight with Charlie. He lived at my house on the East Side with me and my family. He liked company. He has always been accepted everywhere. He had just as many white friends as colored. Everyone adored him. We used to discuss white musicians who played so much better than other white musicians and we wondered, why couldn't the rest play that well?

Once in Baltimore there was a rhythm section that was so bad no one wanted to play with them. They approached Bird, and he said, "I'll be glad to play," and he did. I asked him how he could play with such a pitiful trio, and he said, "All you got to do is make the wrong chords; don't try to play the right ones because there'll be three playing wrong and one playing right—be with them, play the wrong chords with them." If a guy would blame his instrument about a performance Bird would say, "A great musician never complains about his tools."

Everyone loved him so much, they spoiled him. I loved him but would never take any jive from him. I was pretty tough at the time anyway; I was a hood when I was a kid. I boxed professionally. I always stood up to him. If he refused to share something I would take it and threaten to destroy the whole thing. If he got wise, I'd challenge him and tell him I'd whip his ass, and he would back down—not out of cowardice but just out of his own good sense.

When he was leader, I'd always intercede for the fellows when they wanted to draw on their pay. A guy was permitted to draw up to sixty dollars advance, and Bird was a little reluctant about giving out much advance. He was not shy about taking. He was never hesitant about letting people, who love him, give. I asked him about this, and philosopher that he was, he said, "What good is love if you can't take?"

He wasn't the most reliable guy for making sets. One club owner in Philly hired him by the set. The fans were loyal and patient. If he didn't make the first, they would wait till the second or the third. Sometimes he would be at the bar drinking a double while the band was on the stand. The owner would be sore as hell. He would want to fire the band, but what could he do? The people were there. They came to see Bird, even if just to see him at the bar.

My lip went bad after a year in the Earl Hines band. They swung so hard and played so much. We rehearsed so much that every man knew what everyone else was doing, and, if you fluffed a note, someone else would play something that swung it into line.

The Earl Hines band had no cliques in it. Everyone hung out together. It was a real close knit organization. There was never any animosity. We used to get to Bird when it looked like Earl was going to fire him for goofing; fourteen of us ganged up on him in one room. We said, "You just don't want to straighten up, and the man has promised to fire you." And with that we would start punching him around the shoulders—not maliciously; just so he could feel it. "You're not gonna straighten up are you?" And he said, "I'm mad enough to kill someone." "Well if you can whip the fourteen of us, go ahead. If you want to fight, Bird, take a shot at someone and get your ass kicked in."

He behaved after that.

I got the same treatment myself when I started on a crazy kick of taking nembutals. Those yellow pills kept me real goofed. The guys pushed me against the wall and started nudging and poking and keeping me frustrated. You can't lash back, cause if you did, then they would really hit you. Their therapy worked too.

Musicians love things much quicker. People are attracted to each other. Bird loved Sonny Stitt, and Sonny loved Bird, though they had never met each other before. Bird was a very funny person. He would do things opposed to what he thought to keep you from knowing where he was at. He would always try not to show too much affection. I guess it was to keep from getting hurt. He would say to me, "C'mon, you are my guest," and I would reply. "Certainly, if you are spending the money."

When a young fellow goes on the road, he feels this way about sex. He says, "I won't be a trick." They feel it's a disgrace to be a trick (a customer for a prostitute; a whore turns so many tricks a night). An older, experienced cat will tell him, if he wants to cop, it's better to ball a professional than to ball around with a girl and then have her father come in and tell her she had better get home. The young one will say, "Be a trick? I won't be a trick for nothin' in life; I'm too hip to be a trick." The older cat will tell him, "I'd rather be a trick than clipped. Why should I romance this chick when I can go around the corner, spend five dollars, and be in my bed. I got to take her to a bar and spend this and that; and then when I hit on her, she says she's sick. Why should I spend $29 when I can spend $5 and then say, 'Well, you can get up and go now.' "

Girls like the lack of pretense in musicians. A fellow can come to town and call up a girl he hasn't seen in months and tell her he'll be up to see her after work, say five o'clock in the morning, and she'll say, "Call me up a half-hour before you're coming, to wake me up." Or, a chick says to a cat that plays music, "What's on your mind?" and he'll say, "Some work, Babe." [Intercourse]. If he wants work, he comes right out, without bullshitting.

At times, Bird really gave his wife Jerry a hard time. He would always be taking her wedding ring and pawning it or use it as bait to make chicks. In extreme cases, he would marry girls in strange towns to cop.

K.C. was a metropolis for drugs. I wish I knew the real answer to why people goof so I could help a lot of people. Part of it is that they all think they are much smarter than the next fellow. They think they can beat it even if nobody else has beaten it. Three out of five hundred actually beat it.

Taking drugs was not part of being in the in-group as far as getting jobs was concerned. No, strictly ability. If my own brother wasn't good, I wouldn't hire him. Drugs do tend to make a tightness—it is something in common.

I believe Bird destroyed himself. He was told he had acute peptic ulcers and wouldn't live unless he stopped drinking. I mentioned to him a few times about the way he would eat. One day we had been drinking quite a bit. We were sitting down talking. He said, "You know, the doctor says I'm going to die eventually. I don't believe him. I believe I can beat this." We talked about beating destiny.

You could never get him to do anything he did not want to do. You could get anything from him if he liked you. Once he asked me if he could borrow five dollars, and I said no, even though I had twenty on me; and he said why and I told him, "Because you don't intend to pay me back."

He fired me one day in Philadelphia and hired Clifford Brown. He had come in two hours late, and we played hard to cover for him. I had let some guys sit in and there was one on the stand who played awful. "Go up and get him off the stand right away," Bird said to me. And I answered, "Being you are the leader, you go up there and get him off the stand right away." Well, then he said, "You are through." That evening we had a few more words. "I shouldn't pay you," he said. We didn't speak to each other for weeks, but two months later I was back again, playing with the group. He had felt rather hurt about the incident.

Earl Hines

Earl Hines, the world-famous pianist and bandleader, was born in Duquesne, Pennsylvania, on December 28, 1905. The early records he made with Louis Armstrong are jazz classics. He is affectionately called "Fatha." In the 40's his band contained such great modernists as Diz, Benny Green, Wardell Gray, Bird, and vocalists Eckstine and Vaughan.

I don't remember exactly when Charlie Parker joined my band. I do know it was in the forties, because it was in wartime, when we needed a tenor man. One of my musicians used to go down Minton's quite a lot, and he wanted me to come down and listen to a saxophone player, and maybe he might fit the bill. But they said he plays alto. I said, "That's not goin' to help us much." He said, "But he plays tenor, too." That was Scoops Carry, our first alto man—he's very prominent now; he's a lawyer in Chicago. His word was the authority, because he actually knew what it was about when it came to reed men, so I went down one night. Incidentally, Basie was with me, and we sat back in the corner until the young fellow came up. Meantime, he'd been playing so much horn that I said, "Well, who's that man?" The guy said, "Well, that's the boy I wanted you to hear. That's Charlie Parker!"

Actually I had heard Charlie Parker in Detroit with a band out of K.C., Jay McShann's band, but he only had about a chorus and a half. That was at the Paradise Theater. He said to me, "Gee, I'd like to get in your organization sometime."

"Right at the time, things don't look too good."

"If you have an opening, I'd like you to give me an opportunity." I said, "Oh, first chance I have."

Well, that was the first time I heard him, and I never thought any more about it. It was months later when we needed this tenor man. So after hearing him, I talked with him a minute, and I said, "Do you play tenor?"

"Yeah!" he says.

So I went down and got him a tenor the next day.

Truthfully speaking, I never heard so much tenor horn in my life, I want to tell you. You know how the guy got all over that alto; you *know* that he was just as bad on tenor.

The remarkable thing about Charlie, he had such an advanced mind that when we rehearsed an arrangement that no one had seen before, we'd run it down once or twice, or whatever time we had to run it down, and we'd put it away. We decide to play it that night, everybody got the music but Charlie;

he's sittin over there on the end with his tenor. I'd say, "Look, Charlie, when you goin' to get the tune out?"

He says, "I know that."

"I mean that new number."

"I know it."

And sure enough, he knew the arrangement backwards. I never understood that guy had such a mind.

Charlie used to take his alto in the theater between shows—and have an exercise book, that's all he did—sit down; between he and Dizzy, they ran over these exercises in these books they're studying up. One day they'd have the trumpet book, and one day they'd have the alto book. They'd change around. And I think that was where actually Charlie got his particular style from, was from the different inversions and phrases in these exercises he had. They'd insert these passages that they would play in tunes that would come up. Whenever a chord would strike them, with the memories both of them had, why they'd just take one of these passages from one of these exercises and insert them in one of these tunes. And I think that is the reason for them to create the style that they got.

And they seemed to be in a little claque all to themselves. They got a kick out of themselves—not to set a style—they just played like that because they enjoyed it, and they continued to do it.

Well, I think by hitting prominent spots, and then playing in jam sessions as much as they did, I think is the cause of that style catching hold. And then all the musicians wanted to find out how fast they could get over that horn, listening to Charles. But you see, many of them made so many mistakes, because so many reed players didn't realize this was *music* he was playing! They thought it was just out of his mind, and whatever they did was all the same as Charlie. And if there's any mistake made, why they blamed it on the style they called bop. "Why that was bop!" But Charlie knew what he was playing, and when he made these flatted fifths and what have you, it was written in those exercises, and Charlie was playing actually what he remembered from those exercises. So many musicians make a mistake by thinking Charlie was picking it up out of the air, and I think that's one of the things that hurt so-called bop—I'm sorry they even named it that. They should have named it something else, because that name added a little extra salty taste, that name. But one of the things that hurt that kind of music was the fact that musicians, instead of goin' to Charlie and askin' Charlie how he did those things, or tryin' to sit around home long enough to know he actually studied these things, they went home and picked it out of the air and played what they thought sounded good. And they were so wrong until it was obnoxious to the average ear, until the people began blaming it all on the particular style. It wasn't actually the style; it was just they didn't know what they were playing. And they were too big at the time—some of the musicians were—to come and ask the man.

The Earl Hines Band: Diz at extreme left, Bird at extreme right. The young lady on piano is Sarah Vaughan.

I think that's the only thing that hurts the average musician today. Years ago—we're not comparing, I don't like the idea—I don't want people to think I'm trying to make a comparison, but I want to make it back to the friendship that musicians had many years ago that they don't have now.

Years ago, when guys like Fats Waller, Coleman Hawkins, Roy Eldridge all got together, we played with each other, together, because we'd get ideas, to keep on advancing. We didn't envy the guys that actually knew more. We tried to find out what he was doin', and we could. Today, it's one of those things where a guy says, "Ah! Who's he think he is?" That's very wrong. For instance, today, every idea I can possibly get—like Erroll Garner might do something I like—I say, "Erroll, some afternoon, come over my house; we'll sit down have a little tête-à-tête. Few little things I want you to show me. Somethin' you doin'—I don't know what it is, but I like it." Same thing, I'll go down to the Blackhawk and say to Oscar, "Oscar, what'd you do with your left hand there?" And they're so amazed to hear me ask that because we did that years ago. And same way with all the other musicians; they passed it on. They kept advancing, and the reason they kept advancing was because we're all friendly. All together; happy to see each other get ahead; if a guy did something, everybody was happy for the guy. Same thing happened to Parker when he joined our band. Everybody was happy for him, in fact all the members of the group. I think that's why they were so successful. Benny Green; Charlie; this guy who's with Louis, Trummy Young; and, in arranging, Jimmy Mundy. They were all happy. I made them stand out because I made them realize that we all appreciated it as much as the audience. "We got a kick out of hearing you play." You see, that you don't find today.

But getting back to Charlie. Charlie stayed with my band, oh, a year and a half. But Charlie was so advanced. And then, too, around New York there was a certain little group of musicians that sort of stayed with themselves. And it seems as though Charlie got with that group—and then besides, settling down as far as marriage was concerned, why I think that's one of the reasons he decided to stay around New York. But I just don't like to say these things as far as musicians are concerned. The man was such an artist. It's too bad that the public doesn't let a man like that alone, so that he can see the other side of good living. He would have been with us yet.

Now sometimes people don't intend to do things, but sometimes you'll find people follow a boy around, and if he hasn't got a strong will-power, why then he's easily to go off on the wrong foot. Well, we just loved him so much, but you can't very well talk to him like that. After all, you're in the same profession, and a few years older, but you're not his father; you see what I mean? so—much as I did—I talked to him as much as I could. I tell him, "You got the world lookin' at you, Charlie, and you're setting a standard. You've done something nobody else has done, and you can go so far."

He was happy to let me know, when I came to New York, that he had a string section with him. Well, that tickled me to death. I thought that was the greatest thing I'd heard in years. And I thought, "He's really on his way."

But the wrong crowd was running with an artist. The wrong crowd was running with an artist, and he was such a good-natured guy, and he didn't realize it. Same thing happened with Fats Waller; the wrong crowd. The wrong crowd with Billie Holiday; the wrong crowd. And we all have our own faults, but the story is this: you don't let it get the best of you. That's the bad part of it. Have a good time! Sure! You got to have a good time in this business! But there's a time for everything, see?

Now Diz, Diz did some fine writing for us. In fact, a little tune, he wrote the number and didn't know what to call it, and I thought, since we're hearing so much about the war in Europe, let's call it "Night in Tunisia"; and he left it like that. That's one of the tunes he wrote for the band. And this "Peanuts." He used to sing that. And a couple of others. I still have them in the book.

Happy go lucky group!

Yeah, we all used to go to Minton's then. If you wanted to hear something, somebody was really terrific, we all went to Minton's.

I'm sorry that's not being allowed today because that really brought the musicians out. When you went there, you ran into some stiff competition, so the only thing you could do was go somewhere in the woodshed and brush up on the horn if you wanted to compete with these guys. I think it made an awful lot of musicians out of these boys.

Of course everything is commercial. The minute that all these proprietors found out that these musicians love to blow, instead of being big-hearted and hiring a few musicians—if they'd hire six or seven boys in the band and then let the others sit-in, it's a different thing—all they do is hire a piano player. But these kids had music at heart, and the proprietor realized that. I had one guy say, "I had eight or ten musicians every night, and didn't pay them a quarter."

But Charlie! Charlie was a very good section man, and a very good reader. Well, that guy reads the best. He's the last one. I mean, he was a *musician!*

I didn't hear anybody else play that way then. They weren't playing out of the books this guy had. And if they could find those books, and find the passages Charlie was doing, they would play like Charlie. Because just like you and I were to study music, and we could look at ninth chords and double augmented chords, maybe we can add a—a sixth in there, and see what happens. And maybe it sounds kind of good. Might sound kind of weird, but maybe that's what you want for the ear. That's the same thing with Charlie; Charlie played them passages in there in his own way; in his style of breathing, being able to go for five or six measures without taking a breath; and his way of phrasing would have a lot to do with it. It was his own idea.

There are things I heard Charlie do, he didn't amaze only the people he was playing in front of, but he amazed the musicians who were workin' with him; nightly that happened. Because we didn't know what he was going to do, and when he did it, it would seem impossible.

His only real bad nights were when he overindulged.

He was very consistent; he had it all the time. But like if we ate too much or we drank too much, why we aren't at our top average. But that was the only thing I found wrong. He was very consistent, because the guy knew what he wanted to do, and he could play that horn automatically. Sometimes even when he indulged too much, you could put that horn into his hand, and once he got the feel of the horn, he could still do all the things he wanted to do.

Cliff Jetkins

Cliff Jetkins is both a vocalist and an alto saxophonist. Jetkins has written words to some of Charlie Parker's solos. An example is "Billie's Bounce" on a 45 rpm Royal Roost record.

I heard about him a lot in our home town of K.C. He was around twenty and considered the greatest then. We used to play at things they called Blue Mondays. They were jam sessions at various clubs which started at six o'clock in the morning and usually continued around the clock. He used to borrow my horn on occasion; but he repaid me many times over, for he once handed me a twenty-five dollar pawn ticket which he told me to redeem and keep what I got. It was an expensive French Selmer tenor saxophone—the one he had with Earl Hines.

His talents did not extend toward craps, for I remember a game with him, me, Billie Holiday, and a few members of the McShann band. Bird was losing, and his credit ran out. He had borrowed and borrowed, but his luck was bad. I had stopped feeding him dollars. He turned to me with a scowl, "You wouldn't lend me no more cash?" I told him, "If I keep lending my cash, how am I gonna win?"

Someone wanted to get Bird from McShann. He called Jay McShann and asked if Charlie was available. "You can have him right now," McShann said. "He just went to sleep in the channel of 'Cherokee.' "

I can understand Bird's feeling about K.C. A mixture of homesickness and hurt. Every once in awhile I get this urge to see my ma and friends, and I go back for a visit. The last time I drove out by car. When I got to Missouri, I stopped at a stand for a Coca-Cola. The girl said I'd have to go around to the back and drink it. "Well," I said, "now I know I'm home."

Ted Joans

Greenwich Village has always been a party area—all kinds of parties, ranging from literary soirees to big sprawling loft affairs. In 1954 and '55, the Elsa Maxwell of the Village was Ted Joans. Ted, out of Louisville, Kentucky, swept into the Village and took over. He is a surrealist artist. Jones, or Joans, as he spells it, was a trumpet player who threw his instrument in the river one day when he felt he was becoming too involved with too many things. Ted threw some of the most lavish parties, not in the champagne department, but in the area of the décor and costuming. Parker attended a few of these wild bashes. One of these was covered by Our World *magazine. The January, 1955 issue contains a picture of Bird among the masqueraders. Its caption read: "Relaxed as cool Mau Mau is bop alto sax man Charlie 'Yardbird' Parker"; in the background is the slogan of the party, "Dada."*

I slept with Charlie Parker, nothing sexual; just that on Barrow Street, we all lived together, Bird, Basheer, and myself, with very little steam heat. We slept together to keep warm a little. We only got steam four hours a day, from six to ten. Bird would yell down at the janitor, "What in hell you think you got up here, Eskimos?"

I had a record player in my room. Bird would never listen to any of his records. We used to sit around in the room, sipping wine and talking. Bird shared my enthusiasm for Dali. He was particularly fond of the painting with the melted watches. He was also interested in African affairs, and he used to call the Mau Maus "the African Minute Men."

Bird loaned me money many times, and he was helping out a lot of guys in the Village. He loved the Village more than any other part of town. He came in unexpectedly to one of my costume parties one night, all dressed up in a new business suit. He said, "B. . . ." He called everybody "B" probably standing for "Baby." Sometimes he called a person Jim, which meant he

116

didn't like the individual; Jim, in all likelihood, stood for Jim Crow. "B, you didn't tell me this was costumes, but, see here, I am going to get with it." He took his shirt off and painted his face and body. He was still not satisfied with the effect, and so he ripped his new pants to shreds. "I can always get a new pair of pants, but we may not have a party like this for years."

He was very humorous and dictatorial at this affair. The purpose of the party—I always like to have a high and serious purpose for my parties—was to hear the poetry of some of the young surrealist poets. One had written "An Ode to a Piece of Vaccinated Bread." As soon as the poet started to read this work, Bird interrupted, "Stop right there. We are all brothers and sisters. This man here is going to tell us about this piece of bread that has been vaccinated. Now you know there's no idiots in the house; and, if you want to hear these poems, you can . . . but, if you are like me, we will continue the party."

He hated photographers, and there were some at the party. They took his picture, which later appeared in a tabloid magazine with a caption about Charlie Parker dressed as a cool Mau Mau. He was sore at this and claimed that it cost him a couple of jobs.

Ted Joans joined the parade of beat poets and has contributed these poems about Bird:

I LOVE A BIG BIG BIRD

When Charles Christopher Parker first appeared in the window on the sill
of the bohemian coffee house known then as the Jabberwock
All the snow storms began at once and young parasitic whores bleached their
cornsilk hair to resemble the falling flakes
and they rushed to their pads to destroy their worthless non-jazz records
and all the silly milly more square than squarest of squares the folk singers
waved their boney banjo-shaped asses in protest of Bird's arrival
They knew he did not dig ricky-tocky, mokey-pokey folk songs
and that Bird like me plans to remain as always free
to eat porky the pig and all his non-kosher kindreds
Bird carrying seven burlap bags of charcoal and baking powder
set himself up immediately as a wailing seer who could cook
he had a Ph.D. in balling from a Park Ave. university.
Villagers who dug Bird did not carry spears, whips, bricks, or unhip diction-
     aries to his jazz sessions held at Bob Reisner's Open Door they brought
     lots of squat pot and free pussy for the overpassionate jazzites.
Bird wore a black-eye pea suit which gave the heebie-jeebies a right to sing
     the blues

because Bird was a master musician his jazz conversations on his horn were
considered subversive

greasy hair New York Italians from the bowels of the village banded together
"as they always do" and planned to attack the Bird

some worse huge zoot hats with Papal insignias on the band and ill-fitting suits
and their chicks inevitably dressed in black

unafraid Bird blew all the daggerdaddiodagos out of his scene forever

hours later Bird could be seen fingering frustrated old women in the East 80's
and he was notoriously known in Harlem.

he had urinated on the Borough President of Manhattan twice

he loved to kiss unsuspecting policemen, priests, business executives and
Southern bus drivers.

Bird could also be seen nightly writing long letters to his father the King of
Ornithology

Bird is not with us tonight but he is a drawing room at the bottom of the ocean

where hipsters like Rimbaud, Appolinaire, Whitman, Eluard and Desnos read
poetry and perform erotic oral sex acts with all the dead European
whores of the classic era.

the Bird is twelve years older since he came to the Village and he was born in
Kansas City not in Greenville, Massachusetts, Mississippi either.

He is the offspring of a liason between Negro-Anglo-Egyptian-Sudanese-Teu-
tonic maid and a giant stork.

The city in which he was born has since been destroyed by a million intoxi-
cated old owls and a herd of stampeding rhinoceroses all drunk from
homosexual sweat from a psychiatrist's couch.

Bird's folks moved to Maine then Florida, Stockholm, Wisconsin and finally
Iwo Jima and this is where Bird ran into his first alto sax it was standing
nude near the body of a dead monkey who had fallen off the back of
the ax.

We all dug Bird. He is not a black Eskimo nor a gingerbread boy but he is the
greatest musician that ever went down on a horn or an inviting hole of
an angry cavity. Bird is a god of good graciousness. Bird was our
preacher. Bird is the way to musical greatness. Bird died four years ago
today but he lives, he lives and now how do you sound?

Bird and Curly Russell.

HIM THE BIRD

Once upon a time, my time, a few years ago now. . . .
There was a young cafe-au-lait colored bird, who blew
sax, and his earth name was Charles Parker
He mounted a small bandstand in Greenwich Village and blew through Bob
    Reisner's Open Door where Bohemian whores used to sit with big-assed
    businessmen talking trade backed by Bird's funky lore.
He lived at flophouse on Barrow and froze with a Moslem and me during that
    winter of my time a few years after '53, eating canned beans, sardines.
    sipping wine and drinking tea
He blew for young Hebrew in mafia-owned joint, where sat James Dean with
    Weegee and some technicolor chicks
He blew for kicks and a few measly bills, those solos he took on his borrowed
    alto gave everybody their thrills
He blew his horn in the Village and wailed for the world
He died a pauper although now his every effort on wax will sell
So the Bird is gone and in the outer world he cooks
Men like me will always have the Bird in their music, paintings, and books.

It should be noted that many poems
about Charlie Parker exist in the
little literary magazines.

Budd Johnson

Albert "Budd" Johnson was born in Dallas, Texas, in 1910. He is a notable composer and arranger. He plays all the reed instruments. Johnson is one of the few men who made the transition from the music of the twenties right up to the present and recently held a tenor sax position in the band of Gil Evans. He is advisor to band leaders. It was he who got progressive musicians into the Hines band, and he assisted in the organizing of Billy Eckstine's orchestra. He watched the career of Parker from Charlie's childhood on.

In December of 1942, Bird took my place on tenor in the Earl Hines band. A lot of us musicians would be practicing every day at George E. and Julia Lee's house over on Euclid Avenue in K.C., and underneath the window was a bunch of kids playing stick ball, among them, Charlie Parker. This was in 1929. In 1931, he was playing the horn and getting chased off the stand. In 1935, he was blowing like hell.

Most of your best musicians were from the South and Midwest. That's because they were all afraid of New York. They strove to perfect themselves after being raised on harrowing tales of the prowess of New York musicians. At some sessions, it was said, Willie "The Lion" Smith would come in and knock you off the bench. They'd tell you that you'd better hide your arrangements or they'd steal them from you. Musicians would come as far as Philadelphia and make little exploratory ventures into New York and scurry out again. It was little wonder that Charlie was afraid to take out his horn when he first came to New York and found himself at Puss Johnson's after-hours place on 130th Street and St. Nicholas Avenue. When he was finally urged to play, everyone took notice.

One day Bud and Miles ran into me and told me that Bird was laying up at the Dewey Square Hotel with pneumonia. We all went up to visit him, the boys first bringing the patient a fifth of Seagrams. When we got there, he was lying with water running off his face like a faucet. He had just polished off a bottle of wine with some person, and his wife Doris was frantic with worry. Our visit produced a burst of energy in him, and he arose and embraced us including the bottle. When his wife told him to get into bed, he put her out of the room.

When Dizzy left Billy Shaw's office to go to Williard Alexander, Billy was sore, and he determined to bear down on Charlie. He gave him a car, told him to discipline himself, and he could have everything he wanted. Billy said, "I'll show everybody that it's Charlie's music."

He inspired a great deal of love and respect. I've seen him approach a knot of strangers and say, "It's getting cold; I need an overcoat," and they would raise the cash for him. If he had the money, he was always ready to treat. If he didn't have the money, he'd treat anyhow. At Birdland, he ordered a few drinks for friends, and he downed five triple Grand Dads. When asked to pay, he said, "Just give me a pencil and piece of paper." He was told that cash was what was required. He made rapidly for the exit, pursuers at his heels. When he reached the stairs, he stopped, took off his coat, handed it to me, saying, "I'll have to rumble" but somehow the thing got settled peaceably. It is my feeling that he provoked fights to counteract the pain that his habit inflicted on his body. He wanted to get hit. I saw a bartender crack him on the head with a bottle, and Charlie said to him, "Are you satisfied now?" Nobody has ever knocked him out.

Buddy Jones

When he was seventeen, William Burgher (Buddy) Jones met Charlie Parker in Kansas City and, under his influence, decided to become a musician. While in the Navy, he studied the string bass. He was born in Hope, Arkansas, in 1924. He has worked with Lennie Tristano, Buddy De Franco, and Charlie Ventura. His steadiest gig has been with the Jack Sterling CBS radio show. He started in 1952 and can still be heard every weekday morning.

I was brought up in a small Southern town where a Negro got out of your way when you went down the street. Through music, I got to appreciate the fine qualities of the Negro people, and I guess I spent the years from eighteen to twenty-eight arguing with my folks about race. I was sent to the University of Kansas City where, unbeknown to my Ma, I quickly dissipated all my money, had to quit, and I got a job as bellhop at the Aladdin Hotel. It was there that I first heard Charlie Parker, playing alto in Jessie Price's band. He was playing occasional jobs with the McShann group then, also, but work with Price was more steady.

He was a hero, then in 1942, to a great many. I used to go to those Monday morning sessions at the Kentucky Club Barbecue they called "spook break-fasts." No one was allowed in except musicians and entertainers, and I guess I was the only ofay cat there. I was told that the reason Charlie got so far so fast on his horn was that he practiced almost twenty-four hours a day. It has been said that no one ever passed his house and did not hear the sound of him playing. Charlie never slept. I once shared a room with him and never saw him in bed. He just would become unconscious after a while for a short bit.

He was playing tenor with Earl Hines's band at a place called Lincoln Colonnade. It must have been an affair sponsored by some officials of Howard University, because Hines was preening and being very smooth with them. They were congratulating each other about the band, and Earl was telling these deans how clean cut, young, ambitious, and high-type his men were—that they were not the ratty kind of musician one sometimes finds. Just then Charlie entered the room, and Hines called him over and introduced him to the prominent educator: "This is Charles Parker, my new alto saxophonist." They were about to shake hands, when, suddenly, Charlie fell down unconscious.

He was my hero—but the preposterous lengths that some of the guys would go. Fellows would take their good clothes and roll them up into a ball to get them creased, because they saw Bird walking around in a suit he had long forgotten to have pressed. There was an alto player, named Leo Williams, who lived in Washington, D.C., and whenever Charlie played the town, he would hock his horn and devote the money to good times with Bird. People believed him to have a superhuman constitution, and with good reason. I have seen him take several benzedrine wrappers, wad them into a ball, and swallow it. Getting high the first time at fifteen, Bird told me what he felt. He pulled out $1.30, which was all he had and which was worth more in those days and he said, "Do you mean there's something like this in this world? How much of it will this buy?"

Bird's grandfather, on his father's side, was an evangelist preacher, the Reverend Peter Parker. Charlie was very fond of the services of the famed Washington, D.C., preacher, Elder Lightfoot Michaux, who leads the most exuberant approach to the Lord with trombones and exultant voices singing "Happy am I With my Religion" which Bird took and which is now quite a familiar bop musical phrase.

Duke Jordan

Duke Jordan worked on and off with Charlie Parker for three years. He was born in Brooklyn, in 1922. Duke has been working as a modern jazz pianist since 1939. He started playing professionally with a group known as The Manhattan Sextet. Later on he played with Roy Eldridge, Colman Hawkins, Al Cooper's Savoy Sultans, and, finally, with Teddy Walters Trio down at the Three Deuces on 52 Street, where Charlie first heard him in 1946.

Charlie was seated at a front table, and I heard him say, "Wow, listen to that guy," and he was talking about me. Then he came over and asked me if I would like to work for him, and I jumped at the chance.

Well, he formed the group in late 1946, and we stayed together for a year and a half, working steady, making the Baltimore, Washington, Boston, Philly, Detroit, Chicago, Milwaukee, St. Louis route. I never went to California with Bird except later with "Jazz at the Philharmonic." The quintet was Bird; Max Roach, drums; Tommy Potter, bass; Miles Davis, trumpet; and me. The group got on very harmoniously except for slight altercations with Miles. He and Max sort of formed a little clique. They were both getting $135 a week, ten more than me and Tommy. Miles was making it at Juilliard, and he was tight with John Lewis, and he wanted Bird to substitute John for me in the group. But Bird silenced him by quietly and firmly saying that he chose the guys and Miles could form his own outfit if anything displeased him. That was all that was heard from Miles.

Working with Bird was one of the tremendous experiences. He always came on with a new musical line that would make my hair stand on end. He used to say to me, "If you do something out of the ordinary between sets, when you come back to play, you will have a different thought, and it will come out in your playing."

One night I saw Bird in front of the Onyx Club during intermission. Nobody was around, and there he was, lying across a garbage disposal steel box, rolling back and forth. I rushed forward, saying, "Hey, Bird! Are you all right? Are you sick?" But he just smiled and said, "Hey, Duke, hey, Jimsey, everything's cool, everything's cool." He was just trying his in-between-sets-experience experiments.

Charlie was given to impulsively generous acts. I was in a cab with Tommy Potter, and Bird opened the door of the taxi and shoved a good-looking girl inside, saying, "Duke, here, she's for you." A present, like. We took her to the hotel, and she laid out for us.

Wherever we would be, Charlie always called his mother long distance quite regularly. I once saw him phoning her during a terrible thunderstorm. He opened the window and stuck the phone out for a minute during the thunder, and then he said, "Mom, do you hear God talking?"

Wherever we would be, the pushers were with us. The grapevine, as far as drugs is concerned, is very quick, very swift; and as soon as Bird hit town, someone would contact him. "I know where something real good is," they would say, sometimes calling the hotel at five or six in the morning, and Bird would go with them. As years went by, Bird started cooling. He went to a doctor in 1948 and was told he had about six months to live unless he took a complete rest for a few years, which he never did. His ulcers were bad, and his whole body was filled with a terrible cold.

Though he was the idol of all musicians, Bird knew the limitations of his success and felt annoyed that he was confined to just playing in night clubs. He also was bugged at the fact that, being a Negro, he could go just so far and no farther. Once he finished a set to great acclaim, ducked out, and went quietly to a bar around the corner on Sixth Avenue between 51st and 52nd Street, called McGuire's. The paradox of his life was brought into focus when the bartender asked him what he wanted and addressed him as a "nigger." Parker vaulted over the bar to teach the fellow manners. The man picked up a bottle and broke it over Bird's head. It cut his dome, and he always had a little scar; but it did not prevent Charlie from blackening the guy's eyes and knocking a few of his teeth out.

And another incident, concerned with the lack of respect a great artist sometimes has to put up with, was this time in Chicago. We were playing at a place called the Argyle on the Northside. Bird came in one night, late and drunk. He couldn't play. He was too juiced. So the quartet, me, Max, Miles, and Tommy, finished out the evening. The club owner figured that he could get away without paying the band. Bird went up to the union to see if he could get money for the sidemen at least. He was in the office of the colored president of the local. A deal must have been cooked up between the club owner and this official, because the man suddenly whipped out a gun and said to Bird, "Get the hell out of here, or I'll shoot you up your ass." Charlie left, saying, "I'll be back." He was about to make good his promise when I stopped him downstairs from the guy's office and told him not to be foolish, that the man would not hesitate to use his gun. He took my advice. We didn't get any money, but our leader was alive.

Sheila Jordan

Sheila Jordan is the wife of Duke Jordan. A professional jazz singer, she has performed in several of Greenwich Village's small clubs.

He kept a little Palomino horse up at the riding academy in the 70's, and we used to go riding often. He visited us pretty often, making all sorts of weird excuses, as if he'd have to. Once there was a fire in the neighborhood, and Bird, driving in from Philly, stopped at the house and said, "I thought my little girl was burning up," even though the fire was a block away. One night he calls late and asks if he can come over and talk. I said yes. When he arrived, he just sat in the cab. I came down. He gave me ten dollars to pay the cab. The bill was two fifty with the tip. I followed him up the stairs, trying to give him the change which he kept insisting I keep. He finally started yelling, "Keep your filthy money. I have plenty," and with that, he starts pulling out wads of money from his pockets, dumping it on the bed.

Another time he was broke, and he called his manager Teddy Blume. He argued with him for a half an hour to come down and give him some dough. Finally, he convinces Teddy. Sometime later a cab pulls up, the manager steps out, runs up to our flat, gives Bird a big four dollars, goes down, and rides off in the same cab.

He was the strangest man with money in the world. He and Harvey Cropper would empty their pockets, stick all their money in a drawer, and the Bird would say, "I'm going to teach you how to live," and for the next few days, they would go down to the Bowery and live the lives of bums, sleeping in quarter and fifty-cent flophouses, eating at Fred Bunz or a salvation house, panhandling.

One day he shows up in a dirty old T shirt. "Come on, Sheila, I'm gonna show you a good time." He took me to a shooting gallery on Times Square. "I'll show you how to shoot." I shot three ducks; he shot none. He quickly tired of this pastime. He wanted to take me into the Turf to eat, me with dungarees and Bird with ruffled feathers. We had an argument. I was ashamed to go in. He said, "You're with Bird." We went home, thank goodness. I prepared a meal, and he took out a special kind of salt he had for his ulcers. He was so careful, but that didn't prevent him from drinking two quarts of wine with the meal. Once he started to make phone calls one after the other. I told him I couldn't afford all those calls, which I couldn't. He picked up the phone and called the operator, "Put all the calls on Sheila Jordan's line on mine," he said.

Lawrence Keyes

Pianist Lawrence Keyes was Charlie Parker's first leader—in a band formed when both were still in high school. As his narrative indicates, Keyes is still very much active in music; at this writing he is house pianist at the Polka Dot bar on 45th street in New York.

Bird went to Crispus Attucks public school and then to the old Lincoln High School. We had a school band of which I was the leader. Alonzo Lewis was our music teacher, and it's to his credit that he saw the promise in Charlie's playing and said so. Bird played baritone horn in the band, but off the stand he was fascinated with the piano, and he used to bother me to show him chords. I was three years older than him. I was a sophomore, and he was a freshman. We became good friends. It was a triumvirate because there was another guy whom Charlie admired tremendously, and the three of us would hang out in each other's houses, practicing and talking music day and night. We never spoke about dates or girls. We never went on double dates together, only music. We each had a girl of our own but that was separate. Bird's girl was named Rebecca. We had our love life but it was very private. The name of the third fellow was Robert Simpson and he played trombone remarkably. To say that Charlie admired him is perhaps too mild, Charlie worshipped him and was in his company a great deal. Suddenly at twenty-one Robert Simpson died, of what we were never sure. A heart ailment was thought to be the cause. Charlie was a complete wreck after that.

My band in school was called "Deans of Swing" and we were pretty damned good. Besides me on piano and Bird there was Freddie Culliver, tenor saxophone (who is now dead), James Ross, trumpet; Franz Bruce, alto; Vernon Walker, alto; and Walter Brown doing vocals.

If he had been as conscientious about his school work as he was about music, he would have become a professor, but he was a terrible truant. It was a surprise if he came a whole week. He was doomed to be a perpetual freshman.

He quit and joined McShann, and soon the Deans of Swing were playing against McShann and Bird in those band-cutting contests which were so popular. We were growing up and apart. Bird had a new and shiny horn which made me recall the sessions at my house with his first one which was as raggedy as a pet monkey, rusty and patched up with rubber bands.

Over the years we would see each other when we played clubs in the same town. In K.C. he might be playing Green Leaf Gardens while I'd be at the Spinning Wheel Club. In New York he was playing at the Three Deuces and I was at the Onyx Club, and he was a constant visitor. He'd come in and sit near me, and if someone came over to tell him he had to get back to his own bandstand he said, "In a little while; I want to hear my home town play."

I have always been tagged with a nickname 88, a name I've never been too fond of. But 88 Keyes identified me in the business, so I let it be on signs. Bird, with his innate sense of propriety, always called me Lawrence instead of 88 or Keyes.

I was the first one who started him out in music. We met sometime before his death at an uptown club and he asked me where I had been keeping myself all these years. I told him that I was out in Long Island in a place called the Club Carousel and had been there for the past eight years. He was impressed with this. He said that this was because I was a moderate man. I'll never forget the words he said to me, "You're doing the best thing, staying cool and clean. Don't you ever change. Anytime a man can play that long in one club and play what he wants to play, he is a great man." I felt so good that I forgot to ask him for fifteen dollars which he owed me from the old K.C. days, when we were getting a dollar and a half a night—and that was good pay.

Henry Kier

On Sixth Avenue and 44th Street, there's a cluttered little store crammed with magazines and books, jokes and star photos. The proprietor, Henry Kier, recalled Bird as a devoted browser.

He was living around the corner in a hotel. This was around 1947, and he'd come in frequently with a tall girl. They both wore berets. He used to ask about the musicians' photos, which ones were selling best. At that time Coleman Hawkins was the most popular, but Parker was always a steady seller. At least one a day on the average. He was a sweet, unassuming boy, and I vividly recall him, in a tan coat with huge wooden buttons, coming in with a hot dog, the sauerkraut dripping down his chin, saying of his photos, "Is anyone crazy enough to buy mine?"

Baroness Pannonica de Koenigswarter

At 8:45 P.M. on March 12, 1955, Bird died in the hotel suite of his friend the Baroness. "Nica" had befriended and encouraged some of the most powerful creative men in jazz today. Parker was her friend for a number of years. The jazz Baroness was the subject of an article by Nat Hentoff in Esquire *(October, 1960). She is an individualist in the most charming sense. I recall her patronage with pleasure when I was in the night club business. Sometimes she wore a casual sweater with a mink coat. She carried a gold flask. She has been written about in both* Confidential *and the* Almanach de Gotha.

Parker's death set off wild conjecture, lurid copy, and rampaging rumor. The New York Times *carried the respectful heading:* CHARLES PARKER, JAZZ MASTER, DIES. *They gave a sober account except, through no fault of their own, they quoted the police as saying Parker was about 53 years old. The New York* Daily Mirror *headed its story with:* BOP KING DIES IN HEIRESS'S FLAT. *The New York* Journal-American *said:* BARE DEATH OF BOP KING PARKER. *The rest of the large metropolitan dailies carried similar stories. All these stories broke on Tuesday,*

March 15th, and Parker had died on Saturday, March 12th.

The scandal magazines found this juicy grist for the pulp mills. Exposé used the title, "The Bird in the Baroness' Boudoir," and followed it with such ludicrous copy as: ". . . Blinded and bedazzled by this luscious, slinky, black-haired, jet-eyed Circe of high society, the Yardbird was a fallen sparrow." Exposé, along with Confidential and Lowdown, tried to intimate in their oblique and pun-ridden way that there was "fowl" play. They brought up questions. Why was the corpse labeled John Parker? Why was the death only discovered through the chance remark of a morgue attendant to a reporter? Why did the story break three days after Parker's death?

All rumors notwithstanding, Dr. Robert Freymann notified the Medical Examiner and atttributed death to a heart attack and cirrhosis of the liver; the body reached the morgue at Bellevue Hospital at about 2:00 A.M., Sunday. Chief Medical Examiner Milton Halpern said an autopsy had disclosed death was due to lobar pneumonia.

The following is the Baroness' account.

I'm sick of this "shipped the body off to the morgue" business and "laid unknown," for how long, for that is ridiculous. The doctor was there within five minutes of his dying, and he had been there a half an hour beforehand. The medical examiner was there within an hour of the doctor; and the moment the medical examiner comes, he takes over everything, and you have nothing more to say about it. All the pertinent facts were given by myself and the doctor to the medical examiner, and I saw him take them down. He had Bird's name, Charles Parker, taken down absolutely correctly; so the story of the false name tag on Bird could not have been so. The doctor gave Bird's age as 53, because that was his impression, for some reason. I didn't say, because I didn't know.

The autopsy said he died of pneumonia, when, actually, he did not have pneumonia. The doctor said it was a heart attack that killed him, but he had terrible ulcers, and advanced cirrhosis of the liver; and he had been told by doctors for years previous that he might die at any moment.

He had stopped by that evening before leaving for Boston where he had a gig at Storyville. His horn and bags were downstairs in his car. The first thing that happened which was unusual was when I offered him a drink, and he said no. I took a look at him, and I noticed he appeared quite ill. A few minutes later he began to vomit blood. I sent for my doctor, who came right away. He said that Bird could not go on any trip, and Bird, who felt better momentarily, started to argue the point and said that he had a commitment to play this gig and that he had to go. We told him that he must go to the hospital. That, he said, was the last thing he was going to do. He said he hated hospitals, that he had had enough of them. I then said to the doctor, "Let him stay here." We agreed on that, and my daughter and I took shifts around the clock watching and waiting upon him and bringing ice water by the gallon, which he consumed. His thirst was incredible; it couldn't be quenched. Sometimes he would bring it up with some blood, and then he lay back and had to have more water. It went on like this for a day or two. When the doctor first came, he asked Bird the routine questions and some others. "Do you drink?" he asked. This brought a sidelong wink from Bird. "Sometimes," he said ironically, "I have a sherry before dinner."

The doctor came three times a day and any other times we would call him. The doctor knew how serious it was. Before he left the first time, he told me, "I have to warn you that this man may die at any moment. He has an advanced cyrrhosis and stomach ulcers. He must not leave, except in an ambulance."

The doctor liked Bird, and Bird, when he wasn't racked by seizures, was in wonderful spirits. He made me swear not to tell anybody where he was. The third day he was a lot better. Dr. Freymann said he might be able to leave in a little while. At first, Charlie Parker was just a name to the doctor; he didn't know of Bird's genius, nor did he know of Bird's weaknesses. Bird wanted the doctor, who had been a musician, to listen to some of his records, and the doctor developed an interest in his patient and wanted to hear Bird's work. Bird and I spent considerable time mapping out a program. First we played the album with strings, "Just Friends" and "April in Paris." The doctor was very impressed. Bird got a great charge out of that. That was on Saturday, about 7:30 P.M. Bird was so much better that the doctor agreed that he could get up and watch the Tommy Dorsey program on TV.

We braced him up in an easy chair, with pillows and wrapped in blankets. He was enjoying what he saw of the program. Bird was a fan of Dorsey's, and he didn't see anything strange in that. "He's a wonderful trombonist," he said. Then came part of the show consisting of jugglers who were throwing bricks around that were stuck together. My daughter was asking how they did it, and Bird and I were being very mysterious about it. Suddenly in the act, they dropped the bricks, and we all laughed. Bird was laughing uproariously, but then he began to choke. He rose from his chair and choked, perhaps twice, and sat back in the chair. I was on the phone immediately, calling the doctor. "Don't worry, Mummy," my daughter said. "He's all right now."

I went over and took his pulse. He had dropped back in the chair, with his head falling forward. He was unconscious. I could feel his pulse still there. Then his pulse stopped.

I didn't want to believe it. I could feel my own pulse. I tried to believe my pulse was his. But I really knew that Bird was dead.

At the moment of his going, there was a tremendous clap of thunder. I didn't think about it at the time, but I've thought about it often since; how strange it was.

It happened on a Saturday night. At one o'clock in the morning they took him away, and, from then on, it was out of my hands. I said nothing to the papers, because my first concern was for Chan, his wife. I did not want her to hear it over the radio or read it in the papers. I wanted to get to her first. I had attempted to find out where she was when Bird was at my place, but he said she had just moved into a new house, and he did not know the address.

Some people said that I had the body "shipped to Bellevue where no one identified it for forty-eight hours." Actually, Bird's name, Charlie (Yardbird) Parker, was entered on the death certificate that was made out in my apartment at the Hotel Stanhope. The one thing we couldn't find was Chan's address, who was known as Bird's wife. Also, somebody wrote that I was at the Open Door, your place, where you had those bop sessions in Greenwich Village, and that I was talking to Art Blakey and other friends of Bird and I didn't tell them of Bird's death. Actually, I wanted to find Chan before she got the news from the radio or the press, and I went to the Open Door to see if anybody there knew her address. Finally, I thought of Teddy Wilson, and his lawyer, it so happened, had the address of Chan's mother. Chan was finally contacted Monday evening and was told.

I did not know Bird too many years, but we did have a wonderful friendship going, nothing romantic. He always dropped in unexpectedly anytime during the day or night. He was a relaxed type of person, and you sometimes hardly knew he was around. He liked to play peggity with my daughter. That game actually superseded his love of chess. We'd talk about everything under the sun. Bird knew about everything, and then some.

I'd sit around and play him records. He loved Eddie Heywood's "Begin the Beguine." It fascinated him; he used to play it ten times around. Another thing he loved was Billie Holiday doing "You're My Thrill."

For all the adulation heaped upon him by fans and musicians, he was lonely. I saw him standing in front of Birdland in a pouring rain. I was horrified, and I asked him why, and he said he just had no place to go. He was wont to frequent a few of his friends' pads and just go to sleep in an armchair. This night he couldn't find anybody home. He said, when this happened, he would ride the subways all night. He would ride a train to the end of a line; then, when he was ordered out, he would go to another train and ride back.

Bird was a very trusting person with friends. He'd put himself completely in the hands of the people he loved. In sparing his wife the shock of a public announcement of his death, I felt I was carrying out something he would have wanted.

> *Following is a statement from Dr. Freymann, who was attending Bird at the Baroness' apartment:*

I refused to sign the death certificate. He had been definitely off the drugs, I could see by his eyes. He had no veins left to inject anyway—all had been used up. To me he looked to be in his early 60's. When he died, the hotel wanted him taken away quickly. I saw him for three or four days. The second day he was in terrible pain. I gave him penicillin, and then he seemed to improve. No temperature. We begged him to go to the hospital, but he would not have it.

Dave Lambert

> *Dave was one of the founders of bop singing. The success of the Lambert-Hendricks-Ross trio is based on a sound formula, that of taking inspired instrumental solos and putting words to them. David Alden Lambert was born in Boston, in 1917. He, at one time, was a tree surgeon and a paratrooper. He is a talented arranger who does background arrangements for singers, TV cartoons, and commercials.*

I first met Bird around 1948 under pretty weird circumstances. I was living in Gil Evans' pad on 55th Street. It was a one-room, basement apartment, and it was shared by around nine people. There was Gil, myself, my wife and daughter, Specs Goldberg, the drummer, and Gerry Mulligan. Being right near 52nd Street which was swinging at the time, Max, Miles, and Bird would fall by, and, as soon as someone would get up from a bed, another person would jump on it. The people would lie crosswise so they could fit more bodies. It was a struggle, but fun. I remember Gerry Mulligan was rehearsing a band in Central Park, because he had no money to rent a rehearsal studio. They would play in the grass till the cops came and chased them. To get to this one-room apartment with one bathroom, which had to be shared in turns, you had to go down a short flight of stairs, pass a Chinese laundry through a boiler room, and there it was—home.

Sometimes, when I went to hear Bird, he'd be on the stand with his group of about four men, but there would be maybe another four or five waiting to sit in and jam. Bird never was discourteous to a musician. He never told them verbally to get off the stand, instead he would call a number—"All the Things You Are," in the key of E—and start off *pow* in a ridiculous tempo and in a tough key, and the guys would just walk off the stand. The piano player would be quaking trying to keep up with all the changes. The terrific tempos, the keys that no one ordinarily played in, just created a situation like Hayden's Farewell Symphony, only in up tempo. The musicians petered off, and the men were separated from the boys. One of the very fast tunes sometimes played for this weeding-out process was written by Bud Powell and was a variation of "Cherokee." The number was aptly titled "Serenade for Squares."

Jerry Lloyd

Trumpeter Jerry Lloyd (Jerry Hurwitz) is little known to most jazz fans today, but, in the early days of bop and even before, on the 52nd Street scene, he was one of the most respected trumpeters among a group of musicians who later went on to greater fame. He was born in New York City in 1920. He studied piano and gave a concert at Steinway Hall when he was five. His brother got him interested in jazz when he was eight and sneaked him off to the Apollo Theatre in Harlem once in awhile to hear the great rockin' bands of Cab Calloway and Erskine Hawkins. Jerry says, "My brother was not a musician, but he had a discriminating taste in music. My folks got me a trumpet for twenty dollars a couple of years later, and I was launched." Jerry was started on trumpet at the age of thirteen as therapy for a collapsed lung. He joined the union at that age and has kept up his membership to the present. He was out of music for six years due to attacks of arthritis but returned with Zoot Sims's group in 1956, staying for a few months.

I was fourteen years old, and I took a job in a hotel near Liberty, New York. It was one of those "kuchalein" places. One night I walked into Liberty and was just looking around when I spotted some Negro fellows coming out of a drugstore. They were all wearing big hats so I figured they were musicians, and I was right. They were heading for a bar which they had left for an intermission soda. I followed them in. I had my horn with me. I asked them if they would let me sit in. They said sure. They dug my playing. I never went back to the hotel except to get my shirts. This was it for me. They got me on salary with the bar. My folks came in one night, looking for their little boy, and there he was, having a ball. You can't learn playing that kind of music with white people. My people went through the motions of what parents are supposed to say, but they knew how I felt and, in their hearts, knew it was something that had to be. When summer was over, I went back uptown with these fellows. I left home and school. I soon became a familiar figure on 52nd Street.

It was Benny Harris who first told me about Bird. "You know there's a saxophone player out in Kansas City who plays more horn than any other horn player you ever heard." To show me the way he sounded he put on a Lester Young record called "Shoe Shine Boy." He had a machine that could speed up the revolutions until the tenor sax sounded like an alto. "That's a rough idea of how he sounds." Not much later, he was in town, and I met the man in person. He was different. He was skinny; he had bad feet—he could hardly walk at the time.

He was staying at the Woodside Hotel. He wanted a place to blow, so Benny Harris and I took him down to play at MacDougal's Tavern in Greenwich Village. There were two guys, I remember, playing with Jarvis and Skeets. I thought I could play with anybody at the time. We went down and started playing; played a couple more tunes; he started playing. I started listening. I walked off the stand. I put my horn in the case and zipped up the zipper. Those guys in the rhythm section used to work hard for me but they really were working hard for Bird. My ego went down about forty percent. He blew about forty choruses.

I got Bird one of his first jobs in New York. He was desperate. Some days he'd go without eating. I got him a job in a joint called the Parisian Dance Hall

On some days when he'd go without eating, he'd sit at the White Rose bar chiseling drinks. When I first met him through Benny, I was working on 52nd Street. It was daylight and people looked at us—we were a weird-looking trio.

He was pretty frantic about things like borrowing money. One time he slapped me in the face for refusing him. "If I didn't respect you so much as a player, I would beat the hell out of you," I told him. He used to walk a little bent over, but when he fattened up, he also straightened up. He could eat four times to your one.

Julie MacDonald

Julie MacDonald is a sculptor who met Charlie Parker during his stay in California. They became friends, and he often visited her studio. During these visits, she made a series of studies which she later developed in several sculptural portraits of Parker; one of these is now in the collection of Robert Reisner.

In sifting through my memories of Charlie Parker, I find one particular thought recurring—the wonder of his ability to perceive. At times his awareness seemed sensitive enough to make mechanical radar and sonar equipment obsolete! Bird truly listened, with mind and heart, and he observed the same way. He could discover meaning in a cowboy ballad, no matter how insignificant the song might seem, or in a simple nursery rhyme. He was never disparaging or condescending towards the creative efforts of others.

One spring morning, amid cacophony of birds and insects, he remarked, "If we could hear all the sounds existing, we'd soon be mad."

Seeing one unrestrained, free gesture of a child, he would chuckle and become pensive.

He listened to Shostakovich, Stravinsky, and Bartok; looked at art from Egyptian sculpture to Picasso, with the same intensity; and he remembered! Bird's memory was uncanny. With that combination of perception and memory he translated experience through his horn. He caught the pulse of our times, the pressure, confusion and complexity, and more: sadness, sweetness, and love.

Bird's intellect, though happily untrained, was prodigious. Directed in great part towards the discovery of the "inner meaning of life," he felt nature held the key to understanding. Although raised in Catholicism—he mentioned once that he had been a choir boy—he rejected the Church. At one time, around 1953, he tried Yoga. He was interested in extrasensory perception, the theory of past lives, mysticism; he was also frightened of these ideas; He said once that the pursuit of this kind of thinking was responsible in part, for his trip to Camarillo State Hospital, in 1947. He said about his stay at Camarillo "The old Bird died there," and he seemed relieved at this "death." Bird's belief in the omnipotence of the human mind was shaken drastically when the news of the death of his daughter Pree reached him. It was then that he questioned his rejection of religion. And it was then he said he never cried; that he was taught tears were unmanly. His tears were shed through his horn. And his anger, too.

He told me of his fear of the rage inside him. Fear that once unleashed, he could not control. No wonder many who heard Bird play recoiled from his brilliant exposure of human emotions and found his music too painful a mirror of their inner selves. Yet those who listened more carefully found identification; they found release in knowing their anxieties—rage, even,—were shared; found comfort in hearing their longing for love played back to them.

Once, when we were talking about his beginnings in music, Bird mentioned with a big grin: "I used to stand outside the club in Kansas City where Lester Young played—I was only twelve at the time and couldn't go inside—and would listen for hours. Then I went and got an alto. I didn't get a tenor because I didn't want to copy Prez."

Also, about music, he advised me to start my son on piano before he went on to learn to play a horn.

He admired Johnny Hodges, commenting on his lyricism in particular. Never did he mention either Rudy Vallee or Jimmy Dorsey.

Bird always spoke of his four children (before the death of Pree). The older son Leon, Baird, and Kim (a daughter of Chan's by a previous marriage, whom he considered his own too). He referred to his four wives, never mentioning the legal technicalities of divorce. I think he had a grand disregard of law and courts, most probably stemming from the miscarriages of justice towards the Negro. I remember a violently heated argument once on the subject of law in which he denounced it thoroughly and passionately. He tried to make his own law.

But I think if he were alive now, he would be most unhappy about his past disregard of it in this instance . . . and full of remorse. When speaking to me of his wives, he readily pointed out that the failure of his various marriages

was his fault, becoming most remorseful, wondering how any woman could cope with being his wife! I remember after Pree died, just before taking him to the airport, he said, "I hope I can be a good husband . . . at least until after this is over," referring to the funeral.

He didn't return to dope after Pree's death, for he was using it just prior to it, out here on the Coast. The night he heard of her death, he got very lushed on quadruple Alexanders; then, upon sobering, poured a bottle of Scotch down the john, gave away his heroin, and finally departed for the East a sober man.

Did I ever mention the story of Bird's actions that led to the trip to Camarillo? One day he told me this, as he would tell a rather amusing tale. He said that he was living in a dank downtown L.A. hotel, that he had to make a phone call. The phone, unfortunately, was downstairs in the lobby; so down he went. When he got there, the clerk at the desk looked horrified and told him to get the hell back to his room, for he had neglected to wear any form of pants! Back to his room he went, then returned downstairs to complete his mission. Upon reaching the lobby, he was met by further exclamations, followed shortly by the arrival of the police. It seems he had put on his coat and again lacked pants! From there he was taken to the police psychiatrist and so to Camarillo.

Above:

Stone sculpture of Bird by Julie MacDonald. (Collection of George E. Geisler.)

Below:

"Things like this shake me up," said Bird when shown this photograph of a XXVth dynasty Egyptian bust with its remarkable resemblance to him.

Edward Mayfield, Jr.

Edward Mayfield, Jr. was one of Charlie Parker's schoolmates. A musician in his teens, Mayfield is now the owner of a candy store in Kansas City.

He was kind of a bully. He was kind of a mean boy. He pushed you aside and got his horn first out of the music closet in school. If you didn't like it . . . you liked it anyway. He was larger than we were. He didn't stand any kind of pushing around. He didn't pick on you, but he would pop you in a minute. He was not a regular attender, maybe one day out of three. He was a good reader both words and the dots. He managed to make his music classes pretty regular. He was that type of four-flusher. He mostly associated with older fellows. He was smoking and that sort of thing, and we didn't smoke. He was just an older type guy. He knew me pretty well, and I would say he liked me.

I had an encounter with him when he was in McShann's group when I was at Lincoln University. He spent the night with me in the dormitory. We spoke of music all through the night. He played a baritone horn in high school. I played a woodwind. I asked him, "When did you start playing alto?"

"I just picked it up," he answered.

I always have a few of his records on the jukebox in my candy store.

Howard McGhee

Born in Tulsa in 1918, McGhee moved with his family to Detroit when he was six months old. He was too young, I guess, to stay behind. He took his first music lessons on clarinet at Cass High School. He left school, packed a tenor sax, and lit out for California where he joined Gene Coy's band. In 1935 he switched to trumpet, which he was struggling to master while in Art Bronson's band. Admiration for Armstrong caused him to change horns. He almost immediately evolved his revolutionary method of playing more notes and crowding a lot of melodic passages into a given chord structure. He did a lot of traveling with territory bands from 1936 to 1940. In 1941 Lionel Hampton picked him up. In 1942 he was part of a trumpet section in Andy Kirk's band, which contained Bill Coleman and Harold Baker. At this time he met the master of the fast horn, Diz, who influenced him deeply. Stints with Barnet, Auld, and Coleman Hawkins followed. He fronted his own combo from 1945 to 1947. In 1947 he joined JATP. He had his own group at the Paris Jazz Festival of May, 1948. In the heyday of bop in the 40's, he was the second, best-known modernist. He then had his own big band, featuring a lot of Afro-Cuban arrangements with Machito. In the winter of 1951-52 he toured the Pacific, Korea, and Japan with Oscar Pettiford. His discography runs into hundreds of sides.

In 1942. I'm pretty sure it was then, I was playing in Charlie Barnet's band. We were at the Adams theatre in Newark, sitting around backstage on a Sunday afternoon. Chubby Jackson, the bass player, turns on the radio to catch a show from the Savoy ballroom, and who should pop out from the speaker but Charlie Parker playing "Cherokee." Well, nobody knew who it was at the time, but we all flipped. Who could that possibly be to play such a horn? He played about ten choruses on the air. After we got finished with our show that night, we went to the Savoy and asked the band leader, Jay McShann, to play "Cherokee," which he did. Charlie got up to do his solo, and the mystery was solved.

We all stood around, practically the whole Barnet band, to wait to meet this guy. In 1941-42 Charlie Barnet had one of the greatest bands around. Oscar Pettiford. Al Killian, Peanuts Holland, and Ralph Burns were just some of the guys in the organization. We talked to Bird and found out where he came from, but I didn't see him again till later when he joined Earl Hines' band. I was still with Barnet, and by coincidence I stopped at the same hotel in West Philly where Bird was staying. Well, we used to jam at this hotel all through the night, Bird and Diz, me and a guitar player. Then the bands moved on in different directions, and I didn't see Parker again until several years later when we both happened to be in California.

Diz and he had split up. Gillespie went back to New York, and Bird stayed on scuffling. He used to come by where I was playing at a place called The Streets Of Paris, and I used to give him a little bread to keep him going. I stayed at that club for six months and then went to San Francisco for a while. When I got back, I first learned that Bird was very troubled. I asked him about the troubles with Ross Russell, and he said that Ross figured that he was put away for a long time and that there would not be much of a chance to record him further. And so he released the records that Parker felt were no good. I personally was there at the "Loverman" session, and Bird was really disturbed. He was turning around and around, and his horn was shooting up in the air, but the sound came out fine. There were no wrong notes, and I feel that the records are beautiful. After that, he went to Camarillo.

Bird came out in six months from Camarillo, picked up his horn, put it to his lips, and he went up from the top to the bottom of the alto with an authority that had never left him. As soon as he saw me, he grinned and said, "Let's play." We went to work at a place called the Hi De Ho Club, and we each were getting a couple a hundred a week. Bird drew his whole salary the first night, and, on the second night, he wanted to draw two hundred more. The owner said, "I can't do that," but he did give Charlie another fifty dollars on his next week's pay. Bird still must have been a little shook up, because he used to line up eight doubles of whiskey and down them before he hit a note on the job. The average man would be flat on his back after that. In fact, the bartender once induced Hampton Hawes, our pianist, to try to emulate that feat. Hawes accepted, and that night we played without a pianist, except when Bird and I alternated at the keyboard. Yes, Bird could play piano. The owner was very angry at the bartender for letting the incident happen.

A lot of Bird's trouble in California which led to his commitment—besides artistic frustration, because the people out there were not ready for the music at that time—was the fact that without money you cannot buy drugs. The price was much higher than in New York. When Bird was with Billy Eckstine, that's the first time I knew of him using drugs. He had a clarinet case full of those little capsules. I said, "Gee, what is that?" He said, "Man, you don't want to be bothered with that." Diz and I were roommates, and we used to be concerned and talk a lot about him. Diz would say, "Bird is doing something way out." I knew that he was using it, because when we got to a theatre in Chicago, Bird was always late, and he'd be constantly falling asleep on the stand. But in some strange way, he knew when he was supposed to solo and he'd cut loose.

Bird was an extremist. Whatever he did, as far as he could go, he would go there. I saw him drink a quart of whiskey and take a handful of benzedrine tablets. A handful of them, and swallow them, and drink whiskey and smoke pot, and do the other thing he was doing besides, and *stand up like a man*.

And you could never figure him. Sometimes he would fall asleep, but the minute you said Bird, he was wide awake. What I saw him take would kill an average man; the average man couldn't stand up under that. Taking a handful of Benzedrene itself would knock the average man down. Bird, I guess, by using so much different things would counteract some of the effect. Maybe the heroin counteracted the benzedrine; the juice counteracted the heroin. I don't know how he did it, but he did it. I can't drink half a quart of whiskey and make sense. I saw him drink a whole quart. I was amazed. How can a man consume all this and have all this other stuff inside him and still be able to make it?

The last few years of his life, he was not very talkative. We used to play at a place that Bird loved. It was called Christie's, twenty miles west out of Boston, in a place called Framingham. It has been sold now, but from 1950 to 1955, everybody in modern jazz played there. It overlooked a lake, and Bird played his most relaxed horn in a separate little wing, while the rest of the band was in the next room.

Jackie McLean

Bird saw great promise in Jackie McLean, and he treated him almost as a son. Born in New York City, in 1932, he played in a neighborhood band that contained the young sidemen Sonny Rollins and Kenny Drew. He worked with Charlie Mingus in 1955 and 1956 and with Art Blakey from 1956 to 1958. He played in the off-Broadway drama The Connection, *and he also had a few lines to deliver, which he did with great histrionic skill.*

I was listening to a record by Trummy Young called "Seventh Avenue." Dizzy Gillespie was on that record and so was Charlie Parker. I had never heard him before. It was just a little part, but that was enough. It was in 1946, the year that I started playing. I was studying with Foots Thomas. The first time I saw Charlie in person he was playing in Dizzy's band at a place called McKinley Ballroom, in the Bronx. I used to go by Bud Powell's house; he used to show me things—chords, changes. One night we went down to the Royal Roost together, and he introduced me to Bird. This was 1948.

In 1952 I had a gig with Miles at Birdland, and Bird came on the stand. It was the first time I played with him. He was always kind and appreciative of my musical efforts. One evening he kept applauding my solos loudly. I know, because there was not much other applause. When I was through with the set, he rushed over and gave me a kiss on the neck.

Sometimes, when he got through jamming at a small club, there were many musicians crowded around or sitting nearby, but he would pass his horn to me as a gesture that he wanted me to continue. We took walks, and I remember him, looking at a plane and saying how nice to be free of the earth or standing in front of a fish store, admiring the light on the scales of the fish, creating color. He told me to emulate the straight cats. One night, in a bad mood, he ordered me to give him a good kick in the behind: "A good kick may knock some sense into me." One day he suggested that we go to the funeral parlor and see Hot Lips Page, who was laid out there. The place was empty. Bird stood a long time before the body, finally saying, "Damn, his big wig sure looks good."

The last time I saw him was not too pleasant. I got sick one night at a place in the Village called Montmartre. Ahmed Basheer took me home, and Bird said he'd mind my horn. He hocked it, and I was quite angry with him. I managed to get it back in time to make a Sunday night job at the Open Door. Bird was there at a table, and I wouldn't talk to him. At closing he was outside, and he said, "Going uptown? I'll get a cab for us."

"I'll get my own, Bird," I said and did.

Not long afterward I was sitting on a bus. I opened a paper and read it. I had to get off that bus. I didn't know what street, but I walked down it, crying.

Jay McShann

Jay McShann was the leader of the band with which Parker made his record debut in 1942. His band, featuring his own blues piano, included musicians like Parker, Gus Johnson, and Gene Ramey, and was considered the best in Kansas City in the years after Basie and Andy Kirk left for the East.

In addition to being a formidable down-yonder blues and boogie-woogie pianist he had an unerring ear for good musicianship. It is to his great credit that, although Bird's style was quite different than that of the rest of his men in the band, he realized that Parker had something and kept him as long as he could.

Bird first played with me in the year of 1938. I came to Kansas City in 1937 from Oklahoma. When I first came here, the guys around K.C., they didn't want to play with him. Bird didn't have his coordination together; they didn't know what he was trying to do. The neck of his sax was always coming unscrewed, and he played everything offbeat; he had it in his head long before he could put it together. They would get up and walk off the stand. One time a leader said to him, "Man, you just hold your horn." That must have hurt, but he didn't show it. He was a pretty cool cat. He didn't show no outward reaction. But that was a challenge. Made him determined. He said he would go into the woodshed. He went with Prof. Buster Smith and George E. Lee to the Ozarks. It was his first gig with older fellows; it was there that he woodshedded. He slept with that horn in the Ozarks and learned about chords in all keys from Efferge Ware, who was the guitarist in the group. After Bird came back—it was less than a year—well, no one said that to him again. Nobody could believe it was the same guy blowing. Bird said it was his coordination. Bird was the man.

It's a fact that Bird used to like Prof., who was working at a place called Lucille's. We used to listen to them broadcast. Prof. and the lady had an argument, and they had to get someone to replace him, because he didn't show up one night. It was Bird. Prof. was one of his strongest influences. Bird also used to talk about Jimmy Dorsey and Frankie Trumbauer and Lester Young.

He liked to jam. He'd go to different places to jam. Bird opened up with me in 1938 in the Plaza in Kansas City. I had six pieces at the time. We worked there for about three or four months and that is when I realized that he was on this wild kick, because he was always late showing up for the job. So we had to let him go.

He hoboed his way to New York. He was always looking for adventure. He stopped off in Chicago and sat in with the King Kolax band. They helped him along to New York. He loved New York. He just looked at the different places, and the different places amazed him. He washed dishes in Jimmy's Chicken Shack in Harlem for a few months, while out front, Art Tatum was gassing everybody. Several months later he got a job with a group at Monroe's Uptown House.

Bird came back and he started up and started playing a horn in Harlan Leonard's band in the last of 1938. During that time Tadd Dameron was writ-

The sax section of the Jay McShann Band: Bob Mabane, Bird, John Jackson, and Freddy Culliver.

ing for the group. Harlan's quit the business now. He's in Los Angeles, California, working as a mailman. In a sense he's still carrying the message.

There were two big bands, Harlan's and mine. I went up from six pieces: myself, Gene Ramey, bass, Gus Johnson, drums, Buddy Anderson and Orville Minor, trumpets and Bob Mabane, saxophone. Bird said he wanted to blow with us. He told me he was all straight. "I've stopped goofing, I want to blow with you cats." He didn't start blowing with us till late 1939 or 1940. The way we rehearsed, one guy handled the reeds, and one guy rehearsed the brass, and then we put the whole band together. I could always depend on Bird to handle the reed section because he had straightened up. He'd get mad if anyone was late. He was also doing some writing at the time. He had some numbers in the book. He had "Yardbird Suite." There were twelve pieces in the band; we added a guy whenever we found what we wanted.

We had a little fellow in the brass section, Buddy Anderson. Diz would pick this particular fellow out when we met, and they would go to a room together and practice. Anderson had what Diz wanted. He played in the same style as Bird only on the trumpet. Diz was playing like Roy Eldridge at this time. They would go up to the hotel and blow. He didn't have it with the lip, but he had it here, in his head. He went as far as his lip would take him. He and Diz got real tight. He's in Oklahoma City now. He quit playing the trumpet. He took sick and switched to piano. He's making it in Oklahoma City. He was a modernistic player. Bird always admired the guy. Bird had a soul, that he played like he had been hurt. To me Anderson's soul didn't hurt like Bird's. Bird had a crying soul.

Bird introduced this nutmeg to the guys. It was a cheap and legal high. You can take it in milk or Coca Cola. The grocer across the street came over to the club owner and said, "I know you do all this baking because I sell from 8 to 10 nutmegs a day." And the owner came back and looked at the bandstand and there was a whole pile of nutmeg boxes.

We always had this cat who acted a little feminish. There were two horns that always had to be gotten out of hock. Bird's was one, and Bird got this Harold Bruce to hock his too. I guess Bruce was expecting something to happen. One night, some pretty girls were in the house, some fine chicks; all these cats were getting them a chick. Harold Bruce and Bird had a room together; Bruce couldn't stand it when he seen him take the chick to their room, especially because he had no place to go to sleep. He hit Bird in the head with a bottle, and Bird conked him with a bottle. When I saw them on the bandstand that night they both were playing with towels wrapped around their heads like swamis. "Look at you looking like mummies." I gave them the devil about it. But you couldn't make Bird mad about nothing.

He was very straight at this time—saved his money and everything. He was eating a lot of food then.

Once he told me "I won't be able to be here for rehearsal but I'll tell you what, I'm going to the woodshed. This cat (John Jackson) is makin' a fool outta me. If I miss a note at the performance you got the privilege of fining me." He didn't make any mistakes. We threw the book at him but he cut it.

We made some records in Wichita, Kansas, at a radio station there. I think we used Buddy Anderson, Little Joe Taswell, Charlie, Bob Mabane, Orville Minor and the rhythm. Fred Higginson liked the band, and he asked us if we wanted to make some acetates at the station. We made five or six numbers; I remember "I Found a New Baby," stuff like that. Everybody went for them.

It wasn't too long afterward when we went to Texas to make our first recording for Decca. We were playing a lot of stuff like "Yardbird Suite," which Bird called it later on. We had another name for it then, but we were playing all sorts of numbers like that. Dave Kapp, who was in charge of the session, didn't want it. We played fifteen or twenty numbers before we got him to accept something. I think we made "Hootie Blues." (The fellows used to kid me about the bottle, and call me Hootie. I used to like the bottle a lot. Anything to drink was hootch then, and anytime we'd see somebody who looked a little full, we'd say, "Look out! He's hootie.") And we made "Confessin the Blues," "Vine Street Boogie," "Swingmatism."

We started to do a lot of college dates. Bird got his name when we were going to Lincoln, Nebraska. Whenever he saw some chicken on the menu, he'd say, "Give me some of the yardbird over there."

We were in two cars and the car he was in drove over a chicken, and Bird put his hands on his head and said, "No, stop! Go back and pick up that yardbird." He insisted on it and we went back and Bird got out of the car and carefully wrapped up the chicken and took it with him to the hotel where we were staying and made the cook there cook it for us. He told him we had to have this yardbird.

We were on the stage in the theatre one time, and I see a guy that I know is a pusher—I could tell it. I don't know it, but I could recognize him. I gave orders to the backstage doorman that no one was to see anyone in the band. I did everything I could to prevent his buying stuff, because Bird had proved himself proficient many times, the way he rehearsed the group and always came up with new ideas.

Bird left the band the last of 1942. We had to go to Detroit. He had a little too much that day and we had to carry him off the bandstand and lay him on a table. We couldn't feel no pulse. He had an overdose. This happened at the Paradise Theatre. We left him there all night. We were afraid to call the doctor because we were afraid he might be, you know. . . . When he came to, I told him, "Bird, you done got back on your kick again, and so I've got to let you go." Andy Kirk gave him a lift to New York.

Charlie Mingus

Charlie Mingus, one of the most distinguished and creative bassists in jazz, was born in Nogales, Arizona in 1922. He has written over one hundred compositions. He is one of the few real innovators since Parker. He owned his own record company, Debut, and recorded Bird under the name of Charlie Chan. It was a concert they did on May 15, 1953, in Toronto, Canada. The album is called "Jazz at Massey Hall." The feeling between them was that of brothers.

Bird paid me the dubious honor of borrowing five dollars from me back in 1946, when I was in the Lionel Hampton band. In 1951 he borrowed another ten dollars. The next year was a tough one for me in music; so I took a job in the post office. One night I get a phone call from Parker: "Mingus, what are you doing working in the post office? A man of your artistic stature? Come with me." I told him I was making good money. He offered me $150 a week, and I accepted.

When the first pay day came around I asked him for $165 dollars. I reminded him of the old debt. His eyes rolled back in his head in amazement. "Yes, I remember. But do you remember when I lent you fifteen dollars in front of Birdland?" (An event which never took place.)

I decided to gorilla him. "I was making almost as much money in the post office with overtime, and it was steady. You pay me or I'm going to try you. Great as you are, I'll kick your ass in." He paid.

We used to get into long, involved discussions between sets about every subject from God to man, and, before we realized it, we would be due back on the stage. He used to say, "Mingus, let's finish this discussion on the bandstand. Let's get our horns and talk about this." He used to refer to me as a composer more often than a bassist. "I know you write; you are really a great writer."

I was once rehearsing something with some musicians. One of them was an altoist in the Philharmonic. He was having some fingering difficulty on a certain passage. Parker, who happened to be sitting in the last row of the empty hall, came up front and helpfully suggested finger manipulation that solved the problem. To be aware of the notes and the fingering from that distance was an amazing thing.

I loved the man so much I couldn't stand seeing what he was doing to himself. I decided I was going to talk to him like a human being. It was during

151

that fateful engagement at Birdland which got so much notoriety. Everyone has different versions of that hassleous weekend, but here is the version of one who was on the stand.

Friday was perfect. Everybody was normal. No goofs. Bird was great as usual and even played fresh things. The second night Bud Powell is very unruly. Bird is late. The set starts off with me and Art Blakey. Kenny Dorham is late, also. Charlie comes up to the bandstand and tells us to hold everything. He then calls a tune and starts counting a tempo and Bud plays a different tempo. This goes on a second time. "Come on, baby," Bird says to Bud; he goes over to the piano to set the tempo for him.

After intermission, Bud starts doing the same thing again. Bird walks off in disgust, and proceeds to get drunk. It was then that I decided to talk to him. "Bird, you are more than our leader, you are a leader of the Negro race. Don't set a bad example."

Art Blakey lent me support. "Bird, a great man like you should have us walking around in Cadillacs."

I told him that if he jumped out of a window, twenty kids would jump out too. Kenny Dorham chimed in, "I wouldn't jump out of a window." We told Kenny he could go.

Bird was listening for the first time. Next thing I know, tears are running down his face. "You know," I continued, "you lost the poll this issue."

"No I didn't," he said. "I got the banner home to prove it."

"That was the *Down Beat* poll. I'm talking about the *Metronome* poll. You came in second; Paul Desmond was first."

The rest of the evening was no better than the first two sets. Bird's watch must have been off, because he took the strains of the theme to be the beginning of the set instead of the end, and we played a lot without him. Oscar Goodstein and Charlie had words. Oscar ordered him out. Bird reminded him who he was talking to and strode out, only to return later, walk up to the bar, put a wet cheek next to mine, and say, "Mingus, I'm goin' someplace, pretty soon, where I'm not gonna bother anybody."

Most of the soloists at Birdland had to wait for Parker's next record in order to find out what to play next. What will they do now?

Bird is not dead; he's hiding out somewhere, and he'll be back with some new shit that will scare everyone to death.

Orville "Piggy" Minor

From Kansas City, Orville "Piggy" Minor is a family man who never wants to leave. He started professionally in 1936, playing in a seven-piece combo, led by a girl pianist, Countess Johnson. After the Basie band left Kansas City, Minor was considered the best trumpet man left in the city. He and Bird were in the McShann band together and lived in the same neighborhood. Orville was part of the greatest service band in World War II. Willie Smith, the alto player, was the leader and the aggregation also had Clark Terry in it. Orville Minor also plays vibes and valve trombone. When I visited him he was beginning to investigate the guitar.

My wife once saved him from getting burned up. She looked out the window and said there was smoke coming out of Bird's window. It was 1942, in the Woodside Hotel in New York. They investigated and found Bird asleep in bed with flames all around him. He had fallen asleep with a cigarette and dropped it on the floor. Another time my wife noticed the hypodermic apparatus lying around in his room. At that moment an agent came in and proceeded to search. With great presence of mind, she placed a towel over it and then sat down on it.

He would get your last dollar. He was too charming to refuse. People went out of their way to pacify and please him. "I don't want the man to close the place," he'd say, just when the man was ready to close. He wanted to play an hour more. It was always just an hour more. And do you know—the man would keep the place open. He also called me Orville. When he called me that lovingly. I knew he was after something. He used to steal my solos.

Alan Morrison

Alan Morrison became New York editor of Ebony *in 1948. He has met, dealt with, and written about jazzmen for years. In World War II he was a U. S. Army correspondent for* The Stars and Stripes. *He was a close friend of Parker from 1947 until Parker's death. He has been a* Down Beat International *jazz critic. An article on Bird by Morrison appeared in a French jazz magazine called* Blue Star Revue, *dated* Noel, *1948.*

I met Bird in June 1947. He had returned from California and was living at the Dewey Square Hotel over on West 117th Street. One of his records is called "Dewey Square," by the way. I went over to the hotel to ask him to play at a benefit to be sponsored by an interracial veterans' organization whose purpose was to strengthen Negro veterans' rights. Bird was wild about the project, and adding to his enthusiasm was the fact that the guys playing the benefit were Max Roach, Dizzy, Bud Powell, and Curly Russell. While I was telling him about this, the sweat was pouring off him, and his temperature was over 100 degrees. The man had pneumonia.

"I'll go. Just take me in an ambulance," he said. The heart of the guy was so big that he wanted to disobey all medical orders, and he kept repeating that I should call an ambulance for him and he'd make it. Needless to say, it was too impractical and too inhuman a thing to do. Another hotel he frequented was the Marden Hotel; and whenever I visited him there, he'd be listening to Hindemith and Schoenberg over and over. Another of his favorite composers was Mozart. He especially enjoyed *Eine Kleine Nachtmusik.*

Bob Newman

A 34-year-old tenor saxophonist, Bob Newman also has a formidable reputation as an arranger.

I became acquainted with Bird when he was playing at the Downbeat Club in Philly, my home town. Sometime later I approached him about lessons, and he graciously consented. The price was five dollars per lesson, and they usually took all afternoon, except for minor intermissions to a bar for a few drinks. The place of instruction was at the late Lord Buckley's pad. Bird used to stress playing loud, "Blow through your horn, play loud, keep your throat open." He wanted me to control my vibrato with the different parts of my mouth. The vibrato that Bird used was from the back of his tongue. Physiologically it wasn't, but he felt the sensation at the back of his tongue. The idea of playing loud is not too acceptable with most teachers for beginners, but

Bird felt that a horn man should make his statements strong. "Blow through your horn as if you were blowing out a candle." At that time he was playing his plastic horn. He used a reed which was so stiff that I could hardly get a peep out of it.

Around 1949 a musician named Gene Roland, who formerly played trumpet and trombone with the Stan Kenton orchestra, started a band built around Bird. There were twenty-seven pieces; eight saxophones, eight trumpets, and six trombones. I can't recall all the guys, but there was myself on baritone; Al Cohn, Zoot Sims, Charlie Kennedy, and Donald Lamphere on tenor; Joe Maini, alto; Al Porcino, lead trumpet; and Kenny Dorham, Red Rodney, and Eddie Burt on trombone. The band rehearsed for two weeks. Bird led and supervised the aggregation superbly. He used to appear formally and formidably every day, carrying his arrangement brief case with dignity, which I later found out only contained a bottle of gin. That was a dream band. The format of the arrangements were just about the same on all the tunes. The band would play the first chorus ensemble; then Bird would play a solo with the rhythm section; then the backgrounds would build up section by section, with the saxes coming in pianissimo first; then the trombones a little louder; volume would be building up all the time; finally, all the trumpets; by that time, the volume was tremendous and almost unbelievable; and on top of it all, you could hear Bird screaming, penetrating all that brass.

The band was to open at the Adams Theatre in Newark. Lord Buckley arranged the date. He brought the owner down to listen to the band. He did and he liked it, but was frightened by its size. He said, "I like your band but it's too big. If you can knock it down to a quartet, I'll buy it." After that the band just melted away. I have a tape made on a poor machine which is the only remaining souvenir of Bird's great orchestra that existed for two weeks.

Anita O'Day

Anita O'Day is a child of the depression. Poverty had her working in her early teens. In the 1930's she made money dancing in "walkathon" contests. "Sometimes I'd dance without sleeping forty-eight hours at a stretch. Brother, you get tough that way." In 1938 she worked as a singing waitress at Kitty Davis' Café in Chicago's Loop. Carl Cons, then editor of Down Beat, *heard her, and was impressed. When he opened a night club of his own, he hired her. From there she joined Krupa early in 1941. She has recently made a fine comeback after a long period of absence.*

In the winter of 1950 I was working at a place called the Show Boat in Philadelphia. Buddy De Franco and a small group were backing me. One night I was up to the third number in a set, when in back of me, I hear a beautiful alto solo, propelling and inspiring me. I went through the number but was too scared to see who it was. When I finally did, there was no one there. I asked Buddy, "Am I crazy; who was that?" "That was Bird," he said. "It sure was," I answered, "because he flew out as quick as he flew in."

That was the only experience I ever had with Charlie Parker until an evening in 1954. I was appearing at the Flame Show Bar in Detroit, and in between sets, I went over to a place called the Crystal Lounge where Parker was playing. When he spotted me, he made the following little speech—although he did not know me. "I would like to acknowledge the presence of my good, friend Anita O'Day, but please do not ask her to sing because she is under contract to another establishment in this city." I came back to hear him a second time that evening, and this time I sang a few numbers with his group.

Mrs. Addie Parker

Mrs. Addie Parker, Charlie Parker's mother, has lived for twenty years at 1535 Olive Street in Kansas City, Missouri, in a two-story house with a lawn and backyard which she bought with money she earned herself as a cleaning woman at a Western Union telegraph office. She spent all of her life in the two Kansas Cities. In her forties, she began to study to become a practical nurse, and she now works in a Kansas City Hospital. She still does all her own housework, which now includes caring for four boarders in the upstairs rooms which she had hoped would one day be a home for Charlie and his family.

Charles was a fat baby and a fat child. At eleven months he walked, and he began to speak good at two. He graduated Crispus Attucks Public School at eleven years old and always got fine grades. In Lincoln High School he was the pride of his teachers, especially Miss Bridey, who said, "Your boy is going to amount to something." Only once she did send him home for fighting with another boy. Charles licked him for making fun of his face, which was broken out with pimples. School was too easy for him in a way; he could reel off his lessons without much effort. He quit in the third year and put his age up four years to get into the musician's union. School did one great thing for him; he was given a tuba to play. I didn't go for that; was so heavy and funny coiled around him with just his head sticking out, so I got him another instrument. He started playing at thirteen. He was never interested in sports. All he cared about was music and reading. I used to find loads of books in the cellar.

He was sixteen years old when he married Rebecca Ruffing, who was a few years older than he was. He came to me one day and said, "Mama, I think I am in love, and I'm old enough to get married." He may not have been old enough but he was big enough. I told him when he felt he was sure, then it was alright. A short while afterward, before their marriage, Rebecca's mother and six children moved in upstairs.

They were married two years, and then she got a legal divorce. Rebecca has been married several times since then and now lives in California.

John, who is two years older than Charles, is his half-brother. They have the same father but different mothers. John never knew the difference because

I treated them both equally. John is a post office employee and lives in Kansas City, Kansas. John has always loved Charles.

They collected $11,000 at the benefit fund for Charles. Uncle Sam took a thousand. I never saw a penny of that benefit fund.

I can hardly talk about Charles, it hurts so much. If you break an arm or a leg you can fix it, but there's no mending a broken heart. Whenever the band was playing in Tootie's Mayfair Club they would take me out in a car. I'd get out of my uniform, dress up, and the cats would call for me. I sometimes stayed up a whole night to hear Charles.

Bird was the cutest and prettiest child I ever saw.

A month ago this girl comes up the stairs and told me who she was. The girl arrived with a man who I remembered. He had grown this moustachious thing all around his chin but I remembered him.

She had fiery red hair, so red, it looked about to catch fire. She came up the steps, and I said to her, "What is it, Girl?"

"I want to talk to you."

So she came in the house. She had on yellow moccasins, bare legs, and a pink set of sweaters and a red skirt.

"I got into this trouble because of Charlie," she said.

"Charles didn't get you into any trouble."

"Did you get his burial money?"

First I talked on not heeding her question; then she asked again, "Did you get his burial money?" Then I answered, "I'm his mother, and my name is on that death policy."

She said, "I'm still his wife." And I'd never heard of her!

Charles's father was from Memphis. When I met him, he was playing the piano and singing on the vaudeville stages around Kansas City. He died when Charles was seventeen. Some lady stabbed him during a drunken quarrel. Charles Senior drunk terrible. I got a hold of Charles and brought him home for the funeral. His father and I had been separated eight years. He was on the railroads as a chef. He could cook anything. He could dance; he was a good scholar; he could play the piano; but he was a drunkard. I tried so many times to get him to stop but all he would say was "Ten years from today I will stop drinking."

When Charles was sixteen he sold my electric iron and got 50 cents for it. He needed a cab to get to an appointment, he said. He always loved cabs. Rebecca did not have any money around, so he grabbed the iron and sold it to a furniture store. I went to the store and got it back from the man without paying any more than 50 cents because I told him what had happened. The electric iron prank was the only one I remember him doing. He used to phone for money, and I always had $150 to $200 around the house for his emergencies. He always paid whatever it was back with interest. If he borrowed $100 I'd get back $150. When I graduated Nursing School in 1949 he sent me

Charlie at fourteen months.

(Opposite page)
Above:
Bird's birth certificate, establishing the date of his birth as August 29, 1920, thus disproving wild rumors as to his real age.
Below:
Charlie at a year and a half.

$300 and told me it was for uniforms or whatever I needed.

I told Charles the best way to go on living, the way he was doing, he'd better get out of town. (These girls were coming up to the house in cabs.) They give you a book of matches with a name or a number on it. It would burn me up. One of those girls had a pocket full of reefers. I imagine she's on narcotics now.

As I say, Charles's father died when he was seventeen, I got ahold of Charles, who was in Chicago, and brought him home for the funeral. Charles could hardly recognize the body it was in such horrible shape from loss of blood. We had been separated for years.

"Mama, what made him do it?" Charles asked.

"He liked the lady, I guess."

They put her in jail till he was buried, then they let her go. She drank herself to death a year later.

I got him his instrument in 1936. Robert Simpson, his friend who played the trombone who died of an operation at nineteen, was his inseparable friend. They once tried to make a job playing at the Orchid Room at 12th and Vine but they came home a little sad and declared, "They threw us out."

"Charles, if you get into trouble you've got to tell mother."

They sent me two plaques. I rewrapped one and sent it to his boy Leon in California. I raised Leon until he was ten, and then his mother stole him away from me and took him to Baltimore.

In a year or two from now I can take these things. It hurts too much to look at them.

He was born in 852 Freeman St., Kansas City, Kansas. He was reared at a Catholic day school because I was working all the time. The way they teach you, it stays with you. I was a Baptist, but he'd say, "We don't do things that way," talking about his Catholicism. As a child he had a gang of friends and just loved movies and ice cream sodas. He never was in the draft. The only work he ever done was going to Chicago blowing his horn. He was not spoiled through, because I think a spoiled child never leaves his parents. Charles would go away weeks and weeks. He liked to see things and do things.

I think Kansas City is a little Southern. Charles would take his watch to the pawn shop, and the pawn broker, who was friendly, would say to me, "Tell Charlie Parker to stay out of Kansas City; it's a stinkin' town. They don't want him to have a chance. Never." They paid musicians very little, and there's no record companies. After he went to Chicago he said, "Mama, it's different, I want you to come here and I'll take care of you."

But I told him, "You go ahead and live your life." He lived like he wanted to.

If they saw you running around with white girls, they would take you downtown and kill you, and they did. They take you to Swope Park and kill you. I was glad that he left.

Charles got into serious trouble one night when he kept a taxi for six or seven hours and ran up a $10 bill which he couldn't pay. The taxi driver tried to snatch his horn, and Charles stabbed him with a dagger. They took him off to the farm. I told the police, "How dare you treat my son like that. Bring him back!" He came home the next day. They'd taken the dagger away from him.

Charles never let anything go to his head. "You don't have to 'mister' me," he'd say. He couldn't get along with Rebecca; they were school sweethearts. He wanted to remarry her after they were separated five years. She went up to St. Louis with him. "She don't know how to act or talk; she just wants me to sit in a room all day, and I have to go out with the boys." You know how the girls pull on a man.

He was the most affectionate child you ever saw. When he was two he'd come to the door and say, "Mama, you there?" And I'd say, "Yes, I'm here," and he'd go on playing. Since he could talk he'd say, "Mama, I love you."

Chan called me and said, "Did you know that Charles had passed?" I answered, "Yes, I know," because Doris had called before and said, "Parky, sit down, because this is a shocking thing. Are you alone?," and I said, "Oh no, Charles isn't dead?"

He was stuck down in some white morgue. Doris asked them at this morgue, "Do you have a fellow going under the name of John Parker?" and this attendant, "All I want is my money for some work on the body I've done." He advised her to put him in a burlap bag—how could they put my child in a burlap bag?

Doris had called me and said, "We found him; I've taken care of everything." It was Dizzy and his wife who was with her. She stayed out at Tommy Potter's house. She called me every evening. I thought it wasn't nothing but an overdose of dope. I talked with them (Charles and the Baroness) three days before he died. She said, "How are you? I hope to meet you sometimes." I said to Charles, "If you're sick in any way let me know." He said they wanted to give him an electric encephalogram. "Charles," I said, "don't take it. Come home to mother. I work in the finest hospital in Kansas City, and I will have it done if it is a necessity."

I worked night and day for two years. Nights in the Western Union, cleaning the office, and days, cleaning and taking care of babies. In the hospital you never know what days you get off. I have to look at the bulletin board.

In 1953 Norman Granz gave him $1,000 one night. I said, "Why do you have to spend it all?"

"Mama, it's high living; it costs to go with the cats."

"There isn't anybody a big shot," I told him. "You spend your money, and what do you get? A kick in the teeth."

"Mama, if I saved my money, the wives would take it away from me."

Chan once called me up and said, "If I didn't get him, I think I would die." Once when Doris was sick, Charles told her to go home, stay awhile, and then come back. He wanted more children.

"Mama," he says, "after I'm gone, the Parkers will still live." When Doris left, Chan moved in. I think the world of Doris. I run my telephone up to $25 that time trying to get him to live right. "Mother wants you to treat Doris right."

Bird had a white friend here in town named Charlie. He said to Bird, "When you get ready to go, I'm gonna fly you to New York." The Southern in him showed itself when he came to Charles's home in New York. He was greeted warmly by Doris, but when he saw that it was a white woman, he left quickly, and that was the end of their friendship. I told Charles, "You spoiled everything bringing him to your home."

A girl in town here started Charles on reefer stuff. "I found some in his pockets. "What in the world is this stinking stuff?" I said.

Charles smiled and said, "Don't destroy any of that, mama, it's too good." She had this long pretty brown hair. She was a pretty girl, she's mixed. She was in that world around those night clubs. She lost her mind twice. I went and saw her in the isolation ward. She's around here now, right in the neighborhood. She's fat now. I saw her once years ago when she came out of this house. She had nothing on but her dress; my goodness, that is just like that girl! She never worked. She used to see things (crazy). She came into the house once and said, "Didn't you see anything?" Then she said, "Don't tell him I'm here."

I would always have to give him $20 to $25 to help dress himself. I wanted him to study in the conservatory. I put away $500 for the purpose, but the bank closed and I lost the money. He wanted to be a doctor. He paid alimony to Rebecca, $5 a week.

Did you read in *Coronet* *"She Lived Nine Hours In Hell"*? If you can't pay and you keep coming around begging, they snuff you out with an overdose when you become a pest. There's a boy in the neighborhood who is an addict. I told him, "Why don't you quit that."

"Oh, Mrs. Parker, you feel so good when you take it."

They brought a boy into the hospital. They had to tie him down. They put a thick strap acros his chest. The doctors didn't know what it was, but I knew what it was and wouldn't tell. I just told them it'll take three days, and then he'll be all right. They asked me how I knew but I wouldn't tell them. The doctors always say that I have that "old-fashioned mother wit."

I told Charles, "Don't bring any company here; I have my house filled up." Finally he found some chick here. All the roomers would ask me about it. "Where are you going?" I asked him.

"I gotta take this chick home, she likes me."

The girl was white, red-headed and good-looking. She pushed dope, and he had met her through one of those numbers on a match cover people were always slipping him. She was driving a great big 1952 Cadillac. She kept coming to the house. I told him to go to a hotel with her.

"It don't look nice."

One night at five o'clock in the morning he knocks on my bedroom door and says, "Wake up, this chick wants to go to sleep with me."

"You'd better go to the hotel."

"No!" he shouted.

"You tell her she's gotta go."

Anyway, they went. When they came back I had his bags in the hall. She worked for the Italian.

He was about seventeen and in New York when he took those drugs. We had some terrible quarrels, and I said, "One house isn't built for two nasty people. You know mother loves you, but you've got to obey mother or else you've got to leave here."

He was all I had, and all I wanted to put money in. Twenty years I've had a telephone line, not a party line, for that boy to call me. He once asked for some money for a parking fine which had him in jail. He had parked on the wrong side of the street when he was high. I told him he would have it in an hour and a half, and I ran down to the telegraph office.

He has always been a good boy. The most he cost me is when he went to New York. When I graduated in 1949, he sent me $300 for a uniform and a cap and so forth. All that stuff was given to us. I went out to the Medical Center in 1950 and I was hired. I was just in two towns in all my life, the two Kansas Cities; I never cared to go any place either.

His father was musical, but I've never done anything of a musical kind.

I just cried when I saw what they had written, "Charlie Parker was 53 years old." He was older than his mother! They finally straightened it out, because all you have to do was to look at his picture and you'd know he was a young man.

He first started playing out at the old Gaiety Theatre with Lawrence Keyes and all of them. I don't remember him playing with Harlan Leonard, but I remember the Gaiety Theatre; it was a white club and they all took an interest in him.

Charlie was married when he was only sixteen. Rebecca was four years older than he was and wanted to be his mother to him. He wouldn't stand for that and started beating up on her, you know. I told him that wasn't right and it would only cause a lot of trouble and the best thing to do was leave, and he went to Chicago.

Jay McShann used to come over to our house and play on our piano, and those two used to have a time together. It was some other fellow's band at the Gaiety, and he had Charlie and Lawrence in it with him.

I didn't hear him play before he left Kansas City, but when he came back here in 1952 and was out at the Mayfair, I went out there every night. Several people would call for me, and we'd all get dressed up and go out there and have the time of our lives. I was so dead the next day I didn't even want to get up.

My nurse supervisor, Mrs. Driscoll went to New York after Charles had passed and she said, "Oh, Mrs. Parker, that Birdland is the prettiest place in New York." She used to go to all the colored dances when she was a student nurse, to hear Bennie Moten and all of them, you know. In those days they didn't want colored and white people to mix, but it's not like that now.

He always thought he could make it here, but after he and wife disagreed he had to leave and went to Chicago for awhile and from there to New York.

You know he wanted to be a doctor and I was going to put up the money for his schooling. When Charles got put here at Lincoln, they didn't have good teachers, and he didn't care for school, and after a while he asked me to get him a horn and I did, and he forgot about being a doctor then. When he left here he put the horn in pawn, but I finished paying for it, was some 200 odd dollars, and that was in depression times. The first horn I got him only cost me $45 at Mitchell's down on Main Street, but I had it overhauled, and it ran into money. But that other horn was just beautiful, white gold with green keys. Just beautiful.

I don't think I'll ever get over it, but I do feel a little better now. He was my heart, you know. I just lived for Charles. I used to tell him when he'd come home that he could have the upstairs, and I'd take the downstairs, or we'd go down south somewhere and buy a home. He was a dear child, just lovely.

Sunday was his day to call, and he'd call me every weekend. He called me just before he died. He called that Sunday and said he was fine. I had heard he was supposed to go into a hospital and have an electrocardiagram. I told him if he had to have that to come home, because I was in the hospital all the time and I could be near him.

He did say that he wished Jay would come to New York again. He liked Jay, and Jay always lifted up his bands. When he met Dizzy, of course, things changed. He was an Eastern boy but he had been out here before. He didn't like Father Hines, because he was older, and he didn't care for Duke Ellington. When Norman Granz wanted to make those records using oboes, flutes and those, he knew he was going to the top. He'd say, "Mama, I'm going to the top, my name's going to be in lights, and you're going to be there to see it," and I just couldn't hold him. Norman used to take such pains with him and talked to him for nearly two hours on the phone, and when they were finished, I asked Charlie how was he going by train or by plane? He said he was going to fly.

All the people would be crazy about Charles's music, but they wouldn't know what he was playing. I used to tell them, "You'll just have to listen."

One of the announcers on the radio would announce just what Charles was going to play and I have a long list of it somewhere. He announced that when Charles's birthday, the 28th, came they'd have several hours of his records. All the boys used to call me and ask to be sure to call them if it went on. It never did because the announcer was away on vacation when that time came.

Ernest Daniels, the drummer, got hurt with Charles when they first started out, you know. Charles got two broken ribs, and Ernest got all his teeth knocked out. The old man playing piano was killed. Ernest was driving on that ice, and the car got turned around.

They didn't have very many bands around here after Bennie Moten died. The Clouds of Joy left, and then Jay came along and fitted right in. Charles was still in school when Count Basie left, and even then he used to tell everyone he was nineteen. He was always a big boy. A lot of them didn't ask, and I didn't tell them, and those that did ask, like Jay, I'd say to them, "What difference did it make?" He wanted to play; give him a chance. If he'd waited a couple of years until he got older he might have been out of luck and had to do something else.

I never went to any of the dances until Charles had come back home. I heard all the other bands, Clouds of Joy, etc. Charles had some white friends who used to pick me up at the hospital and take me out to the Mayfair.

Did you see that story in *Playboy?* Doris sent it to me. I was so hurt I couldn't even finish it, haven't read it yet. They certainly told some big ones. Said he looked like a scarecrow and all that. Whenever he needed anything, all he had to do was to call, and it was there. That's what I worked for and what I lived for, that boy. He called me all the time when he was in California. He said, "Mama, our music doesn't go over so fine out here."

One day he called me out at the hospital, when his little girl Pree died.

Chan wrote me a letter after my boy passed. She claimed her boy was Charles's, and I know that wasn't so because he was four or five months old when Charles met her. After he passed she wrote me that she meant that it wasn't Charles's but that he accepted him. That's different.

I just loved Doris. I never saw Chan in my life, but she's got little Bird, and the money is coming in, and I guess she doesn't mind.

I don't know where he got his nickname Bird from. Another thing, in those books they wrote Charles Christopher Parker, Jr. I don't know anything about any Christopher; his daddy wasn't Christopher. Just plain Charles Parker. He was Senior and Charles was Junior. I got a subpoena when Chan wanted all of Charles's furniture. The question was whether they were married. Charles's car, Charles's horn and all of Charles's clothes, and his ring, the one he had when he was married to Doris. Chan said Charles hasn't been married to no one but Geraldine. I never heard of her.

They almost buried him in Potter's Field. But I'd have had him dug up and brought here. Norman had the body sent to me, and I didn't have to pay a penny; he was swell. I can't understand why he didn't get his horn. I wanted

Bird's Second wife, Geraldine.

Below:
Rebecca, Bird's first wife, with
her second husband and Teddy
Blume, Bird, and Leon Parker.

his horn, and I'd love to have it. Norman was in California and couldn't transact business the way he would if he was in New York. I'm sure he would have gotten it for me.

All my friends at the hospital, white and colored, said they never saw anyone put away as nice as he was and I really appreciate what Norman did for me.

A lady wrote me and said she had some pictures of Charlie Parker that she was going to send me. I didn't want to hurt her feelings but those things hurt me so that I was going to write her and tell her not to send them. I never did.

Everytime I see a picture or a letter from him, it just hurts. They're all locked up in that trunk of his. I washed all the pictures and frames and wrapped them up and put them away. I can't look at them.

I had an experience once. Some fellow came to the house in a cab and asked for Charlie Parker. Charles was asleep then and I asked what it was all about. He said Charles owed him a bill for $15. I asked what for and he said that was his business. He said if I paid the fifteen he would go on home. I said, "Without a bill?" He would come around the next day and ask for more money. That peddler was the first one to meet Charles at the airport when he came back to Kansas City. I told him I didn't want him around Charles because of what he had done. I always said that if someone was going to do something not to do it at home, and that was what Charles tried to do.

He brought two pills around and said they'd cost Charles $10 and that I was to give them to him. I was studying to be a nurse at that time, and I knew what they were, and Charles never got them, because I put them in the fire. He should have known that I would know what they were, because I had a dictionary that listed all the narcotic and drug names, and I knew what they were. I saw him on the street about three months ago, but I never want to speak to him again. And he was one of Charles's friends.

I hate that fellow. He brought some of that stuff here. "When Charlie wakes up give this to him," he said, handing me some white squares of paper with something wrapped up in it. I didn't know what it was at the time. A friend of his was at the house, and he noticed how Charles had changed somewhat. My Charles was asleep, and this boy said to me, "Look how Parker is breathing; Charles is loaded with something." His eyes were open at times, his breathing was heavy, and his tongue was lolling out of his mouth. In Camarillo he bit a little side piece of his tongue off. I told that fellow who sold dope as long as he's black not to put his foot on my porch again. "Why does your mother hate me?" he used to ask Charles. I told Charles why I hated him. "He's the first one to meet you at the airport. I hate him cause of it— no good junks who go everywhere you go."

Once he made away with a little more than his share and the Italian had him half whipped to death. I used to get some of Charles's records in the mail from New York. They sent a bill for $25 for them. I just turned them over to my lawyer. I didn't even open the package because I didn't have anything to play them on. Their lawyers used to write me, but I sent the records back and had the receipt for them, insurance and everything. I wrote him that I didn't want them, and that they had been sent back. I didn't hear from them again. They tried again and had a school kid write me that they cut the price of records to $14, and I wrote back and said I didn't care what the price was I didn't want them. I went to Mr. Zee's record store to get one of his records after he passed, but he didn't have it and told me to write to several different shops, and they'd probably send it to me free, but I never did do it. I guess I picked the wrong profession, because there's so much suffering. Every day when someone is hurt or needs help it takes something out of you. They'd tell you someone needed help, and you'd go to help them, and they'd be dead, and that's always a shock.

Doris Parker

I first met him through a girl friend of mine who was going with a musician. A little while later I got a job as a hat check girl on 52nd Street. This was around 1944, and I got to see a lot of Charlie. Charlie and I lived together for some time before we were married in Tia Juana, in 1948. I really had no strong desire for marriage, but Charlie was going through a jealousy period, a romantically insecure stage with me; so I said yes. He was with the Norman Granz JATP package in Los Angeles. We drove to Tia Juana, and we were back that night so that Charlie could make his gig. We separated in 1950, but we were never divorced legally at any time. The parting was a combination of things. I was in no physical condition to cope with the erratic life of a jazz musician. I was nervous and bothered by low blood pressure and anemia. I just couldn't take the anxiety of wondering where he was the nights he came home very late or not at all. Visions of him hospitalized or in jail would come into my mind. I went back to my mother in Rock Island, Illinois.

In the beginning of our relationship, the differences in our psychological make-ups and upbringing were very cementing, and we had some real good years together. We lived at 411 Manhattan Avenue, New York City. Argonne Thornton lived there, too. I am very punctilious about bills and allied responsibilities, and some of this rubbed off on Charlie. Also, I had a very wonderful childhood, and Charlie had no childhood whatsoever; and it was fun taking him on picnics and ball games and to try to give him some of the childhood he missed. His kind of fun at fourteen was going on benzedrine parties with

Chan, Charlie, and stepdaughter Kim.

his friends. At fifteen, thanks to some character in Kansas City, he became a drug addict.

My mother was very fond of him and was prone to side with him when arguments came up between us. The fact that it was a mixed marriage troubled her not one bit. Bird was a source of both grief and pride to his own mother; and to make up for the grief, I insisted that he be buried in Kansas City, because I know he would want to make her content in that. He admired his father, who is a person shrouded in mystery to me. As far as I can gather, he was a small gambler and pimp. When Bird was in his late teens, his father was stabbed to death by some woman.

I attended a memorial concert a few years ago given at Roosevelt College in honor of Charlie. A young alto man got up, and it was announced that he was to play "Lover Man." I turned to some friends and said, "How much do you want to bet he copies Charlie? Even to the mistakes he made on that record he never wished released." It happened as I said it would, and that incident is typical of the countless people and musicians who aped him at the expense of their own personal expression.

Letter from Doris Parker to Bob Reisner, December 31, 1956:

Got _Playboy_ last evening, and there were many things I liked in your article, but many I had to take exception to.

No. 1: Charlie was not always deeply in debt. From the period when we came back from California until late 1949 or 1950, Charlie was doing well. We had money in the bank. I just wish Billy Shaw were alive so you could talk to him. The story about the friendly manager who bought him the Cadillac that he pawned two weeks later is not true, unless this happened after I left. The Cadillac we had was paid for out of the money we had saved that Charlie made, and it was never in pawn. This can be checked at Shaw's Agency, because that is who Charlie was with at the time. Billy Shaw was more like a real person than a manager; you had better talk to his wife, Lee Shaw.

People sit and tell you Bird stories for hours. That is true, but probably half of them never happened, because I've heard people tell me some fantastic stories that, comparing the time and place, I know didn't happen. I'm not excusing Charlie, but I do believe from your story that you spent a great time talking to Chan—and Charlie had begun to deteriorate in 1951 and 1952. The Charlie who was at his best was when he played so much during the late '40's. He did not adopt weird outlets; he had many suits, went to work always neatly dressed, and on time.

Try talking to Dizzy Gillespie, Tommy Potter, and Max Roach—fellows who knew him and played with him—Duke Jordan, Al Haig, are but a few.

I really can't believe that Charlie was ever intentionally rude to any musician just starting out, because I know of many fellows who came around and Charlie would ask them to sit in. He was always most kind. In fact, I was usually hard on them, and he would tell me they were trying. These same fellows would say that other fellows in the group didn't really want them, but Charlie would insist. Even when Charlie went places where Dixieland was played he'd always tell the "cats" they were "wailing."

All I can say is Charlie must have changed very much after I left him. He certainly was never vulgar about sex. And as for calling friends in to watch and photograph—these friends I'd have to meet. Sounds like another Bird legend. Who is this friend who recalls Bird with two or three women at a time? This really, to me, is unbelievable. This certainly was not true during the period when I was with him. I would be with him twenty-four hours a day, so I can't understand that. This must have happened during the period he was with Chan, because it didn't happen before. So, curiously enough, in his wailing years, he was a one-woman man.

No. 2: Big point! Please spell my name right—Sydnor! (Smile.)

No. 3: A big point! He was never married to Chan.

No. 4: Charlie was born in 1920. His mother should know. His mother would have to be much older than she is if he weren't. Charlie was thirty-five when he died. Charlie's childhood did not ruin Charlie—he had no childhood. He got caught in the web that held him very young, and he never had a chance to do all the things most kids do. You better reconstruct your thinking, because, when Charlie came back from the Coast, he was really on his feet. Check the records he made. Perhaps he did act far out in Europe, because he would get off on tangents; but there were some years in there when he was pretty relaxed and straight. Ask Miles Davis, who was working at the Three Deuces with Charlie when he first came from California, how Charlie was trying to stay straight when every night the same "cat" or "cats" were there offering him the free ones.

When Charlie was straight, all across the country the pushers never gave up. They were always around. Don't forget—Charlie didn't always go looking; they came looking for him. One musician, in particular, kept after him and after him when he was straight, always with a few free ones. You know Charlie always talked against and never for narcotics. He would never offer to buy you any. If you asked him for some, he might take your money, but come back and say he couldn't get it. Of course, he didn't have your money. (Smile.)

Charlie may have been weak, which I agree he was; but he never wanted to hurt anyone but himself. He always felt if he got caught he'd pay his own "dues," and he'd never implicate anyone else.

The rest of his life from the time he came back from California was not departures from and reconciliations with Chan. That really isn't true. No. 1, he did not go to live with Chan until July of 1950. So there is a four- or five-year interval she left out.

Norman Granz did not conceive the idea of Charlie working with strings. This was Charlie's dream, and, perhaps, it bugged him later. But Norman did it only to please Charlie. On all their sessions, Charlie's ideas and consideration were always first to Norman. Norman never imposed his will on Charlie; Charlie had dreamed about playing with strings. He went on a date when Mitch Miller was there or had something to do with the date, because Charlie came home raving about how wonderful these fellows could play, and he was crazy about Mitch Miller—also a violinist named Sam. Can't remember for sure his last name—Katz, but I'm not sure.

As for Charlie humiliating Bud Powell, I know that must have hurt him very much, because many times he had defended Bud when Bud was doing ridiculous things.

Also, when Charlie died, he died of lobar pneumonia. They mentioned nothing to me of cirrhosis, because I went to find out about the autopsy, and they gave me a run down.

Who told you that Charlie did not want to be buried in K.C.? This is something Chan said, and I'm really getting tired of reading it. The implication is very plain. Charlie loved his mother very much. In life, he brought her a great deal of unhappiness. I'm sure Charlie would be the last person in the world, knowing how much his mother wanted it, to have said no. Perhaps Charlie did say at times that he didn't like K.C. But he said many things at times about people involved in his personal life that were not true. But Charlie did love his mother, and it was his mother's wish that he be buried in K.C. The services in K.C. were beautiful—they played "Repetition," and it was really a beautiful service. There were old men and young there. People who knew Charlie all his life and people who grew up with him. It makes me angry—every article I read speaking of Charlie not wanting to go to K.C.— well, it makes me furious.

Ask Dizzy about when I came to New York. I was willing to promise Chan anything to have his funeral in peace with no scandal, but Chan wouldn't have it that way. Perhaps you didn't know, but I made arrangements for Chan to be there. She sat in front, not I; so I feel that she brought all the unhappiness on herself. That whole scene was unnecessary. I am not a vindictive person, because I had all the good years—the years when Charlie was the straightest. I had many tears with Charlie, but we had some grand moments, too. In time you forget the bad and only remember the good. So, you see, I don't sit up and tell people I was wronged; even though when we broke up, I was very sick, and Charlie never sent me a penny. I had to depend on my family for help. But I don't cry the blues well; I'm no martyr. I loved Charlie for what he was—good or bad, musician or not. He was not Bird to me. His genius was only incidental. To me the name was nothing; I didn't know any-

Doris and Charlie.

Teddy Blume, Bird, and Chan.

thing about jazz when I met Bird—so it really wasn't his music, only him.

I'd suggest you talk to Teddy Reig, Eugene Ramey (he's around New York), who knew him in K.C., and some of the other fellows I've mentioned in this letter. I really didn't mean to write you such a long letter, but that is the way it is. Also, you should contact Maely Dufty; you can reach her through Bill Dufty on the *Post*.

I realize what a big job you have undertaken, sifting and trying to talk to everyone and giving a true composite picture of him. I hope you won't be too influenced by the notoriety brand of stories but will delve even deeper into his friends' minds. Ask Tommy Potter about the time the fellows in the group heard a new little bass player, and they decided he'd fit into the group. Charlie listened and decided the fellow wouldn't be able to keep the tempos the way he should. But he didn't say anything to the band, only had the fellow come over and sit in. Of course Tommy was drug, because Charlie didn't defend him, but the fellow came over and sat in and Charlie played a normal set. He didn't have to say a word. The fellows heard for themselves that Tommy could play the tempos and the other fellow couldn't.

I've probably ruined your eyesight for life, trying to read this scribbling. But I wanted to tell you some of these things while they were fresh in my mind. I hope, in your book, you won't see fit to make anyone a martyr. Not even Chan, 'cause anyone who knew Charlie had to pay their dues. And if I knew the way it would turn out, I'd do it again. I hope you get to talk to these people Dizzy and Lorraine Gillespie and some of the others. I think you'll get another view of him then.

Perhaps I should write a book—looks like I'm well on my way. (Smile.) Take care.

Sincerely, Doris

I didn't go to the Coast with him; but when he went to Camarillo, I went out there in September, 1946, and visited him three times a week. The place near Oxnard, California. He had some work done on his teeth out there and was very proud of them. The place was all right. Just the route to it was so depressing—flat, brown, almost nothing. When I first saw him, he was coherent. He knew where he was. He didn't have much to do. He was undergoing analysis. He had an Austrian doctor; I never knew his name. Charlie was very affectionate. He would meet me when I came out and kiss me, then kiss me when I left. We'd go on picnics a lot on the grounds. There were main buildings and a lot of smaller houses, all stucco, regular California style. Sometimes his words and actions were . . . guarded, held in. There were a lot of people there who spent all their time going to the edge of the hospital grounds and staring out into space. Charlie used to laugh at them, but he got like that too. Just standing out there, staring. The place looked like statues had been placed all around. I was there six months while Charlie was in the

Charlie and Chan, from which combination came his *nom de disque*, Charlie Chan.

Leon Parker

Below:
Baird Parker

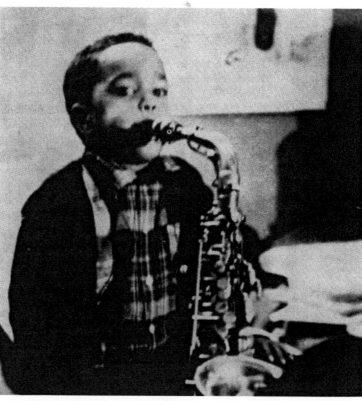

hospital and went on that long ride three times a week. I stayed until he got out. He played some gigs in Los Angeles; then we came back east together. He played a date at the Persian Ballroom at 64th and Cottage Grove in Chicago.

Oscar Pettiford

The late Oscar Pettiford was a pioneer in modern jazz and is unquestionably one of the great bassists in jazz history. He was born on an Indian reservation at Okamulgee, Oklahoma, one of thirteen children of Harry 'Doc' Pettiford, who led one of the most successful territory bands in the Southwest, a band in which most of his talented children started playing. Pettiford worked with Charlie Barnet's band, and in 1943 he and Dizzy Gillespie led a bop group, the first on 52nd Street, with Don Byas, George Wallington and Max Roach. Pettiford has worked with Duke Ellington, and led his own groups, large and small.

I got started at six, when I used to dance with my father's band. When I was seventeen, I had a bit role with Olson and Johnson in Minneapolis. Before I settled on bass, I played piano, trombone, and trumpet (which hurt my jaws), and I studied tailoring in case the music business ever got tough.

When I first met Parker he was with the Jay McShann band, and they came out to Minneapolis where I was playing in my father's band; that was around 1940-41. I was around sixteen years old. Everyone, Jay and the band, respected and loved Charlie Parker; he wasn't called Yardbird or Bird then. Everyone dug his playing; he had a happy sound.

I saw him again in Earl Hines' band in 1943; they were in Chicago, and Diz was in the band, too. I got word that time that I could be in a jam session with Bird and Diz, and I walked two miles carrying my bass without gloves in ten below zero weather to the Ritz Hotel. It was a fine session. I remember a fellow named Red Cross taped the session. He works for Billy Eckstine; maybe he still has it.

In 1943 I met Bird again. I was with the Charlie Barnet band, and we were playing at the Capital Theatre. Bird was with the Earl Hines band playing at the Apollo Theatre. We were both registered at the Braddock Hotel on 126th Street and 8th Avenue. This was a hotel where a lot of musicians stayed in town. Bird and I did a lot of jamming at the hotel. He was writing a lot of things then.

Dizzy Gillespie and I went looking up and down 52nd Street for work in 1943. We turned down $75 a week apiece offered by Kelly's Stables. I had worked at the Onyx club before, and I was good friends with the owner, Mike Westerman, so I asked him if I could be re-engaged. I was welcomed back gladly. I said, "Make it a Diz group." And Diz said, "Make it your group because you got the job." So we made it the Gillespie-Pettiford group. We wanted Bird to come in the group, but he didn't have a union card. He never seemed to have a card. He didn't stay in town long enough. There's a local 802 regulation that says a musician must wait in town six months for his card. For the first three months he may be able to work at a steady job with union approval as long as he is in town.

Bird was always broke, and he would have to work jobs out of town to make quick money. He continually borrowed. Dizzy always allotted part of his pay to him. Nobody ever expected it back—never got it. Nobody ever did. One musician said laughing, "To know Bird you got to pay your dues." I never knew Bird to lend money to anyone. Anyone. Once when I was flat, I asked for some of the money that Bird owed me. I never got it. He was so likeable that you didn't mind being generous with him.

At this time, Billy Eckstine and Dizzy Gillespie were Bird's closest friends. Bird dug Eckstine's singing very much.

Tommy Potter

Tommy Potter played countless gigs with Parker and was with him quite steadily between 1947 and 1949. He was born in Philadelphia, in 1918. At sixteen, he was stricken with a heart attack that kept him on his back for two years. For someone who was told he would have to ex- pend very little energy, he did very well. He became one of the first and finest Bop bass players.

I first played with Bird when we were in the Billy Eckstine band. He had known me previously, when I played in Washington, D.C., with a small group

at a place called Crystal Caverns. He was very easy to get along with. He craved attention, lots of it; but, then, he needed a lot of everything. He'd force guys to get along with him. He'd cajole and soothe. He seemed to be very proud of the group, and he always plugged the individual members on the bandstand or on radio interviews or to people he met. He'd say, "Have you heard my bassist, Tommy Potter? You haven't! Where have you been?"

In 1951 we played a date in Chicago, and, then, found ourselves with some free time before the next date in a nearby city. Bird told us to send our luggage on to the town we were to play and come home with him. He wanted us to meet his Ma. We spent two wonderful days there. We woke up every morning to big meals. His mother was very kind. Bird looked a lot like her. A friend of Charlie's owned a small plane and offered to take Bird to the next job. So Max, Duke, and I took the train, and Charlie and Red Rodney went by plane. Red told me that Bird asked if he could take the controls; his friend said yes. Now, Charlie never flew a plane before, but there he was, blithely flying the ship, a broad smile on his face. Suddenly, Bird leans left, and the plane banks to the right. The guy grabs the controls real fast. Red was shaking with fright. Bird said he just wanted to hear the motor when he banked the plane.

Bird always wanted to play the big places, but his reputation for being unreliable kept him limited to the small night clubs. In Europe, he had the chance he wanted. I was with him in 1949, and the reception in France was lavish. Autograph-signing parties in record shops and lots of press coverage topped by a press party in Bird's hotel room. Charlie ordered a bottle of champagne, and he tipped the waiter generously; and well he might, because he had that waiter make five trips for five buckets of champagne.

When he was a young musician, he would sometimes be chased from the bandstand. He never forgot that, and I think it may account for a lot of his erratic behavior. He used it as a test. I feel he said to himself, "I'll be so good that no one will chase me from the bandstand no matter what I do. I'll be accepted, no matter what."

On record dates he could compose right on the spot. The A. & R. man would be griping, wanting us to begin. Charlie would say, "It'll just take a minute," and he'd write out eight bars, usually just for the trumpet. He could transpose it for his alto without a score. The channel of the tune could be ad libbed. The rhythm section was familiar with all the progressions of the tunes which were usually the basis of originals. For example, "Ko-Ko" is based on the same chords as "Cherokee"; "Ornithology" derives from "How High the Moon"; "Scrapple From the Apple" is a mixture of "I Got Rhythm" and "Honeysuckle Rose" in the channel.

Tommy Potter, bass, Bird, and Miles Davis.

He could be a suave con man at times with little regard for the club he was playing at. He'd spot a mark or a sucker. It was usually a person who was hanging around the bandstand looking at him in a worshipping way. The person would call him over. "Hey, Charlie, come over here and have a drink." Then Bird would really put him on. He might introduce one of the members of the band, "Have you met my percussionist?" Then he might mention something about a party later that night. The fellow would be glowing. Bird would follow up with, "By the way, have you got any money on you?" or still stronger, "How much money do you have on you?" He would explain that the club owner was out for a while, that they had money coming to them, and that he would pay it back in an hour. Here was a chance for the person to buy his way right into this enchanted circle, and he'd fork over twenty dollars or so. Bird would then cut out for the night. The fellow would hang around and finally start to worry the fellows with, "Have you seen Charlie Parker? Where did he go?" And to tell the truth, we never knew.

We flew to Los Angeles to do a concert at the Shrine Auditorium for Norman Granz. When we got there, all of a sudden, Bird disappears. Norman dramatically offers a reward of one hundred dollars for anyone who locates him. Teddy Edwards, our tenor man, finally located him after a few days and got the reward. Charlie had eloped to Mexico and married Doris, wife number two.

Gene Ramey

Bassist Eugene Ramey was born in Austin, Texas, in 1913. He played sousaphone in the band of George Corley at seventeen. In 1932, he moved to Kansas City. He first met Parker in Kansas City when Bird was still a schoolboy. Walter Page taught him to play the string bass. He became one of the best bass men in the Middle West. He was with McShann from 1939 to 1944, Luis Russell from 1944 to 1945, and then went on to 52nd Street and small combo playing.

I was like his guardian; being a little older, I had to keep my eye on him. Once, in later years, he said to me, "Gene, I'm gonna punch you in the mouth to get you off me; you're too much like a daddy."

We first met in 1934. In those days, there were a lot of mock band battles. They were judged by enthusiasm and loyalty rather than musical ability. When you played in your home town, you won. Charlie was in a group from K.C., Missouri, and I was in one from K.C., Kansas. The leader of Bird's band was a pianist and singer named Lawrence "88" Keyes, who later became well known in the East. It was the first band Bird had ever worked in, and he seemed to me then just like a happy-go-lucky kid. In fact, the whole outfit was a school band, and Bird was hardly fully grown at the time—he was barely fourteen years old!

Bird wasn't doing anything, musically speaking, at that period. In fact, he was the saddest thing in the band, and the other members gave him something of a hard time. About a year later, I saw Charlie again. He played regularly at a place called Green Leaf Gardens in K.C. He was very antisocial and belligerent; he would fight with all the guys about music. He was an only child, sheltered and coddled, and he was not used to getting along with people. At this time I was about two blocks down the street from Count Basie at the Reno Club, and Duke Ellington was on the other side of the street. All of us had a regular habit of running from one club to another during intermissions. Bird was a little bit downhearted, because everybody would be holding jam sessions, and he was one of the few musicians who was *never* allowed to sit in.

He played a whole year at the Green Leaf Gardens, and I was playing at a nearby place called Bar-le-Duc. I got to know him real well and could see him start to develop as a musician and a person. In K.C., there was an institution known as "spook breakfasts." They were jam sessions held every morning. The ones Bird and I attended faithfully were held at the Reno Club, where Count Basie was playing. Basie had a nine-piece band, and they worked a touch schedule—from 8:30 to 5:00 in the morning. After that, the jam sessions would begin. People stopped by on their way to work, and there was the "sportin' life" set who never worked, and musicians of any big band that was in town—like Dorsey or Garber. Sometimes there would be as many as a hundred musicians waiting to get on the stand. In K.C. there is a wonderful tradition where a more experienced musician tries to help a new one. An alto player called Prof. Smith used to help Bird get to his horn better. Efferge Ware, a guitarist, coached a whole group of us, teaching us cycles, chords, and progressions. We would sit in the park, practicing all night long.

Jam sessions in a sense were constant trials of manhood. Different sections of the band would set difficult riffs behind a soloist, and, sometimes, they would see if they could lose each other. Usually it was one man who became the goat. He might then come in for some kidding. Charlie would shoot back to his teasers' and censors' remarks like, "Play your own horn" or "Stick to your script." I remember one night in particular when we were to jam with

Basie, and Charlie made no answer. Jo Jones waited until Bird started to play and, suddenly, in order to show how he felt about Bird, he threw a cymbal across the dance floor. It fell with a deafening sound, and Bird, in humiliation, packed up his instrument and left. Major Bowes was popular then, and Jo Jones had given contestant Parker the gong, like The Amateur Hour maestro used to do.

However, this gave Bird a big determination to play. "I'll fix these cats," he used to say. "Everybody's laughing at me now, but just wait and see."

In the summer of 1937, Bird underwent a radical change musically. He got a job with a little band led by a singer, George E. Lee. They played at country resorts in the mountains. Charlie took with him all the Count Basie records with Lester Young solos on them and learned Lester cold, note for note. When he came home, he was the most popular musician in K.C. He had gone up in the mountains; and when he came back, only two or three months later, the difference was unbelievable.

He lost his Sweet Lucy sound, which is like a combination of a man talking and drinking wine at the same time (Sweet Lucy was what we called wine). His style had completely changed. He became the darling of K.C. Unfortunately, it was at this period he acquired the "monkey" and frequently was strung out.

Naturally, after this sudden development in his style, Bird began to get lots of work. He was always an aggressive youngster with lots of ideas and suggestions. At that time, there were lots of jam sessions going on in night clubs and in various private houses. One night Bird suggested that we go out to Paseo Park; so after that, every once in a while, all the cats would get out there in the middle of the park, and we'd play all night. The cops very seldom bothered us; in fact, they used to come out there to enjoy the music themselves.

Bird was the most receptive being. He got into his music all the sounds around him—the swish of a car speeding down a highway, the hum of wind as it goes through the leaves—and he also absorbed some environmental evils. Naturally we petted him and babied him, and he traded on this love and esteem we had for him until he developed into the greatest con man in the world. His own wolf cries tripped him on occasion, for he later said to me, "I'll never forgive you. Once you refused me when I was really hungry."

The Jay McShann band, in which Bird and I worked together for so long, was the only band I've ever known that seemed to spend all its spare time jamming or rehearsing. We used to jam on trains and buses; and as soon as we got into a town, we'd try to find somebody's house where we could hold a session. All this was inspired by Bird, because the new ideas he was bringing to the band made everybody anxious to play.

Bird kept everybody on the stand happy, because he was a wizard at transmitting musical messages to us, which made us fall out laughing. All musicians know certain musical phrases that translate themselves into "Hello Beautiful" or, when a young lady ambles to the powder room, "I know where you're going." Well, Bird had an ever-increasing repertoire of these. During induction days, he'd salute a band member who got tagged with a phrase which translated said, "Bring enough clothes for three days." Everything had a musical meaning for him. If he heard a dog bark, he would say the dog was speaking. If he was in the act of blowing his sax, he would find something to express and would want you to guess his thoughts. When we used to take carriage rides during our free hours, we would sometimes roll along the country roads and look at the trees and the leaves falling from the branches; he had notes to explain all these phenomena presented by nature. Sometimes on the dance floor, while he was playing, women who were dancing would perform in front of him. Their attitudes, their gestures, their faces, would awaken in him an emotional shock that he would express musically in his solos. As soon as his tones became piercing, we were all so accustomed to his reactions that we understood at once what he meant . . . he could look elsewhere, but soon as he repeated this phrase, we all raised our eyes and grasped his message.

We were at a club in New Orleans on one occasion, playing a one-nighter, when we were informed by Decca that we were due for a record session in a couple of weeks. McShann suggested that we do something real quick. It was one of those real warm days in New Orleans, but we got together and had a little session, and the ideas came across. After beginning with a little jam session, we began to improvise. I believe we succeeded in less than forty-five minutes in completing "Jumpin' Blues." It had been entirely orchestrated by Bird, and now in this record appears the first great solo ever waxed by him.

Bird was one of the reasons McShann's was such a happy-go-lucky band. Jay McShann gave him latitude, because as Bird explained to Jay, "If you let me act a little happy, you'll have me playing a few good notes for you." When McShann criticized his appearance once, he answered, "How would you like me looking like a doctor and playing like a doctor?" Bird used to say, "If you come on a band tense, you're going to play tense. If you come a little bit foolish, act just a little bit foolish, and let yourself go, better ideas will come."

Bird was also responsible for that sort of private joke which is repeated on the slightest pretext. For example, I remember that a cartoon in the newspapers had drawn our attention. It showed a fellow who seemed sad and hungry. This cartoon was particularly expressive, and whenever Bird saw it, he would always repeat, "Huh, me worry?" Therefore, whenever we were not paid or whenever someone in the band seemed sad or drunk or any time we didn't get paid, we would all use this phrase, "Me worry!"

When I look back, it seems to me that Bird was at that time so advanced in jazz that I do not think we realized to what a degree his ideas had become perfected. For instance, we used to jam "Cherokee." Bird had his own way of starting from a chord in B natural and B flat; then he would run a cycle against that; and, probably, it would only be two or three bars before we got to the channel (middle part) that he would come back to the basic changes. In those days we used to call it "running out of key." Bird used to sit and try to tell us what he was doing. I am sure that at that time nobody else in the band could play, for example, even the channel to "Cherokee." So Bird used to play a series of "Tea For Two" phrases against the channel, and, since this was a melody that could easily be remembered, it gave the guys something to play during those bars.

I don't remember exactly what Bird was telling us in his "Jumpin' Blues" solo, but I do remember that we all used to start joking from the very first bars. It was, I remember, a simple phrase that we already had had occasion to use before, but which later became a sort of leitmotiv like "Ornithology."

Bird was not the only alto soloist in McShann's band. In certain of our blues numbers, John Jackson was the soloist. He began on sax with McShann, and Bird used to say that he was the soul of animation and that he had the best tone on alto he had ever heard. At the time when Bird and I were members of the band the best composer was William Scott, a good musician who later retired to become a radio technician. He was the composer of "Dexter Blues" and "Swingmatism" as well as numerous other numbers we played. By a strange coincidence, some days before Bird's death, Scott was killed in Kansas City. Most of the musicians who were a part of this band are now dispersed. Gus Johnson, the drummer, was still with Basie's band a few months ago. McShann and certain others are still around Kansas City. Al Hibbler, who was our vocalist, is now a big star in his own right, while Walter Brown, who made our famous singing record, "Confessin' the Blues," later retired from business. Bird left the band for some time in 1939, but he returned a little later and remained in McShann's band until 1942, at which time the whole group began to disintegrate. In 1941 I am quite sure we were at the Savoy ballroom in New York. That was the time when Dizzy Gillespie was working very hard with the band. We always reserved a place for him on the stand, as well as for Chubby Jackson and Big Sid Catlett, and they used to come almost every night when they were in town. Bird was so far ahead of his time that nobody really appreciated just how radical his ideas were. I think it will be a long time before those of us who were a part of that scene will forget the spirit and freshness of the Jay McShann orchestra and the great inspiration that was lent to it by the immortal Charlie Parker.

In later years he was leaning on me too much. So I told him and we had a verbal agreement that he would not call upon me unless in serious trouble. One night he came over to the Apollo Theatre where I was working. He looked like an unmade bed. It was six degrees above zero, and he was wearing a T shirt, no socks, and a black, expensive overcoat. He asked me for two dollars, which he said he needed. I gave him the money, and he went to Braddock's bar and set up some people with drinks. He did this to make peace, for he had been promoting himself a beating by the following: the bar had a two-for-one policy during the hours of six to eight. Bird would come in, reach for a person's second drink, and polish it off—this with guys who didn't know him.

On another occasion he came to the Apollo and wanted to borrow Sonny Stitt's horn. Sonny said no. Bird replied, "You stole my horn in Detroit when you were strung out. I never said anything to you. You've got three horns on stage." Sonny said, "This is my band, and I'm featuring three horns." Bird turned and said, "You have your day; I'll have mine."

But he didn't leave it at that. He went around to the back of the theatre, climbed up the fire escape in an attempt to sneak into Sonny's room. He was drunk and fell into the wrong dressing room, where some girl was changing clothes. She gave a yelp. I came in and so did the manager. Bird was lying on the floor. He groaned, "I think I have broken my ankle." We all became a little concerned about him, which is what he wanted so that his crime would be forgotten. When I took off his shoe to examine his foot, he winked at me—"I was doing my best to steal Sonny Stitt's horn."

I helped him into the hall, and, there, the theatre manager asked him what it was all about. Charlie told him that he wanted to see him, but he never could get to him in his office. Bird's fanciful alibi did not wholly placate the man, and a few unpleasantries were exchanged, culminating in a dramatic pose of Charlie's in which he removed the fire axe from the wall and threatened to hit the guy over the head with it. I unruffled everyone and led Bird outside. I said to him, "You are acting awful mean today." He was okay by then. He said, "There's nothing else for me to do. These other guys say less than me. They have good work. They will only give me $800 to go out on the road, which I hate." I told him that, if he wished, and if he thought it would make things pleasanter for him, I would give up my job and go out on the road with him.

Jimmy Raney

Jimmy Raney, a gifted guitarist, was born in Louisville, Kentucky, on August 20, 1927. He began to play the instrument at ten. In 1944 he left home to play in Jerry Wald's band. He gathered experience with Woody Herman, Buddy De Franco, Artie Shaw, and Stan Getz. He toured Europe in 1954 with Red Norvo. Strong influences of Parker and Tristano are heard in his fluid and inventive playing. Of Bird he said, "I went to 52nd Street and heard him a lot there. His records were my greatest inspiration."

I talked to him some; he was always an enigma to me. I could never tell whether he was kidding or not. He always had a strange personality to match his music. I could never figure him out personally. Up at the Prescott Hotel, I asked him, "What do you think about when you're playing?" He got serious for a moment; he said he felt like everything disappeared when he put the horn to his mouth; he forgot the outside world, the girls. He said, "Sometimes I look at my fingers and I'm surprised that it's me playing. I get an idea, and I try it till it comes out right." And then he returned to a gayer mood, to the party spirit, and said, "Let's celebrate. We have Bartok and gin—what else do we need?"

One of the manifestations of his genius was that he took inspiration from anything. He could transform the driest things, even saxophone exercises. He picked up odds and ends and used them. He'd go hear Chopin and come back playing quotes. He'd pick up tunes nobody else would play, and they became standards.

Bird's appearances at clubs on 52nd Street were always erratic and eventful. At some clubs he was actually paid by the set; it was that risky a thing that he would show. His horns presented a problem—they were in hock so often. At the Three Deuces the porter had a job assigned to him, to go to the pawn shop every day and get Bird's horn for the job, and then return it to the shop after the job.

One night Bird was scheduled to play at the Deuces, and a crowd started to assemble in the club. Bird walked in and went right to the kitchen and started to make himself a few sandwiches. He was doing a magnificent job, building them very big and garnishing them with all sorts of condiments. The managers of clubs had a very easygoing attitude with Bird. He had a way of stimulating expansive spirits in the hardest people. But this was a hectic evening, and the full bar was waiting for Charlie. The manager came into the kitchen and told Bird that he was on. Bird, his jaws champing, kept on eating. The manager waited a bit and then said, "Please, Bird, finish later; the crowd is getting restless." No response from Bird. This went on until the manager was almost in tears, imploring him to go on, and Bird turned around and said, "Man, why don't you try one of these sandwiches? They're crazy."

What amazed me about his playing was that he was one of the great creative people on that higher level of creation that has something mysterious about it. There are many who play creatively, but in their cases, you can always trace where they learned and how they were formed. With Charlie Parker, it was as if he had come full-grown from the head of Zeus. I never could figure out where what he was playing came from. Sure, there were small things you could trace back, but his main creativity was on that mysterious level, the greatest level of all. In classical music in this century, Bartok had it. In jazz, it was Bird.

Teddy Reig

Teddy Reig is an A. & R. man who has enough sense to let the musicians do what they want on a record date. He arranged some of the earliest bop disc makings. He worked for Savoy Records and later had his own label, Roost.

He was an angel. That man was so abused that anything he did is excusable. People say that some differences arose between Bird and Diz, and it is possible that Charlie was a bit jealous of Diz's commercial success, but Parker could have had it, too, if he had had the self-discipline for it. Bird once spent his last two dollars. bought a bouquet of flowers, and brought it backstage to the Strand Theatre. He gave the flowers to Dizzy Gillespie as a token of his love and best wishes.

During one show a singer and dancer called Baby Face Lewis brought Bird on with a flourish. At the conclusion of his act, he cued in the band and said, "Take it, Charlie Parker." The spotlight swung on to Bird fast asleep in his chair.

On a night he was to do a concert with Diz he was out in a bathtub. We went to his room and broke down the bathroom door. We got him out of the tub. dried him, dressed him, got him in a cab, stuck the horn in his hands, and pushed him from the wings on to the stage. The result, which was recorded, can be heard on a record today (Birdland label). It is unbelievable in its speed, ideas, and artistry.

Jerome Richardson

Jerome Richardson was born in Oakland, California, on December 25, 1920. He plays the saxes, woodwinds, and also sings. Among the people he has worked with are Lionel Hampton (1949-51), Earl Hines (1954-55), and Quincy Jones.

There was an after-hours place in San Francisco called Bop City. A lot of us used to go there after our regular jobs. One evening in 1952, Bird was there. He was very drunk but was persuaded to go up on the stand and play. There was only a rhythm section, a powerful rhythm section. Art Blakey, drums; Curly Russell, bass; and Kenny Drew, piano. These guys were miffed at Bird at this time. As Art said, "Bird had messed up our money on the last date we played together." They were out for revenge. "Anything you want to play," Parker muttered. Blakey said, "52nd St. Theme" and with that he started a rhythm at a murderously fast tempo. Bird was all tied up. False starts, uncoordinated fingering. He stopped. "Give me an hour, I'll be back." No one knows how he did it, but in one hour, he returned cold, deadly sober. There was no tune too fast, too slow, too unfamiliar. He played till seven in the morning.

Above:
Singer Jackie Paris at a 52nd Street club with Bird, Potter, Roach, Davis, and Jordan.
Below:
Massey Hall, Toronto, on May 15, 1953: Bud Powell, piano; Mingus, bass; Roach, drums; Gillespie and Bird.

Max Roach

In modern jazz every session is a trial of manhood. Max Roach developed his speed, technical precision, and variety of beats in the early grueling night-after-all-night bop sessions at Minton's and Clarke Monroe's Uptown House. He credits Charlie Parker as the major force in his development. To watch him work is to see a man calmly beating the hell out of various drums, paying special attention to the cymbals, so as to get a legato feeling rather than the old heavy bass-drum sound. He graduates tones to such a fine degree that I have seen him execute a few strokes upon the air at the end of a solo and you imagine you are hearing something.

He was born in Brooklyn in 1925.

One night long ago, when I was playing at a place called Georgie Jay's Tap Room in a little band led by Clark Monroe, Victor Coulson came over to me and said, "Tomorrow night the world's greatest saxophonist is going to play with you." It was true.

Bird was kind of like the sun, giving off the energy we drew from him. We're still drawing on it. His glass was overflowing. In any musical situation, his ideas just bounded out, and this inspired anyone who was around. He had a way of playing that affected every instrument on the bandstand.

Even the way I play drums. You can say Bird was really responsible, not just because his style called for a particular kind of drumming, but because he set tempos so fast, it was impossible to play a straight, Cozy Cole, four style. So we had to work out variations. But it was a logical idea anyway, because the bass drum is the worst sound. One of the things I liked about the old Basie rhythm section was when Jo took his foot off the bass pedal behind the ensembles and just used the high hat. I'd rather use the high hat as a back beat and break up the bass drum rhythm. You get a more definite sound, as though the drums are really contributing something instead of just filling in.

Bird had all sorts of musical combinations in mind. He wanted to make a record with Yehudi Menuhin and, at least, a forty-piece orchestra. He mapped out things for woodwinds and voices, and Norman Granz would holler, "What is this? You can't make money with this crazy combination.

194

You can't sell this stuff!" He seemed to have a nice relationship with Granz, though. One time he took a tape we had made of the Massey Hall concert in Canada with Bud, Mingus, and Diz. We agreed to split it right down the line, twenty per cent to each. He asked Norman the reasonable sum of $100,000 for it and was politely refused. Mingus issued it on his own label, Debut Records.

If Bird were to clear $750 a week, he would spend it in a day. He would always take the easy way out. I found that out when I worked in his quintet later on. Because of some of his irresponsible acts, the rest of the men would be docked or the owner would try to get out of paying the rest of us anything. I would start beefing to Bird, "I was here all night and working for you." I would chide him about his responsibilities as leader. "I hope you are going to give us some money." Then Bird would anger and say, "You mean to stand there and tell me, etc." But he'd come across and pay us. Or he'd say, kidding, "Put up them big fists," when we'd reproach him.

After he'd just come out of Camarillo, I promoted a session in Brooklyn, starring him. I promised him $100 for the engagement. The place closed at 2 A.M., and Bird arrived at 12. He plays one tune, comes off the stage, and says, "Max, give me my $100."

"I don't think you deserve anything," I said and walked off into the office of the owner. Bird followed, to talk it over. When we were in the office, Charlie orders the man out of his own room. "Now, Max, give me my money." I repeated that he did not fill his part of the agreement.

"O.K.," he says, and he goes through elaborate preliminaries to a fight. He clears the room and bars the door. I was mad, but then I had to laugh at all this big thing he was staging. I gave him $50, and it was settled.

The way he treated his manager, Teddy Blume, was pretty bad at times. Blume is a humble and sincere guy who was doing everything he could to build Charlie up. But Bird would really carry on. "This is my boy," he would say and pat him on the head like a dog. Or he would call the police on Teddy and cry, "This man is stealing my money."

I once asked Bird how a certain chick was, after I had seen him with her, and he politely replied, "She's soft as taffy candy and as warm as little sister's ass." A favorite expression of Bird's was, "How much money would you give me on my face?"

He had a secret love life. He would get that loving sound that would come out of his horn. Everything else is incidental to one thing, and that is that Bird contributed more and received less than anybody.

Ross Russell

Ross Russell became a convert to the new sound in the mid-forties and soon afterward started the Dial record company, for which Parker made some of his earliest and finest recordings. His novel, partly based on his experience with Parker, is entitled THE SOUND.

My background had been the jazz classics—Jelly Roll Morton and Louis Armstrong. Just after the war I opened a record store in Hollywood, intending to sell these kinds of records. Without going into the background, the store became a battleground between "mouldy figs" and hipsters, with the hipsters coming out on top after a few months. We ended up selling a lot more records by Dizzy Gillespie and Charlie Parker than we did of, say, Duke Ellington or even Benny Goodman. The Dial label was an outgrowth of the store. Actually, it was an attempt to emulate what Milt Gabler had done at Commodore, starting with a store, selling only jazz records, and then branching out into a label. We were trying to do the same thing.

The first Dial recording date was ot be the Dizzy Gillespie-Charlie Parker band which had come into Billy Berg's club in Hollywood, during the first month of 1946, I believe. We planned to have a rehearsal before the date. It took place at sort of a little offbeat studio in Glendale, California, which was part of some kind of a religious network. It was actually in a wing of a church in a little park—almost a Grey's "Elegy" setting. But it certainly didn't look the way the owners intended when this rehearsal got going. The word had gotten around over the hip grapevine, and the studio, which was fairly roomy, was jammed; nobody could move around. It was full of these hip types—they were something pretty new to me in 1946.

The band at this rehearsal was not exactly the one at Berg's. There were a couple of changes; Charlie Parker, Dizzy, Milt Jackson, and Lucky Thompson formed the front line, just as they did at the club. Al Haig was pianist at the club, but George Handy, the pianist and arranger, had come to this rehearsal. He had signed the contract and was getting the musicians together. Then the band was filled out with Ray Brown on bass, Stan Levy on drums, with an added starter in Arvin Garrison's guitar. Lester Young was also supposed to be on the date, but he never did get there.

At this rehearsal, we had the studio for at least three hours, and during that time, we actually recorded one thing that was later released on Dial, a version of "Diggin' Diz." But the confusion was terrible. The hippies who jammed the studio kept interfering with the musicians and the engineers, and I was too inexperienced to get the situation under control.

One other little incident impressed me at this rehearsal. One person who

196

came to the studio was a man with a reputation in Europe as a concert artist, I believe a violinist. He knew quite a bit about recording, and he had agreed to come over as a friendly advisor to help me over the rough spots of my first recording. He was standing up there in a monitor room looking out through the glass, scowling, and trying to dig the scene—all the musicians tuning up and all the hipsters walking around. Bird finally got the horn unpacked and got his strap on and put the horn in his mouth. I remember my classical friend was standing there, and, all of a sudden, these notes started to fly out of the alto saxophone like machine gun bullets, and the man sort of staggered —he took two or three backward steps as if someone had suddenly shot him. And he cried out, "Who is that?" He'd just never heard anything like it.

When we made the actual date a few days later, Bird didn't show up at all, and George Handy didn't make it, and Lester Young didn't make it. And at the very last minute—I mean the last, with the studio standing by and all that sort of thing—George Handy called me up and said he couldn't get hold of anybody and just couldn't make the date. Luckily I reached Dizzy Gillespie at his hotel, which was in another part of Los Angeles altogether, and Dizzy said, "Well, man, why didn't we do business between ourselves all along?" He asked if I still wanted to make the date, and I said, "If we can." He said all right, he'd have everybody out there. And less than an hour later they were out there, in Glendale, over fifteen miles, and this included Ray Brown's bass, Stan Levy's drums—and I guess the biggest hassle of all was Milt Jackson's vibes, which was roped on the top of somebody's automobile. Bird wasn't on this date at all.

The first official Charlie Parker date for Dial Records, which produced "Ornithology" and "Night in Tunisia," was done at a different studio, Radio Recorders. The third date, we found another studio with an extremely high ceiling, C. P. MacGregor on Western Avenue, with an engineer named Ben Jordan. We did "Lover Man" there and the "Cool Blues" date and the "Relaxin' at Camarillo" date.

We did the first official date with Charlie Parker, the "Ornithology" and "Night in Tunisia" date, two or three months after the date with Dizzy. Meanwhile, Charlie Parker had signed as an exclusive artist with Dial Records, a regular one-year contract, with option to renew for an additional year.

As a matter of policy, as far as I was concerned and Dial, the leader on the date had full authority to make decisions on the personnel that he was going to use. We felt that this was a matter of utmost importance. Just one wrong guy on a date can ruin it. As a matter of fact, it might be as out of place to have a very able drummer, like, let's say Buddy Rich on a date with Parker as to have someone like Baby Dodds. On the "Ornithology" date, we had Lucky Thompson again (we were very fortunate), and Bird felt very happy in having Miles Davis, who must have been in his very early twenties at the time. Miles had come to Los Angeles with one of the traveling bands—

probably Billy Eckstine's band—and, as I recall, he had left it there. I remember Bird telling me with some delight and anticipation that Miles was coming, and, later, that Miles was here, and that he was the man he particularly wanted to use when we recorded. The rest of the men on the date were Arvin Garrison, again, guitar; a bass player who hasn't been heard of very much since, Vic MacMillan, who I think is quite a good bass player; Dodo Marmarosa, a pianist I've always liked very much; and Roy Porter, Howard McGhee's drummer. Roy was a bomb dropper, with a driving beat.

"Night in Tunisia" took two, possibly three, hours to get pulled together and to record. It proved to be very difficult for everyone in the studio except Bird. We made five takes and a number of false starts. After we made the first take and Bird took that wonderful alto break, we listened to the playback, and we knew that the rest of it was so ragged we couldn't possibly release it. Bird said, "I'll never make *that* break again." Actually, he didn't make it quite as well, or at least not with the blinding brilliance and wonderful sense of suspense and climax he had in the first take. Later on, we released that little fragment, that first break, on an LP intended only for collectors.

On this date, there were no other people in the studio at all. We had learned our lesson, and it was a very workmanlike date. Bird was in full possession of his faculties; he was extremely interested in the date and trying to have every detail perfect. And I think the date did produce some very well-knit, well-organized music.

As to the difficulties in recording "Night in Tunisia," these seemed inherent in the musical material, changes of format, or harmony, or something. They had an awful time with it. And Dodo Marmarosa was a man that could play practically everything, anything.

Parker was a musician who solved problems so quickly that logic often seemed dispensed with and sheer intuition called forth. His insight, concept, and execution were far above the already high professional level of jazz recording stars. He played his finest solo on the initial take, well before the other musicians had worked out their own concepts, let alone digested the ensemble parts. Because Parker often blew his finest on early takes, much wonderful Parkerana has been lost to the public.

The date that we made with Errol Garner and Charlie Parker came about in a curious way. These things just seemed to happen with Bird. My feeling about Bird, if you want to put it in a sentence, was he was a cat that hung everybody up. The "Cool Blues" date happened this way: Bird had collapsed on a record date, the "Lover Man" date, in August; and he wound up in Camarillo State Hospital. He stayed there for six months. Finally, by a certain amount of pressure and string-pulling, the use of a private psychiatrist, and many trips up to Camarillo, we got him released. Actually, he was released in my custody. The fact that I had a store gave me some sort of middle-class status in the eyes of the authorities, and they agreed to release him if I signed him out.

The famous Bird's Nest date, Los Angeles, 1947: Left to right, Harold Doc West, drums; Parker, alto sax; Errol Garner, piano; Red Callendar, bass.

While we're on the subject, I might say that the Dial contract had reached an option point while he was in Camarillo. Before he came out, I discussed this with him, and I told him that I thought in view of the fact we only made one record date that produced four sides that were considered very good, that he ought to renew the contract for a year. He agreed to this, and that's the way that went. Some people have kinda put me down on this, I guess, and Bird had another version of it later on, but that's the way it was.

In any event, he was out, and he was in marvelous shape. He looked really healthy, bubbling with energy, nerves calm, and in good humor. He just couldn't be better. The one thing he wanted to do was to get back to New York. He'd had enough of Los Angeles, and I think he had some good reason for feeling that way.

He didn't have any money and he wasn't working and he didn't want to take a job—so we ran a benefit for him. There was Maynard Sloate, who now owns a night club in Hollywood. Also, Eddie Laguna of Sunset Records; and the late Charlie Emgee, the *Down Beat* man at the West Coast at the time; and June Poole, who was doing booking then. We got this benefit organized, and we got all the leading jazz instrumentalists to play for free with union blessing. We raised possibly six to nine hundred dollars, and this was all turned over to Bird. He bought some clothes, and he bought two plane tickets back to New York. Doris Parker was with him; she'd come out while he was in Camarillo.

Parker had agreed to make one record date before leaving, sort of the parting bit for the Coast. Naturally we wanted to make this date as good as we could, and we very carefully selected the musicians that were to be on it: Howard McGhee seemed to be the best man on trumpet available; a new tenor player, a very interesting, exciting tenor player who showed up locally, Wardell Gray—so he was on the date. A young guitar player named Barney Kessel. We had Dodo Marmarosa on piano again. We had this all-star date in mind. We had the time set for it and the studio reserved and all the rest, and Bird was supposed to be writing tunes, originals, and he had written one, the one that was called "Relaxin' at Camarillo." So a great deal of preparation had gone into this date.

Well, about ten days beforehand, but right when all these preparations were going on, Bird showed up with a vocalist named Earl Coleman, in whom he had suddenly taken an interest. He had decided, in an arbitrary way, that Earl Coleman should be on this date and that instead of making four instrumental sides there should be extended vocal choruses. This was something I felt that Dial Records needed like a hole in the head. I'd never been very strong on vocalists anyway. But Bird was adamant, and the upshot was that I agreed to make a separate date built around Earl Coleman, provided Bird would sort of throw off a couple of quick alto choruses with a rhythm section. I figured that maybe these would get us off the hook if the vocals weren't so good.

Erroll Garner came in to the picture by the back door. We had a singer; we had an alto saxophone player; but we needed a rhythm section, and I was a little bit afraid of trying to assemble one or use some of these bomb droppers or wilder pianists, particularly, since Coleman had a very bland sound . . . he was on a Billy Eckstine kick. The happy thought occurred to me that Erroll Garner was in town. Erroll was working as a single, but he'd been experimenting with a trio. They couldn't make it, because nobody in the clubs around there wanted to pay for the trio. The clubs could pay the single scale and a few extra bucks and get by, but, when they had to pay three musicians, it sent the cost up. So Erroll didn't have too much luck with his trio.

However, the men were still around: Doc West on drums and Red Callendar on bass. I figured, well, let's just use the Erroll Garner trio. So I went to Erroll, and he had eyes. So we worked out a deal. He wanted a little extra money. I said, "Well, all right, that's cool, but can you make two trio sides, sort of throw them in, after the alto solos had been thrown in?" That's the way this date came off.

Of the three hours, about two hours and twenty minutes were allotted to making two vocals with Earl Coleman. At that point, Earl had had about enough; his pipes were beginning to give out on him. So Charlie Parker kinda cranked up, and they tossed off a blues. They did three takes—bang, bang, bang. The first two were too fast. Garner didn't like the tempo, and we gradually slowed the takes down a little. One of the fast takes was released as "Hot Blues," and the slow, "Cool Blues." As soon as that was finished, they made an ad lib improvisation on "I Got Rhythm." Three takes on this— bang, bang, bang. This all happened in the last forty minutes of the date. The interesting thing is that Bird played a little differently with Erroll Garner. Some of the very hip people didn't like what happened; but I think a very interesting performance resulted on this date.

The "Relaxin' at Camarillo" date was the all-star date we had been planning and came about a week later, without the vocalist. We held a rehearsal two days before the date. Bird showed up about an hour late. He was supposed to have written four originals. He arrived with a line for a twelve-bar blues that he'd scribbled in a taxicab on the way out. The entire rehearsal was spent in everybody's trying to learn this sinuous twelve-bar line. Actually, they didn't get it down anywhere near cold by the end. I remember driving Dodo Marmarosa home later that night. He kept talking about this line. It was still bugging him. He hadn't been able to get it straight. It was only twelve bars, but he just couldn't get it. He kept talking, talking, talking about it. He said the next day, he hadn't been able to sleep; this thing bugged him all night. It's indicative of the sort of thing Bird created. When you consider that the musicians on the date were some of the best men available, and they couldn't quite pick up on it, it's pretty remarkable. Bird was that far ahead of the most advanced musicians of his time.

When you read the music that's been transcribed from Bird's records (assuming these transcriptions are right, and they probably are) the lines are not really so far out harmonically. They're very close to the fundamental and the tonic and all that sort of thing. It's just a masterly rearrangement of basic elements, with a great deal of rhythmic implication always.

The Camarillo date was the last Hollywood date. Bird was an hour or two late. Everyone else was there, waiting, hung up. Howard McGhee finally found him in a rooming house. Bird had passed out, naked, in a bathtub, and had apparently been lying there all night. A very few days later, maybe even the next day, Bird went back to New York.

Dial Records moved to New York within a matter of months. We resumed recording Bird in the fall that year, almost right up to the Petrillo record ban, which began about January, 1948. These dates were made with Miles, Duke Jordan, Tommy Potter, and Max Roach.

I was always interested in the trombone, and I thought that J. J. Johnson was just the end. I liked the idea of getting him into a date, and Bird thought it was a pretty good idea. So J. J. made the last date, the "How Deep Is the Ocean" date. That was December, 1947, and one of the three dates that Dial did with Charlie Parker in the fall of 1947—the last three we did with him. There were six tunes made on each of these dates. They were all done at the WOR studios with a very fine engineer named Doug Hawkins, and there was a certain uniformity of sound, I think. The working conditions over there were always very good. Hawkins sometimes seemed as important as another musician because he was so fine technically. He was a Juilliard graduate, and he also had a great deal of patience and understanding of what jazz musicians were trying to do. We felt that we had the sound we wanted—not just the sound I wanted, but also the sound the engineer and the musicians wanted.

There are two takes on "Klactoveedsedsteen," which is the title that Charlie Parker gave me. He wrote it out and gave it to me and said, "That's it, man." It was rather baffling. I talked to different people about it. I remember I asked a psychiatrist if he could read anything in it; he couldn't. I found a man with a background in philology. I thought maybe he could come up with something; and he couldn't. Then, I finally got around to asking some of the cats, and they said, "Why, it's just a sound, man." And that's what it is.

The most important thing about the records we made in New York, I think, is they were made by a working band, Bird's own band, men that he had selected by choice, and a rhythm section that would be hard to surpass even today. It had a very light, airy, almost frothy sound, and, yet, it had a great deal of lift. And, of course, there was almost complete one-mindedness among the musicians so that everything they played had a lot of cohesion and was very supple.

George Salano

I knew him real well during the last three years. He made these frequent trips to Boston, my home town, and used me as his drummer. He was erratic, unpredictable, and given to a good deal of goofing, but he was also gracious, very kind, sensitive to the feelings of others, generous with his talents (which included being a good cook, especially with leftovers), time, and money. Once I remember in the Hi Hat club, there was a young man with some books under one arm and a clarinet case under the other. He was obviously a European by the cut of his hair and clothes. He had a picture taken, and he got into conversation with Bird when he asked him to sign it. He was an exchange student from Switzerland, and he had flown from New York to Boston just to hear Parker. Bird invited him to come backstage and played Debussy and Ravel on this fellow's clarinet with amazing proficiency—and this was an old clarinet with a different fingering system. He then invited the young man to sit in on a set. He gave instructions to the club's camera girl to take a lot of pictures. He paid for and signed all of them with stuff like, "It was a pleasure to play with you." He sent the fellow back to Europe with a memory he'll never forget.

There was no set pattern to his dissipation. Sometimes he would go for two straight weeks without touching a drop of liquor; he'd be so healthy it was ridiculous. We would take long walks in the park before and after jobs, and lots of times we hung around Boston Common until dawn making bird calls with little gadgets you get from the Audubon Society. They are small round wooden objects with a little handle and resin inside, and you can manipulate them to simulate a thousand different bird calls. At work, on the stand would be a glass of water. But at other times, Bird would be juicing up a storm. He'd have a bottle in his coat, one in the band room, and drink up his pay at the bar. And as for the drugs, he hated it and subjected me to long harangues against it even though I never messed with it. He made valiant attempts to shake himself of the habit in the last years. I spent one night trying to keep him cool. I finally gave him an old army ampule of morphine I had laying around the house as a souvenir of battle days. They gave you this little glass thing which you could shoot into yourself if you were painfully wounded. Charlie broke the thing, spilled the contents into a glass of water, and fell right off to sleep.

Everybody loved him, there was an old colored woman who worked in a bake shop below a café called Wally's Paradise, and, whenever Bird came to Boston, this old lady would bake cakes for him. He had special cake boxes which he brought to her and which she filled. When you were in his company, you might be subjected to some very far-out experiences. One friend of mine accompanied Bird on a strange expedition. Parker read in the papers of some unidentified bodies, and he decided to visit a morgue at night. He told the attendant that they might be friends of his. Bird and my friend spent an hour that evening silently viewing the corpses.

Frank Sanderford

Sometimes the vibrations are right, and a devoted fan is given an inside view by the musicians who dig his personality. Such a man is the Chicago author, Frank Sanderford.

I went to see Charlie Parker play when he had his now-famous group in 1947-48, consisting of Duke Jordan, piano; Max Roach, drums; Miles Davis, trumpet; and Tommy Potter, bass. My jazz tastes then were rather old— Lester Young was the last innovation. I had listened for a few times to a couple of Bird records. The first time I heard "Now's the Time" I wondered if the musicians were "birding" me, if they were having a private little joke of their own. Of course, I later found out that that was an important part of the whole thing. But aside from any wry humour and sardonic wit, there emerged a beautiful sadness, tinged with anger at times, all clothed in an exactness of craftsmanship that had never before been expressed in jazz.

I went to the Argyle Show Lounge with some of this new awareness within me. The place was packed, but I somehow managed to get a seat at the bar, directly facing the band. Bird was tired, only occasionally playing a short solo. A few times, it seemed to me that he might fall over backwards. The fellows with him would shoot side glances his way, look quickly at one another with guilt not quite being covered by hastily formed masks of derision. It was difficult to tell if they were concerned or fearful and, if so, for themselves or their leader.

Soon I noticed Bird watching me. I told myself that it was just my imagination. Then he touched Miles's sleeve slightly, and they both stared at me. I began to feel conspicuous and had to remind myself many times that others in the audience looked and dressed in more unconventional ways than I. But it was small solace, for their stares became more noticeable, and they were smiling and whispering together. Before the number they were playing was over, Bird left the stand and walked uncertainly to the back, down the aisle between the stand and the bar, circled the bar, and came slowly toward me and stopped next to me. He didn't look at me, and he said nothing. Finally, in a sort of desperation, I said hello.

When nothing was said, I continued, "I hear the kind of jazz you play was started by Dizzy Gillespie."

"He tell you that?" he asked.

I said no, that I had not met Dizzy, and he laughed.

"Come on back to the back room after this set," he said, then walked away.

I managed to squeeze through the crowd to a small, dark room where the musicians lounged. As I came in they looked surlily at me. It was hot, the musicians whispered among themselves, I heard snickers.

Bird demanded that I go out and bring him back a hamburger. I left, confused and humiliated. But outside in the cooler air, I began to think of all I had heard of his genius, the struggles he had to face. I recalled his face, thin and tired-looking, his clothes that seemed to hang on him, giving the impression they had been made for him at a healthier state or for somebody several sizes larger. I went to the closest hamburger joint and got two with everything on and french fries.

Back at the Argyle, Bird wolfed them down as though he hadn't seen food for several days. The other musicians seemed less bitter, more friendly. Suddenly, the manager appeared and demanded in querulous tones for their return to the stand. Slowly, resentfully, they went out. All except Bird. "Stay here," he ordered.

Nothing was said. We just remained in a sort of stupor. I heard the music begin and people mutter. The manager knocked on the door and Bird signaled me to open it. Very few times have I seen a man as angry as the manager. He seemed to be consumed by it, struck dumb by it. All he could do was splutter and point his finger. Bird walked disdainfully by him and toward the front entrance.

"If you don't get back on that stand and give the customers what they paid for, you can leave." Bird motioned for his men to follow. They got up, packed their instruments, and left the stand. "I'm not firing you fellows," the manager screamed. They paid him no mind. "You fellows going to let that bastard get you all in trouble with the union?" the manager pleaded. They paused. Bird said, "You fellows can stay if you want, but I'm leaving."

They followed.

On the street, some young musicians I had just met were standing together talking. Red Rodney, Jim Gourley, Tiny Kahn, and Lou Levy, who was known then as "Count." He touched my arm. "Hello, Frank," he said eagerly. "I'll bet you don't remember me." To me Lou was a marvelous pianist who would some day make his mark in the jazz world. How could I forget him. "Could you get Bird to come with us?" he whispered. The others seemed to hang on what I would say.

I introduced Bird to the fellows, and he got in the car with them. "We're going to have a session at my house tomorrow," I told Bird and Miles, who was just getting in the car. "You're welcome to come."

"Eyes," he said, "give me a ring at the hotel," and he mentioned a hotel on the corner of 61st and a block east of Cottage Grove. Max and Miles said they had eyes too, and they drove off. Up on the El structure, I laughed softly to myself. Well, I had met the fabulous Bird.

The last time I saw him was at the Beehive in Chicago. The owner had asked me to get Charlie to go on. He was in a little room where they stored beer. I went back there; Charlie met me at the door and threw his arms around me, as if I were the only person in the world. He couldn't go on the stand, he said; he was in no condition. He looked bad. The house was jammed. I asked him to take a look and see how many people had come just to hear him play, and I opened the door a little. He glared out. "They just came to see the world's most famous junky," he growled. I will always be guilty, because I did get him to get on the stand. He made a few, awful, bleating sounds. He couldn't play. He was disgusted, afraid, and frustrated somehow. He was a beaten man, and he knew it. He died soon after.

Dave Schildkraut

Dave Schildkraut was born in New York City on January 7, 1925. He made his professional entrance with Louis Prima, in 1941 and worked in the various groups of Buddy Rich. In the summer of 1953, he toured with Stan Kenton and Charlie Parker who was a star with Kenton. He has also played in the groups of George Handy and Anita O'Day. A family man, he has had to take a nonmusical job once in a while. He worked as floor manager for Woolworth's in 1949. He is a superb alto saxophonist in the Parker tradition.

Bird was no goof. He was too active, always on the move, always writing tunes. Even when he seemed to be doing nothing, things were getting done. I had a chance to observe him on a tour I did with Stan Kenton in the summer of 1953. Charlie was a featured soloist with this package. He joined the troupe in Texas, taking the place of Stan Getz.

I had always followed him musically, and this was brought into sharp focus by an incident where the guys on the trip once complained that I disturbed their sleep by playing in the middle of the night. I denied it but didn't seem to convince anyone. I asked around till Bird told me it was he. On one of Leonard Feather's blindfold tests someone attributed a Bird solo to me. Such things never bother me. Everyone derives from someone else, so choose the best.

The trip had us hopping around the country in planes and in two chartered buses. In one Southern town, a restaurant would not serve Negroes, so Bird had to wait in the bus while the rest of us were wolfing down steaks. Finally, after persuasion, the eatery relented. Dizzy and Erroll Garner left the bus, but Charlie held out and refused to go in and eat. I brought him out a big steak sandwich, and he grumbled, "What, are you trying to be good to me?" and he put it aside. But I noticed that, as soon as the bus moved on, he fell on that sandwich and devoured it. His behavior throughout the tour was exemplary and in the best tradition of musical knights of the road. He never missed a performance; his horn, reed, mouthpiece were just right to cope with the ten brass that he had to sail over at times. His treatment of other musicians was always considerate; in fact, he showed greater consideration toward the guys who were having a tough time with their instrument, and he would spend time going over something again and again till the person felt he got it.

He was an old-fashioned crapshooter, the kind that blows on his hands, gets on his knees, kisses the dice, and shouts to them.

His only bit of contrariness occurred when Kenton wanted him to play a selection written for Zoot Sims entitled "Zoot." Bird said the number was too hard for him, and Stan asked me to help Bird. Charlie could do it, and I knew he knew it, but I went over to speak to him to confirm what I felt it was. It was that the composition was so characteristically Zoot Sims that Parker did not feel comfortable playing it. He never did.

I used to run into him many times around town, and, if I wasn't working, he would always spring for coffee or a few dollars. Once, when we were broke, we were strolling in mid-town and we passed Basin Street where Charlie espied two affluent-looking members of the Hampton band. He didn't say anything to them but, in his booming voice, he said to me, "Let's talk about when we were with Stan Kenton on the coast."

Tony Scott was born Anthony Sci-acca in Morristown, New Jersey, in 1921. His first influences were Clar-ence Hutchenrider, clarinettist with the Glen Gray Casa Loma band and Benny Goodman. Tony's father, a barber and amateur guitarist, noting his son's interest in music, bought him an aluminum clarinet. Tony has stuck to the clarinet, even though it has gone out of vogue in modern jazz. He also plays the saxes, piano, and arranges. He went to Juilliard from 1940 to 1942. From 1942 to 1945 he had his own band in the Army. He has played with all the top names in jazz and has led many small combos of his own. Extremely idealistic and vociferous in his love for jazz, he has turned down many lucrative jobs in commercial music. He was a one-man, goodwill ambas-sador, touring Europe and South Africa by himself (accompanied by his lovely artist-wife Fran). In Af-rica, he played before nonsegregated audiences. A close friend of Parker for many years, he appeared on the CBS-TV production called The Mythical Bird *in which he spoke of Parker's musicianship.*

I first met Bird in 1943, and, from the very first, he was always very kind to me. I was a kid in awe of everyone, anxious to sit in and play, or to curl up in the corner of a club and listen. I guess I was lucky. The club owners never bothered me, even though I didn't drink. Well, this first night, Don Byas was playing with Bird. I walked in, and there was Don playing "Cherokee." Man, he flew over that horn; and after his solo, Bird played, and it was incredible. I said to myself, are you going to follow that? But I figured I'd do the best I could. Bird always encouraged me to play. A lot of guys didn't want to play on the same stand, feeling that they would look too bad or be too badly scared by Bird, but I felt I wasn't in competition with the man. I played my horn the best I could. It was a different instrument. Bird tried the clarinet, and he sounded like a twelve-year-old on the thing.

One night he was playing on the street (52nd Street) with Miles and Max, and I took out my clarinet and started to assemble it, when Miles turned to me and said, "Bird don't like no one to play with him."

"O.K.," I said, and sat down. After a set Bird spotted me and said, "Tony, what's the matter with you? Do I have to give you an engraved invitation every time? Come on and play a few with us."

I told him what Miles had said. He said, "Miles and Max have been bugging me lately. I'm going to fire those two guys." And he did. But such a magnificent combination could not be separated for long. They went to California; and several years later, when Charlie was back in New York, I wondered if he would remember me. He was at Small's Paradise. I walked up to him.

"Remember me, Bird?"

"Sure, man, sure." And we started to talk. "Remember, Tony, how we used to jam up at Clarke Monroe's Uptown House? You were in the Hudson DeLange band." He turned to someone and said, "Me and Tony are buddies."

I was puzzled. I had played at Minton's and some other places, but never at Clarke Monroe's. I was never in the Hudson DeLange band. I said nothing. The time he spoke of was 1939. I had graduated high school in 1938 in Morristown, New Jersey.

One day I was called to do a radio show, and afterwards I was walking home with another clarinettist by the name of Artie Baker. He turned to me and asked if I knew of some place to blow after hours, some place like the old Uptown House. I turned to him and said, "You used to play there?"

"Yeah," he said.

"Around 1939?"

"Yes."

"Were you ever in the Hudson DeLange band?"

"Yeah, for a short while."

"Did you ever know Charlie Parker?" And he said, "No." Well, that stopped me for a minute, but then I said, "He was thin and played tenor sax."

He said, "What! That wailin' cat! I played with the guy you described. He was tremendous."

I said to him, "Man, you just cleared up a mystery that was annoying me for years." And come to think of it, this guy looked somewhat like me.

One time I was living above Café Society, and Bird was playing there with Kenny Dorham, and I decided to cook some Veal Scallopine for Bird. So I went down to the butchers and I asked him to give me some good veal. It was the first time and the last time I ever cooked that dish. I put wine and tomato sauce in, and, as I was putting some pepper into it, the lid fell off and a whole lot of pepper fell into the concoction. Oh, God, I thought, this is going to be some hot Scallopine, and I got as much of the pepper out as I could. So Bird finished the set and came upstairs. I had placed the settings on the table. Somehow, in the conversation before we fell upon the food, Bird mentioned something about having ulcers. I said, "You got ulcers, Bird?"

"Yes. But I'm taking pills for it."

I said, "Man, don't eat any of this, because I dropped pepper in it. Man, this will kill you. Boy, I can see me walking down the street, and people will be pointing and spitting at me, saying, 'He killed Bird.' "

Bird laughed, and he said, "No, man. I got some good pills. As a matter of fact, I'll take two."

"No, man. Please don't eat any of this. I'll fix you up some eggs or something."

"No," Bird said. "This smells good, with the wine in it and everything. These pills are a bitch." So he took the pills and ate the stuff, and nothin' happened, and he was straight.

Not long before Charlie died, I was working at the Metropole, a restaurant-bar in mid-town Manhattan that featured continuous music both afternoon and evening, the quality of which was uncertain. It paid good bread and gave a lot of work. The musicians had to play loud and be on public view, something like a freak show in Coney Island. During a break I stepped out in the street, and there was Bird. He asked me if I had seen Charlie Smith, the drummer. Just then, we spotted him coming up the street. Bird greeted him warmly, and then asked him if he had any money. Smith said, "Sure, Baby, I got something," and he pulled out eight cents, his total resources. Bird took it. Then he turned to me and said, "How much have you got, Tony?"

"I only got thirty cents, and I could let you have half, because I'd like to take a bus home." I gave him fifteen cents. After chatting with us a few minutes, Bird gave Smith back three cents, feeling he couldn't take all his money. I turned to him and said, "Bird, are you gonna give me back some of my money, too?" He turned to me with a grin and said, "Now, Tony, you wouldn't want me to walk around New York broke, would you?"

Some friends once made me a birthday party on the thirty-first year of my existence. Bird wandered in around four, and, when he learned of the occasion, he took out his horn and began to wail "Happy Birthday." I'll never forget that as long as I live. When it came time to break up proceedings, Bird had fallen out—that is, he was asleep; and when Bird slept, nothing you did could awaken him. I put his horn in the case for him. I was very surprised to find a pair of baby shoes lying in the case.

I once organized a birthday party for Charlie. It was to be on Tuesday, at four in the morning. Charlie was mightily pleased. He said he had to be in Detroit over the weekend, but he'd be back in time for the party. It was a big success, and everybody had a ball; but Bird was a trifle late, three days late. He knocked, walked in, and asked me, "Where's everybody?"

Bird kind of respected the fact that I was studying legit. He'd drift in some afternoons, just sitting around while I was writing. It was nothing for him to knock off a bottle of scotch and bottle of gin at a sitting. If liquor were not available, he'd drink orange juice. I studied with Stefan Wolpe, a modern, classical composer of considerable reputation. One of Wolpe's works called for a tenor saxophone. I never suggested Bird for the part, for various reasons. I felt that he was too undisciplined to come in time for rehearsals; he was out of town most of the time. So I didn't want to stick my teacher with so risky a performer for his quartet. I got Al Cohn to play the part.

Whenever Wolpe was in my place or at a party with me, I'd play some of Parker's records or sometimes a record of Mahalia Jackson's. Wolpe, on hearing Mahalia's free-flowing voice, said complainingly, "Why don't they sing my songs that way?" He was really sold. I explained to him that Mahalia was completely unschooled. As to Parker, it got so that he would always ask to hear his records. "Play Birdie, play Birdie," he would jubilantly shout. One afternoon I introduced them when Wolpe was in my loft and Parker made one of his unscheduled visits. "This is Birdie—this is Stefan Wolpe." Wolpe, who has the exuberance of a child, exclaimed, "Ah, Birdie, how are you?"

Bird, on the other hand, became very formal. "It is indeed a pleasure to meet you." It was as if he had donned a cape and plumed hat; he even made a little bow. "You know, Mr. Wolpe, I would like to commission you to do a work. I am now associated with Mercury Records. I want you to write for as many men as you care to, seventy-five if necessary. Norman Granz will do it if I tell him." To Bird, seventy-five men meant seventy-five times scale. It seemed a tremendously generous offer. Of course, Wolpe never even considered such a thing. He could write for as many men as the music seemed to demand. He could write for four men or one hundred and twenty.

Charlie Parker opened the door, showed the world, and then he shut the door behind him.

Noble Sissle

Noble Sissle was a drum major in the famous Jim Europe band of World War I. When Europe died, he took over leadership of the band. Sissle was born in Indianapolis in 1889. His band was heard steadily in the 20's and 30's and intermittently in the 40's and 50's. He is the composer of "I'm Just Wild About Harry."

During the war, we had the constant problem of losing men in the band to the Army. In late 1943, we were working in Chicago, a couple of my men had just been drafted, and we needed an alto player. Some of the guys came up to me and told me, "Charlie Parker is outside. He's a great sax man." I said, "O.K. Bring him in. If he can play, we can use him." He looked all right, and he seemed to do okay in the section.

In those days, my band was pretty commercial. We played for the shows, and then for dancing, but there wasn't much jazz. On one number, "St. Louis Blues," I used to feature the soloists. So, as was customary with a new man on the band, I had Parker come up front. I was leading, and when I heard the strange sounds that came from his horn, I must have made a funny face, for some of the guys in the band broke up. I was aware then of the strange new jazz the younger men were beginning to play, but I had never heard anything like this before.

Charlie didn't stay with us long, maybe three or four weeks. He used to thrill me and upset me, one after the other. One thing about him, he was a phenomenal musician. What he played may have been weird, but he always knew what he was doing. Not like some of the bopsters. Whatever he was playing, the harmony was always correct, and he could play his horn.

I've heard about his supposed habits, and of course I know about his tragic end, but I never noticed him doing anything wrong while he was with us. There's one incident I remember, though, which made me wonder about him. We were on a train, at night, and I was sitting by myself reading when Charlie came up to me. He looked frightened. "What's wrong?" I asked him. "I want to get off this train," he said. "The guy sitting next to me has a knife, and he wants to kill me." At first I thought he was pulling my leg, but I was soon convinced that he was quite serious. I calmed him down a little and made him sit with one of the men I knew well. I went back on the train and found a porter and asked him if he had an empty berth on one of the pullmans for one of my men who was sick. As I thought, he had extra space, and I went back to get Charlie, and we put him to bed. The next day he was all right. That was the only time he did something out of the ordinary, other than his playing.

212

When we hit St. Louis, Billy Eckstine's new band, which had all the young bebop musicians, was playing in town, and Charlie left me to join him. I went down to hear them one night, and let me tell you, neither I nor the people in the audience had ever heard anything like that music before.

I think that the war, with all the regimentation and frustrations, had a lot to do with what happened to jazz in the last fifteen years. The young musicians wanted to play for themselves, and to hell with the public. It was musicians' music, and you couldn't sell it. I saw Charlie Parker a few times after that, and we always had friendly words on those occasions. I've heard all those stories about him, but he always seemed like a nice fellow to me. The only thing I ever saw him take was benzedrine. . . .

Buster Smith

Walter Page discovered Buster Smith playing in a speakeasy in 1925. He hired him despite the fact that he could not read music. While he played with the Blue Devils, someone dubbed him Professor because he wore spectacles. The alto man was born in Ennis County, Texas, in 1904, but moved to Dallas as a youngster.

I went back to Kansas City and organized my own band in 1937. We had twelve pieces. Jay McShann was in the band; Odel West, tenor; Hadnott, bass; Willie McWashington on drums; and a guy named Crooke on guitar. Then, there was Fred Beckett, trombone; Andy Anderson on second trumpet; and I don't remember the third trumpet's name. The first trumpeter was Tiny Davis' husband, but I can't remember his name either. And then we had another tenor player that I can't remember. I played alto, and, of course, Charlie Parker played the other alto.

Charlie had been in Kansas City for a long time. I'd seen him running around in 1932 or 1933 when he was just a kid. He came up Tommy Douglas' brothers: Bill played alto, and Buck played tenor. They were pretty good boys, themselves, and Tommy, too. I used to listen to Tommy on alto myself. And then there was Jack Washington. Bennie Moten played a lot of alto, but you could hardly make him play unless you got right behind him. But he played a lot of alto. Eddie Barefield, too.

Anyway, Charlie came up with Tommy Douglas' brothers, Bill and Buck.

Charlie would come in where we were playing and hang around the stand, with his alto under his arm. He had his horn in a paper sack—always carried it in that paper sack. He used to carry his horn home and put it under his pillow and sleep on it.

Well, he used to tell me he wanted to play like me. He'd say, "Buster, you're the king," and I'd say, "No, you're the king." And he'd say, "No, man, you're the king."

Charlie would run by himself. He wouldn't stay with anyone for over a night or two, and then, tomorrow, he would be with somebody else. I tried to get him to join Bennie Moten about 1934, but he wouldn't do it. He wanted to play in small groups where he could solo like he wanted to, when he wanted to. There was a trumpet player there, a white boy named Neal that Charlie ran around with. (Neal played with Charlie Barnet later on.) The two of them used to go out and play all night around the joints.

When I came back to Kansas City to organize my band, Charlie was still there. He had been there ever since '32 or '33, just running around taking gigs where he found them. Charlie was headstrong, but he wasn't a smart-alec kid. He was a good boy; he'd listen to you. When he heard about my band, he was the first in line to get in it. He'd improved a good bit since I'd seen him before, and, of course, I wanted him. The only trouble he had was with his mouthpiece. He had trouble getting the tone he wanted to get. But as for knowing his horn, he knew that. He always knew that, since I first saw him.

He used to call me his dad, and I called him my boy. I couldn't get rid of him. He was always up under me. In my band, we'd split solos. If I took two, he'd take two; if I took three, he'd take three; and so forth. He always wanted me to take the first solo. I guess he thought he'd learn something that way. He did play like me quite a bit, I guess. But after awhile, anything I could make on my horn, he could make too—aand make something better out of it.

We used to do that double-time stuff all the time. Only we called it double-tongue, sometimes, in those days. I used to do a lot of that on clarinet. Then I started doing it on alto, and Charlie heard me doing it, and he started playing it. Tab Smith did a lot, too.

I had that band about two years and Charlie was with me all that time. He was the youngest cat in the band. I'd use the twelve-piece band for dances and tours and things like that and try to keep six pieces, or maybe seven or eight pieces, working steady there in Kansas City the rest of the time. Jay McShann was gone, and we had Emil Williams on piano in the little group. And then Parker, Hadnott, McWashington, Crooke, and me. We worked at a place called Lucille's Band Box on 18th Street. We used to broadcast from there sometime. When I left for New York the band was working at a white place—the Antler Club.

He was a little hot-headed sometimes, and he wouldn't stay with nobody but me. He stayed with me longer than anybody, till he got with McShann.

In 1938 I went to New York to look for work for the band. I thought we might get a break up there. I left Charlie and Odel West in charge and told him I'd send for them when I found something. Well, I stayed seven months and didn't send for them. Charlie got downhearted when it looked like I wasn't gonna send for them, so he just caught a train and hoboed up there, came up there where I was. He sure did look awful when he got in. He'd worn his shoes so long that his legs were all swollen up. He stayed up there with me for a good while at my apartment. During the day, my wife worked, and I was always out looking around, and I let him stay at my place and sleep in my bed. He'd go out and blow all night somewhere and then come in and go to sleep in my bed. I'd make him leave in the afternoon before my wife came home. She didn't like him sleeping in our bed, because he wouldn't pull his clothes off before he went to bed. (Laughs.) He was always like that. He would go down to Monroe's and play all night. The boys were beginning to listen to him then.

He stayed around doing that for a while and then went down to Baltimore for about three weeks, and that's when McShann sent for him. McShann had started his own band he put Charlie on tenor at first.

I didn't see Charlie much after he joined McShann. I was in New York and he was in the Midwest and Southwest with McShann's band.

Sonny Stitt

A week before he died, Bird ran into his friend Sonny Stitt. Sonny was one of the first alto sax men to play in Parker's style with a great deal of cogency. Stitt says that Bird looked very beat. They exchanged a few pleasantries and Charlie said in parting, "Man, I'm handing you the keys to the kingdom." Sonny Stitt was born in Boston, Massachusetts, on February 2, 1924. He played in the band of Tiny Bradshaw. He was part of the Norman Granz JATP for three years. He toured with a band led by himself and Gene Ammons from 1949-51. In 1960 he was part of the Miles Davis Quintet.

I'm not going to throw any dirt on the man. He was the greatest man I ever knew. He would find something beautiful about the ugliest person. When I was nineteen, playing with Tiny Bradshaw, I heard the records he had done with McShann and I was anxious to meet him. So when we hit Kansas City, I rushed to Eighteenth and Vine, and there, coming out of a drug store, was a man carrying an alto, wearing a blue overcoat with six white buttons and dark glasses. I rushed over and said belligerently, "Are you Charlie Parker?" He said he was and invited me right then and there to go and jam with him at a place called Chauncey Owenman's. We played for an hour, till the owner came in, and then Bird signalled me with a little flurry of notes to cease so no words would ensue. He said, "You sure sound like me."

I saw him before he left for Sweden, and I remember he was wearing an all-white outfit: pants, shoes, socks, jacket, except for a big red Lord Fauntleroy bow tie.

Idrees Suleiman

Idrees Dawud Ibn Suleiman (Horace Graham) was, according to Mary Lou Williams, one of the first to play modern jazz. He started in music with the Carolina Cotton Pickers and Fess Clarke in his home town of St. Petersburg, Florida, and has worked with Benny Carter, Cab Calloway, Earl Hines, Count Basie, Lionel Hampton, Dizzy Gillespie, Gerry Mulligan, and Thelonious Monk, among others.

I played with Bird in the Earl Hines band; I also used to jam with him back in 1941 at a place called the Kentucky Club. We would meet there every Monday at four in the morning and play till about one in the afternoon.

The things that stand out the most in my memory of him are the complex moods of the man. Among the men of the Hines band he was looked upon as a jolly fellow, full of buoyant spirits. With me he was a man of infinite patience when it came to explaining a point in music. He seemed at times the most serious person I have ever met, the most intense—without any type of superficiality. He seemed to know the insides of everything. I've seen him stagger into a club, drunk, his head drooping over his horn, seemingly asleep, and then he would come in and play perfectly, constructing masterful choruses and bringing what might have seemed mistakes into line.

I've known the good-natured Bird. Once a group of young kids were jammin' in a club, and they were terrible. Other musicians were yelling for them to get off the stand. Bird turned to them and said, "I hear what they're trying to do," and then he went up on the stand and he demonstrated it.

At another time, after I knew him awhile, I walked up to him once at a place where he was working and asked him if he would play a tune I loved to hear him do, "Embraceable You." He looked me dead in the eye as if he never met or knew me, and he said, "I don't know that song."

"Symphony Sid" Torin

Sid Torin made his start in radio in 1937 at a small Bronx station, WBNX, where someone dubbed him "Symphony Sid." For almost twenty years Sid has made his paradoxical nickname synonymous with the best in modern sound. He was preaching Bird, Diz, and Bud away back. He had all-night shows emanating from Bop City and Birdland. After a five-year absence in Boston, he's back in New York on station WADO.

To disc jockeys, jazz has always been a stepping stone to worse things musically and better things monetarily. The D.J. renegades are many, and it is understandable. All the more credit to Symphony Sid, who has always espoused the righteous sound in his sonorous, off-beat way. This boy can really sell. He started his career as a record salesman. He has been a pitchman on radio for some of the strangest sponsors: a meat-cutting school, a zoot suit pants shop, and he laid down the following spiel for a mortuary account he had. "When fate deals you one from the bottom of the deck, fall by to the Sunshine Fu-

neral Parlor. *Your loved ones will
be handled with dignity and care,
and the cats at Sunshine will not lay
too heavy a price on you. Now I'd
like to play a request, Cootie Williams doing 'Somebody's Got To
Go.' "*

I'm a disc jockey, and I've been around the New York area since 1937. We
didn't have any modern jazz then. We were playing Lunceford, Harry James,
Goodman, Count Basie, all the swinging-type things. In the old days we used
to call him *Feigele* (Bird in Yiddish). One of the last times I saw Charlie
Parker before I went to Boston was at a club called Le Down Beat, on 54th
Street off 8th Avenue. In those days, he was learning how to play golf. He
was big and fat and looked well. He was taking lessons from a pro. He was
very elated about the golf situation. He told me he was going to play golf the
gentleman's way, very leisurely, and his game was improving every day.
I think I know Bird as well as anybody from the outside. I don't know too
much about his personal life.

My close association with Parker dates from the time he came to New
York with Jay McShann. Monte Kay and I used Charlie on our various jam
sessions at the Fraternal Clubhouse on 48th Street. Dexter Gordon used to
play. Tony Scott used to come in and play for nothing, and we used to chase
him off the bandstand—but he was learning—it's just that he got hung up
with too many rhumba bands. In 1942 Monte Kay and I presented the first
Charlie Parker-Dizzy Gillespie concert. It was held at Town Hall, and Al
Haig, Curly Russell, and Max Roach were also featured.

Did you ever happen to hear how jazz went off 52nd Street? Monte Kay
and I were doing promotion, mostly radio, for Irving Alexander and Sammy
Kaye, and we asked for a $25 raise. They refused it. About that time Ralph
Watkins had this chicken place on Broadway right across from the Strand
Theatre. This place was later known as The Roost. Being mad, we went over
and did our first Tuesday night session. We had Dexter Gordon and Allen
Eager doing like a battle of tenors. When the owners saw the type of business—we had people in line waiting to get in—well, that's when we decided
to put jazz on Broadway. Our first big show at The Roost featured Parker and
his group: Curly Russell, Al Haig, Kenny Dorham, and Max Roach. Billy
Eckstine was also on the bill.

I'll never forget one night. Charlie Parker, as you know, was using whatever he was using. We used to do a Friday night remote where we took our
microphones down to The Roost. We usually started with our theme, "Jumping With Symphony Sid." Parker got up and, just about in the middle of the
theme, sat down in a chair and fell asleep—which to me was the wildest thing

in the world. Here in the middle of a broadcast—in the only program that was doing jazz—he falls asleep.

I'll never forget one night Charlie Parker sat in the back room in his stupor and said, "You can't put me on the bandstand." He said, "I'm God," and with that somebody, to bring him around, cracked him right across the jaw and laid him out on the floor. Bird was always giving us trouble, not making dates, but everybody loved Bird—he was just a likeable guy, a sweet guy. If he met you with your girl or with any girl he would always say how beautiful she was, if she happened to be beautiful. There was one particular girl I used to go with that Bird thought very, very much of. He was the one that gave her the name Chi Chi, and he recorded the tune "Chi Chi."

I also remember a night Charlie had just come back from Paris, and someone had given him a beautiful beret. Dizzy had also come back from Europe and was given a beautiful pipe. Tadd Dameron and Billy Eckstine were also in the WHOM radio studio that night, and we were going to discuss the European situation in modern music. All of a sudden, out of a clear sky, Bird grabs ahold of Diz's pipe and steps on it, breaking it. Dizzy grabs Bird's hat and puts a knife through it, and the fight is on. All this while we were on the air—and the knives were jumping, and Eckstine was on the floor, a brand new suit of his torn. I had to segue a lot of records. I think we segued records for three hours straight. I was scared to open up the microphone till we got this scrape straightened out. Years ago Bird and Dizzy were very good friends, but Bird used to tell me that Dizzy didn't deserve to be bigger than he was, since he thought he knew more about the jazz scene. He thought he should be the bigger man. Diz was with the big band and making a lot of money, and Bird was scuffling, because he was negligent in his work.

A while after Birdland opened, Norman Granz made an album of Bird with strings. When I got to the Birdland scene after I left Bop City, Monte Kay and I came up with the idea of bringing in Charlie Parker with strings. We hired him for four weeks, and it was expensive because we had a harpist and oboe. Well, he stayed for sixteen weeks, and that was the beginning of the Birdland success story. WJZ built a studio for me in the club. Some thirty-odd states heard me broadcast nightly.

The whole scene of jazz should be built around Charlie Parker, because he was the character that made modern jazz possible. I do not think it would have been without him. He was the first on. He started Dizzy off. I just feel he was the whole jazz story of today. Every musician I speak to, the young ones coming up today, they all say that Parker was the inspiration to the whole jazz scene.

I saw Bird the summer before he died. He was living in Brewster on the Cape with his wife and the kids. To show you how beautifully this man got along with people—Brewster is one of the most exclusive places—not only is it restricted, but the poor are prohibited. I don't know who Charlie Parker knew there. Somebody must have dug him very much to allow him and his wife to have a cottage on their property. Bird did a gig out there at a place called The Red Barn. It was a dance, and there was Chan with the baby sitting on the bandstand, and that was the last time I saw Bird. He looked beautiful and healthy, and he said, "Say, Sid man, we're havin a ball, the baby's havin a ball. I don't care if I work." He was just having a wonderful time.

There was a period when I would see Charlie six times a week. When he wasn't working, he'd stand in front of The Roost and say, "Man, lend me quarter," or "Sid, give me two dollars." I never asked for these loans back. When I asked him for a favor he always came across. He played that first Town Hall 1942 concert for me for $25. Diz got $25; everybody got $25.

When I was up at Boston he worked at the Hi Hat and Storyville. He always did good business for everyone.

The successful musician is not a junkie. I believe the reason that many musicians made junk in the years between 1940 and 1942 was frustration. The frustration of knowing that they are so great. Every musician knows how great he is, if he is. If he's bad, he knows how bad he is. If he's great and he's not doing what he wants to, if he's not earning the money, it hurts. Parker was never a very successful man in the music business. In the years of modern music, a jazz musician was more or less frowned upon because he was playing a lot of notes that didn't make sense, because you couldn't hear the melody or you couldn't tap your foot to it. The so-called swing era people who still like Benny Goodman still say, "I don't hear the tune." They don't listen to improvisation, they just listen to whether they can tap their foot to it, or if

Above:
Mingus, Bird, and Symphony Sid.
Below:
At the Royal Roost two Apache visitors, Bad Wolf and Swift Eagle, demonstrate their native music for Bird.

they can dance to it. Music outside of that is not music to them. Bird was disgusted with the people around him; he was disillusioned. When he worked, he made scale, and he had a family to support in addition to a big boy back home. After all, what does junk do for a person? It gives him a lift. They forget their unhappiness. When a musician achieves success, he usually gives up junk.

I remember when Bird bought his first car. He bought a second-hand 1949 Cadillac. When he first started to make money at Birdland, Morris Levy advanced him enough, and he bought his first Cadillac. He had no license, he didn't know how to drive, but he wanted that car so bad, and he just drove. He got stopped a couple of times, and somebody had to fix the ticket or square the beef for him. I only knew on the job, in the street, 'cause Parker was everywhere, wherever you went there was Bird.

He was a funny kind of junkie. The ones that I've known are emaciated and look like death, because junk takes away your appetite and your sex. Bird looked heavy and a little overfed. I think he was able to control what he was doing somewhat.

In California, during a concert engagement, Norman Granz hired a detective to watch Bird and to drive him around. The guardian met the same fate that John Barrymore's did. Bird not only slipped away, but he got away during the night in the detective's car and never made another concert in that particular series.

A musician may be using pot and some girl will say to him for example, "Man, why don't you pick up on some of this, you don't have to shoot it but just sniff it (heroin, for example), and you could ball me all night, and you'll never come." And that's how a guy may get started. It takes about fifteen seconds the first time you take it. And the horrible part of it is that it sometimes works the first time. You take a sniff of this jazz, and you can ball a chick all night long. So the buy says, "Tomorrow, I'll make it again," so he goes out and buys a little packet for $25 which will last him for the whole week. If he uses it for more than a week, that's when he gets hooked. And when he's hooked, his balling eyes will be quite dimmed. It's the same with the music. A musician can take a few sniffs, go on the stand zonked, and play his ass off, at least swing hard. But in time he'll be so uncomfortable as he begins to require constant dosage that he will be unable to function on the stand. Panic will disrupt his performance.

Sniffing is much more expensive than shooting. When you shoot, you hit the mainstream immediately, and you feel it immediately. Sniffing, you have to use and sniff a lot, and it doesn't catch so fast. It takes more to keep you high. A connection is usually a junkie. He can't work so he supports his habit by hooking young ladies and turning them into prostitutes to support their habits. Ninety percent of your junkies are women; most of your prostitutes are junkies.

Lennie Tristano

His great and profound respect for Parker once led Lennie Tristano to say, "If Charlie Parker wanted to invoke plagiarism laws, he could sue almost everybody who's made a record in the last ten years." Tristano was born in Chicago, in 1919. At six he suffered a siege of measles that weakened his eyes, which were poor from birth. At eight he was placed in a handicapped class in a Chicago public school. His sight was rapidly diminishing, and from the age of nine to nineteen, he was in a state institution for the blind. Despite some discouraging aspects of this institution, whose rules were rigorous and some of whose occupants were idiotic and feeble-minded, Tristano did a magnificent job of self-development. He studied piano, saxophone, clarinet, and cello. He formed his own band, and they often got beyond the grounds to play dates in town. He romped through the American Conservatory of Music in Chicago, picking up a four-year Bachelor of Music degree in three years. He was one of the honorary pall-bearers at Parker's funeral. At one juncture, they dropped the casket. By some mysterious intuitive process, Tristano stuck out his arm at that precise moment and caught it.

I knew Bird since the time he came back to New York from Camarillo. I can say that he has been nicer to me than anybody in the business. My group was opposite his at the Three Deuces. He sat through my entire first set listening intently. When it was over, the two fellows I was playing with left the stand, leaving me alone. They knew I could get around all right, but Bird didn't know that; he thought I was hung up for the moment. He rushed up to the stand, told me how much he liked my playing, and subtly escorted me off the bandstand.

Before we were to go on together to do a couple of Mutual Network shows ("Battle of Styles"), I was sitting at the piano, playing something. He started playing with me, and he played his ass off. He wasn't used to the chords I played. I play sort of my own chords. In a lot of ways, they were different. I don't remember the tune, but whatever I did, he was right on top of the chords, like we had rehearsed. He has always been limited by the people he played with. If he had made records without a piano. . . . Harmonically, the rest of the band is not with him. The right chord structure is not behind him. Most of the kids who played piano for Bird and played in his style, they always used the same chord progression. It does make it a lot easier for the horn player. It takes a horn player with real ears to make it and play something (meaning to cope with a new progression and even play something good).

One of the main things in Bird's life was that he wanted to be recognized as an artist, not as an entertainer, on a higher level than the night club. He wanted to be recognized by composers. He wanted everyone to know how great he was. Charlie Parker not only provided the life-giving force which is the essence of bop but also adequately expressed the music—the creator and the performer. There is quite a sizeable gap between bop and previous phases of jazz. The most complex aspect of bop lies in the ingenuity with which the melodic line was originated. It was creative. The context of the line breaks up into a large number of precisely thought-out phrases, each of which is an idea in its own right and may also be used in conjunction with any of the other phrases, and on any tune whose chord structure is chromatic or diatonic. This may be compared to a jig-saw puzzle which can be put together in hundreds of ways, each time showing a definite picture which in its general character differs from all the other possible pictures.

In 1949, however, Bird told me that he had said as much as he could in this particular idiom. He wanted to develop something else in the way of playing or another style. He was tired of playing the same ideas. I imagine it was brought to his attention strongly by the repetitious copying of his style by everybody he met. His music had become stylized. He, of course, played it better than anyone else. In his great moments, it was still fresh. It had to be inspired. I don't think he had this inspiration often after a time. It was a question of saying what had been already said.

One night I was sitting in the Three Deuces. Bird was twenty-five minutes late. It was cold out. The place was pretty crowded. Bird dashed through to the stand, slammed the mouthpiece on the horn, and played as great as I have ever heard him, all this without taking off his heavy coat. Besides the moments of great inspiration, he was consistent in that he always could play.

Bird's music is so perfect that it is scientific. Had he been a composer, he could have written hundreds of compositions in the same way composers use their material. He had the kind of material that he invented, on the spot in solos, that could have been transformed into preludes, fugues, symphonies, and concertos. Bird's music is tonal. It is as tonal as anybody can be. His music is so structurally perfect that you cannot change a note in it to make it better.

One evening after he had consumed a fifth of Scotch, he chased everyone out of the room except me. He told me he wanted to start a record company with me. It never happened, but it was a flattering thought; and though he never said anything further about it, I think he meant it at the time. I never heard Bird use vulgar language. I never heard him talk about girls in a lewd manner; in fact, he never spoke much about women at all. He had good manners. He always made sure to introduce a person all around if he came into a room. I have never heard Bird put on his fans. He was always kind and sweet to them, accepting their praise gracefully.

I have found great degrees of hostility in the music business. It is a grueling profession. The world is seen as a bar after a while. The hours, the dulling, deadening surroundings, the competition, hassles, the drinking which either produces maudlin moods or aggressiveness of an ugly sort. It is no wonder that no one can sustain a high level of creativity without stimulants of some sort.

I was sitting with Charlie and some musicians at a table in Birdland when Bud Powell came by and said hello, then, for no apparent reason, he said, "You know, Bird, you ain't shit. You don't kill me. You ain't playing shit now," and went on putting him down unmercifully. I said, "Bud, don't talk that way: Bird's your poppa."

Bird said, "Lennie, don't pay any attention. I dig the way he plays." On the next set it was apparent that Bird was going to teach Bud a lesson in manners, for he played every tune in double time, and nobody could play as fast as Bird. Concerning Bud, Charlie once said to me, "You think he is crazy? I taught him how to act that way."

Ray Turner

Possessed of a strong underground reputation, this tenor man was born in New York City in 1918. Ray Turner "sat in" and was a familiar figure at clubs such as The Famous Door, The Onyx, The Three Deuces, and Minton's. He knew enough about what was happening to be able to jam with Bird and Diz in the very early forties.

I've been on the scene for twenty-three years playing tenor. I played with all of them and with Bird a great many times, but what can I say? The only thing that I remember beside the music was that once I was standing in Charlie's Tavern, and Bird reached over and removed my handkerchief. He wiped his glasses with it, he also may have blown his nose with it, and then he folded it neatly back in my breast pocket. It was the only thing he ever borrowed from me. I never had any money to lend anybody.

Asked if Bird ever loaned him dough, Turner said with a smile that if such a thing happened it would really be something to put in a book. Just then a painter friend of Turner's, Arthur Richer, spoke up, "I lent him twenty dollars and in fact when I go down there, I'm gonna collect it. I'd say he was a grumblin' rude old fart," Arthur said, "but he got to me. It was about seven years ago and I was telling him how disgusted and depressed I was and that I was going to leave New York and go out to the coast in order to shake the blues. Well, I'll never forget the tone of his voice when he said that he had always felt the same as I with the difference that he'd been to the Coast. In fact, he'd been everywhere, and he couldn't shake it. This conversation took place outside Café Society in Bird's Cadillac. We were both juiced and salty, and Charlie was going in and out of the club catching Sarah Vaughan's numbers and insulting people at tables. I guess he didn't want my competition in the insult department, because, at one point in the evening, I found he had locked me in the car and left me banging on the windows. He came back two hours later, drove me uptown, and let me off in the middle of nowhere."

Turner started to remember things.

Oh he was a moody fellow. I heard tell of how he was on the road with a new bunch of guys and they never heard him utter a word. He rode along in another vehicle with someone else, and when they got to the date, they wondered, as they sat on the stand, whether he was going to make it. He showed up, played the engagement, and then boarded the bus with everyone. Just as the bus got started, he said his first words in a booming voice, "Well, how do you like the business?" and fell fast asleep.

Bird was a star, and they sent him out as a single, throwing him in with different outfits. It was like an actor appearing in a different play every night. Bird was under a strain. One night he appeared slightly alcoholic and in a vile mood. The band he was supposed to play with was not of the caliber he deserved, but it was to their credit that they tried hard. Bird just stood off to the side listening, and at one juncture, he tore off the neck of his horn and threw it into the bell. After a little while, due probably to Bird's presence, the band came alive, and they really started to wail. Parker grabbed his horn to join in and for a few seconds he seemed disconcerted and puzzled, for it was a horn without a neck and mouthpiece—he had forgotten, but he quickly assembled it and himself musically.

Bird was once late for a theatre engagement, and the guys started the show without him. In the middle of the second number, he arrived. He did not enter from the stage door in the back, but from the front entrance, and to make it dramatic and memorable, he came down the aisle playing his alto. All heads turned with feverish excitement, eyes and ears following him right up to the stand. A master showman, he would not like to think of himself in any commercial light. Part of this master showmanship stemmed from an unpremeditated sense of the fitness of things—following a situation with the correct emotional and uninhibited actions that his audience felt and appreciated. In 1950 he played Café Society Downtown. Art Tatum was the other attraction, and they alternated on the stand. When Bird's trick was through, Tatum took over. One night Bird stepped down, and Art started to play. Charlie listened a few minutes and was so moved by what he heard that he stepped back on the stand and played right through to his next set. He just felt like accompanying Tatum.

Barry Ulanov

Barry Ulanov is the author of A History of Jazz in America. *He has written books about Duke Ellington and Bing Crosby, and was the editor of* Metronome *for a number of years. He teaches in the English De-*

partment at Barnard College. An unusually perceptive critic, he called all the shots in jazz. He was just what modern jazz needed desperately in the 40's and early 50's, namely a highly-cultured and literate spokesman.

In Down Beat, May 4, 1955, Ulanov speaks of Charlie Parker as a legend: "Paul Bunyan and John Henry had nothing on Charlie Parker. . . . Charlie Parker bent a whole music his way and changed the lives of thousands of musicians." Later, he tells one of his strongest memories. "I guess the strongest memory I'll have of Charlie Parker's playing will be of his playing at the rehearsals and the broadcasts for the "Battle of the Bands" he did with me in 1947, on the Mutual Network. It was a modern group versus a New Orleans combination. . . . It was just a couple of broadcasts. . . . The listeners chose the modern group in a postcard balloting. Charlie was all musician those Saturdays, but never so much as when he suggested that the New Orleans veterans choose the tunes for the "Battle" and let the modernists blow them as best they could. He'd never played "Tiger Rag" before in his life, but that first Saturday he played it and made it come alive in his style and with his great personality."

He was not only the fastest man on the horn, but he could also end a conversation, put out a cigarette, and blow on a horn in the count of one [beat]. I made mention of him in 1941 when I heard him with the McShann band. They were both playing opposite Tommy Dorsey, and I recall someone in the Dorsey camp complaining that I made special of this alto man (Parker) which left that much less space for T. D. In the early days when I knew him he was humble and engaging. When he came back from Camarillo, he was still the same engrossing person but more aggressive. We got along well at all times. He was always cooperative. Whatever state he was in, he always seemed essentially controlled. His early demise was tragic, because he was on his way to greater and greater sustained solo. He was on his way to the half-hour performance. Bird came up in a rough world when it was rough.

Edgar Varese

Varese was born in Paris in 1885. Since the first World War, he has been living in the United States. Varese believes that electronic engineers may write the music of the future. A great deal of his compositions are machine-made in which he leaves gaps for his notated parts. He has a predilection for percussive instruments. He is an uncompromising modernist, and his search for expressiveness has gotten him far away from euphony. He defies classification and says, "Right wing, liberal, left wing applied to any art—what nonsense! I try to fly on my own wings." His music shows no derivative qualities. This, in part, must have been something Charlie Parker admired. One can imagine his receptive mind thrilled upon hearing such compositions of Varese's as: "Ionisation" (1931), with its many different percussion instruments, "Hyperprism," written in the 20's, which contains a sleighbell and a siren, and "Density 21.5."

He stopped by my place a number of times. He was like a child, with the shrewdness of a child. He possessed tremendous enthusiasm. He'd come in and exclaim, "Take me as you would a baby and teach me music. I only write in one voice. I want to have structure. I want to write orchestral scores. I'll give you any amount you wish. I make a lot of money. I'll be your servant. I'm a good cook; I'll cook for you." He was so dramatic it was funny, but he was sincere, and finally I promised myself I would try to find some time to show him some of the things he wanted to know. I left for Europe and told him to call me up after Easter when I would be back. Charlie died before Easter. He spoke of being tired of the environment his work relegated him to, "I'm so steeped in this and can't get out," he said.

Ted Wald

Ted Wald has saved many a session that was hung up for a bass player. He played for kicks so many more times than for cash that he put himself in the hospital. He's in good shape now.

New jazz came to Broadway in 1947. I was just old enough to get into clubs legally. I had just gotten my axe and my ears were beginning to open. Later that year I went to college in Ohio and met Frank Foster. Frank and a trumpet player named Freeman Lee were playing Bird's tunes and trying to swing in that groove. Bird, whether he knew it or not, was taking a lot of cats under his wing.

I first met Parker in 1950. The first greeting I received from his was, "Give me a cigarette." I didn't see him after that night until the summer of 1953.

That summer of 1953 was wonderful. Those of us who lived in the Village got to play with Bird almost every day, either at the Open Door or at Sherry Martinelli's pad on Third Avenue and 4th Street. Al Cohn, Zoot Sims, and another guy who's "left," Ronnie Singer, were around; so, it was pretty swinging. Don Joseph and Bird used to sound nutty together. Brew and Bird used to groove each other, too. I was lucky enough to work a gig that summer with Charlie and Al Haig. It was at The Open Door. When we got on the stand to blow the first tune, I was petrified. It was a real up-tempo tune. Bird had a way, with besides his blowing, that made a guy want to play. He dug I was unrelaxed, and so he called some blues. The second chorus he made me walk the twelve bars by myself. He just stood there snapping his fingers saying, "Walk on." The rest of the gig was a ball for me.

Some put him up almost as a god, others put him down for a goof. I heard him speak as a man and as the most wailing alto player that has been.

Bird and Ted Wald.

Bob Wallace

Bob Wallace contributed some information to piece together the mysterious origins of Parker.

Jay McShann was a tenant when my family had a big rooming house at 1015 Park Avenue, Kansas City. The house was equipped with an upright piano and a large reception parlor. So this was where the band held rehearsals. This was 1940 or '41. At this time Bird was playing tenor and doubling on alto. Bird was a quiet fellow and did not have much to talk about. He had a chance to write music as well as play; and the fellows he had, pushing him to stardom, such as Gus Jr., drums; Gene Ramey, bass; Jay McShann, piano; John "Eggs" Jackson, alto; Little Joe Taswell, trombone; the late Freddy "Southern Fried" Culliver, tenor; Walter "Confessing The Blues" Brown; and "Sing The Blues" Buddy Anderson, a trumpet player who played nice background on Parker at Jay McShann's old jams.

I remember this incident that took place in 1950. Bird came home to visit his mom and rest, if that's the word, and was going from joint to joint jamming. At a club on 12th and Vine, then called The Orchard Room, they had a duo. In walked Bird. They swung a few numbers. Then an unforgettable blues fan staggered up to the bandstand, juiced. This is the conversation.

Customer to Bird: "I hear you are Charlie Parker and in town."

Bird to customer: "That's right, man."

Customer: "Well, play me some of those good ole down-home-in-the-alley blues. And you know what I mean—Memphis Slim style."

Parker looked back at the piano player. " 'White Christmas,' Ted." The tempo was one of Parker's best, and you can imagine the groove. Bird played bar after bar, everyone different. At the end:

Customer to Parker: "Say, here now. . . . Don't they call you Yardbird? I see why now—man, you really fly."

Bird, with darts in his eye, packed up his horn and cut out, cursing.

George Wallington

George Wallington (Georgio Figlia) was one of the first pianists to play modern jazz in the early days. His parents brought him here from Italy when he was one year old. He comes from a musical family—his father was an opera singer—and by the time he was fifteen, he had started

*working jazz gigs in Brooklyn and
in Greenwich Village. In 1944, he
was a member of the first bop group
on 52nd Street, the Gillespie-Petti-
ford quintet at the Onyx Club. His
pieces, "Godchild" and "Lemon
Drop," are well known. He now
plays in New York clubs, usually
with a trio.*

I first heard Bird and Diz in 1942 down in the Village at a place called Mac-
Dougal Tavern. In the years between '42 and '48, the fellows lived only to
play. We were obsessed by the new music. There was such pleasure in the
faces. We would play our regular jobs until three in the morning, then go to
an after-hours place till seven and then wait around a few hours till Nola
Studios would open at nine, rent a studio, and practice some more. Our bodies
were sustained by enthusiasm, and when that alone could not carry through
a weaker physique, a little barbiturate pill helped. But dope never made anyone a better musician. It does something to your coordination.

I remember Bird tapping on my window at five in the morning to get me
up to play. If that didn't do it, Bird would start yelling, like a little boy,
"George Wallington!" under the window.

Bird was the friendliest guy, always wonderful company except once when
he was sick, and needed some junk.

Bird seemed to avoid the topic of race. About the South, he said, "The only
way to get around down there is with a gun. Why should any one live down
there while there's a place like New York?" Statements like those were rare.
Usually, when someone brought up the topic, Bird would smile and say, "Why
discuss these things? Let's get high."

When Clyde Hart died, Bird felt that his friends were getting too worked
up over an inevitable part of existence. "Why should we feel sorry? Let's not
get emotional about it." This was just Bird's armor.

It is tragic that no one ever got the full impact of Bird's genius through
records. Some evenings he was so inspired. One night he blew twenty-five
straight choruses of "Cherokee." One week he played differently every evening. It was at the Deuces, a club where he was once thrown out by an unhip
manager who was going by the holes in Bird's socks. He sort of sat way in the
corner of the bandstand and played like a little boy. He had such a cuteness.

Some weeks before his death, he was walking along Broadway with only
fifty cents to his name. He met a blind man who was playing the accordion.
Dropping twenty-five cents into the unfortunate man's cup, he asked him to
play "All the Things You Are." Some minutes later, when Parker again passed
the accordionist, the latter was still playing the requested number. Charlie

laughed heartily and said to the person who was with him, "This boy makes the right changes." He then took the remaining twenty-five cents he had in his old trousers and gave it to the blind man.

The Funeral, The Memorial, and the Estate

Chan Parker went to the Bellevue Morgue and claimed Charlie's body. It was removed to the Walter Cooke Funeral Home; but after the arrangements were all set, Doris Parker arrived and, after hasty consultations and threats of a lawsuit, had the body turned over to her. Charlie's body was then laid in state at the Unity Funeral Home.

The following is quoted from the *New York Post* column by Murray Kempton of March 22, 1955. It was entitled "Flown Bird."

"A service for Charlie (Bird) Parker was held yesterday afternoon at the Abyssinian Baptist Church on 138th St. The pallbearers included Charlie Shavers, John Gillespie, Lennie Tristano, Louis Bellson, and a number of other musicians who have walked some of the road that Parker had travelled.

"He got the sort of funeral a valued member of the congregation gets at any Protestant church, largely because Mrs. Adam Clayton Powell, the pastor's wife, who is Hazel Scott in professional life, was able to speak for him.

"The Rev. David Licorish, who presided, made a speech about a musician; he said that Parker had been put into the world to make people happy and that, if he were alive today, he would say to those of his colleagues who were present that it was time to be up and doing because life is not an empty dream. The organist played Arthur Sullivan's 'The Lost Chord,' and the Rev. Mr. Licorish read those old words about the search for the chord that sounded like the last amen.

". . . And so Charlie Parker came to the end of his life, as the good ones do in all centuries, pushing against the limits of art. If he had been born lucky as we count these things, he might have run out his life in some academy, using his equipment in a tired, derivative form, and writing proper pieces for

Above:
Charlie Shavers and Bird.
Below:
Hollywood, June, 1952: Left to right, Benny Carter, Barney Kessel, Flip Phillips, Charlie Shavers, Ray Brown, Charlie Parker, Oscar Peterson, J. C. Heard, Ben Webster, and Johnny Hodges.

the journals. Remembering that and what he did, it cannot truly be said that he died badly."

The Blue Note club in Philadelphia held a benefit and raised a thousand dollars. A Swedish magazine organized a concert in Stockholm and sent another thousand, a respectable sum, considering exchange rates. Milling around Carnegie Hall the evening of April 2nd were hundreds of fans who could not get in, for the hall was sold out twenty-four hours in advance. The net proceeds were $5,739.96. A memorial fund was established so that the money would be in trust for Parker's two sons. Bird died broke, save for a thousand-dollar insurance policy. The concert started at midnight and was to run till 3:00 A.M. It ended at 3:40 because of management regulations and disappointed dozens of musicians who did not get a chance to blow their homage to Bird. Jazzbo Collins, Leonard Feather, and Barry Ulanov were among the m.c.'s. The audience stood during a recording of Charlie Parker's "Now's the Time." The 2,760 people who were there heard Diz, Blakey, Monk, Billie Holiday, Stan Getz, Pettiford, Mulligan, Pres, Hazel Scott, Tony Scott, Horace Silver, and so on in jazzdom's *Who's Who*.

The estate, which becomes considerable as time goes on and royalties accrue, is in a hopeless muddle. Doris Parker is the present administratrix. Chan is endeavoring to unseat her. Two-thirds of the estate goes to Leon Parker, 23, who lives in Kansas City. Addie stated: "All I've gotten is five hundred dollars from the estate. I was down on the will, but I'm not down on it any more. They rubbed my name out. I'm down here in Kansas City and I'm pretty far away so I just don't do anything about it. But I just don't think it's right for an older woman to get nothing that her son left." The second wife Geraldine, whom Parker married shortly after divorcing his first, is not involved in the treasure hunt. Bird and she drifted apart after a short while, and it is not even known if they divorced. The unfortunate woman was on drugs, and she brushed with the law frequently and spent time in prison as the result of a habit in which one eventually has to "deal or steal." The *New York Post* of April 16, 1961, contained a full-page article concerning the legal complexities of the Parker estate, which fill three manila folders in the files of Surrogate's Court. His artist's and composer's royalties are supposedly in the six-figure range. Tapes of his music keep turning up. Anything Parker did, whether taken off the air or in a night club or in someone's loft, is a valuable item. One person in the record business named Sam Suliman told me that a person brought in a tape of Bird's music supposedly never before released. Sam recognized it as an old album. The crafty crook had played the album into a tape machine and had inserted noises of glasses and some other instrumental solos and produced an imaginative forgery. Parker who was frequently in need of immediate "bread" would sell his compositions outright. He led a complicated life; *ergo*, a complicated estate.

Chronology

1920   Born in Kansas City, Kansas, on August 29th to Addie (Boyley) and Charles Parker, Sr.

1927   Family moves to Kansas City, Missouri.

1931   Graduates from Crispus Attucks Public School at age eleven.

1933   Begins studying music. Alonzo Lewis is his instructor. Plays baritone horn and clarinet in the school band.

1935   Quits Old Lincoln High School. Plays first professional engagement on Thanksgiving, earning $1.25 for the evening.

Plays regularly at Green Leaf Gardens in Kansas City, Mo.

1936   Marries Rebecca Ruffin. He is sixteen. She is a few years older. They divorce five years later.

Goes with George Lee's combo to play summer resort at Eldon, Mo., in the Ozarks. Studies seriously. The pianist, Carrie Powell, teaches him simple major, minor, seventh, and diminished chords.

1937   First plays with Jay McShann's band in September. Leaves after three weeks.

His son, Leon Francis Parker, is born.

Plays in the band of Lawrence Keyes.

Returns home for the burial of his father, who was stabbed to death in a quarrel.

Plays in the two K.C. bands of Buster Smith. The first, a five-piece combo at a place called Lucille's Paradise and the other, a twelve-man group that has hopes of fame on the road.

1938   Plays a short while in Harlan Leonard's band.

1939   Is introduced to Dizzy Gillespie at the Booker T. Hotel in K.C.

Arrives in New York. Works as a dishwasher. "I played at Monroe's Uptown House. Nobody paid me much mind at first at Monroe's except Billy Moore, one of Count Basie's trumpet players. He liked me. Everybody else was trying to get me to sound like Benny Carter. There was no scale at Monroe's. Sometimes I got forty or fifty cents a night. If business was good, I might get up to six dollars.

"I remember one night I was jamming in a chili house (Dan Wall's) on Seventh Avenue between 139th and 140th. It was December, 1939. Now I'd been getting bored with the stereotyped changes that were being used all the time, at the time, and I kept thinking there's bound to be something else. I could hear it sometimes, but I couldn't play it. Well, that night, I was working over 'Cherokee,' and, as I did, I found that by using the higher intervals of a chord as a melody line and backing them with appropriately related changes, I could play the thing I'd been hearing. I came alive."

1940   Rejoins McShann and in the summer of that year makes first recordings for Decca with Jay's band.

1941   Jams frequently at Minton's in Harlem with fellow habitues: Diz, Monk, Charlie Christian, Bud Powell, Max Roach, Kenny Clarke, and John Simmons.

1942   Very short stint with Noble Sissle's band. Frequently plays clarinet in the band.

Plays first Town Hall concert for twenty-five dollars.

1943   Spends almost a year with Earl Hines, on tenor, because all alto chairs are taken.

Marries Geraldine Marguerite Scott, April 10.

1944   Makes his first combo records with Tiny Grimes in September.

Goes on the road with Billy Eckstine's band of 21 members which includes: Gillespie, Fats Navarro, Sonny Stitt, Gene Ammons, Dexter Gordon, Lucky Thompson, Tommy Potter, Art Blakey, Sarah Vaughan, Tadd Dameron.

1945   Works on and off 52nd Street with Ben Webster and Dizzy. Has his own group at the Three Deuces, where he features Miles Davis.

Meets and begins romance with Doris Sydnor.

Late in this year, is in California with Gillespie, playing at Billy Berg's.

1946   Leads own group at the Finale Club in L.A. Joe Albany and Miles Davis are with him.

On July 29th, is in bad condition during "Lover Man" recording date for Dial. Suffers a breakdown later that evening and is taken to Camarillo State Hospital.

A benefit for Bird is held in L.A., in December. Five hundred dollars is raised to obtain instrument and clothes for him.

1947   On February 26th, records "Relaxin' at Camarillo" after release from hospital.

In April, returns to New York in good health. Is wildly acclaimed by musicians eager to see and hear him.

1948   Plays at the Royal Roost and Bop City until 1949.

Marries Doris Sydnor in Tia Juana, Mexico.

Doctor tells him that his health is in dangerous condition.

1949   Plays at the International Jazz Festival in Paris.

Late in the year Birdland, a club named in his honor, opens.

1950   Plays a great deal in Birdland.

Records album accompanied by strings and woodwinds.

In July, begins a common-law marriage with Chan Richardson. She bears him two children: a girl, Pree, and a boy, Baird.

Does a week's tour of Sweden in November. Goes to play at the Paris Jazz Fair at the behest of Charles Delaunay. Receives advance payment and goes on a sleepless, three-day revel, playing at a few St. Germain clubs and then, without warning, flies off to London without playing at the Salon. Tells reporter of the excellence of Swedish musicians.

1951   Suffers a peptic ulcer attack upon his return from Europe. Is hospitalized and recovers.

Daughter Pree is born on July 17th.

1952   Opens at the Tiffany Club in L.A., on May 29th.

Is stranded in San Francisco for a week. Opens at the Say When, after appearing twice on the Cerebral Palsy TV marathon. Takes up a collection in the club, asks the club owner for a contribution, is refused because owner says he has already given. Bird takes the mike and calls the house "cheap" and is fired.

Son Charles Baird Parker is born on August 10th.

1953   Daughter Pree dies of pneumonia.

1954   Swallows iodine in an attempt to commit suicide. Wife Chan hears his screams of pain and calls police to their apartment on New York's lower East Side at 5 A.M. Treated by the ambulance surgeon. Booked into Birdland for a three-week engagement. Begins behaving strangely by playing one tune while his string band plays another. Birdland's management has a camera girl take a picture of Parker in action, then fires him. Charlie is said to have told a union official that if he did not make good on his current job, he would "jump off the Empire State Building."

Is admitted to Bellevue Hospital following suicide attempt. Discharged ten days later on September 10th.

Returns to hospital on his own on September 28th due to depressed feelings.

Is featured in Town Hall concert on October 30th.

1955   Plays last engagement. The club is Birdland and the date is March 4th and 5th, on Friday and Saturday.

Dies in Stanhope Hotel, New York, on March 12th. Autopsy reveals lobar pneumonia due to visceral congestion caused death.

Funeral service held at Abyssinian Baptist Church on 138th St., on March 21st. Body is subsequently flown to Kansas City.

April 2nd. His memorial concert jams Carnegie Hall.

Discography by Erik Wiedemann

(See page 256 for Key to Labels.)

JAY McSHANN AND HIS ORCHESTRA:
  Harold Bruce, Bernard Anderson, Orville Minor (tpts). Joe Baird (tmb).
Charlie Parker, John Jackson (altos). Bob Mabane, Harry Ferguson (tnrs). Jamy
McShann (pno). Gene Ramey (bass). Gus Johnson (drs). Walter Brown (voc).
New York City, April 30, 1941.
  93730 "Swingmatism"   De 8570
  93731 "Hootie Tootie" (V. Brown)   De 8559
  93732 "Dexter Blues"   De 8585, BrE DeE 03401
  93734 "Confessin' the Blues" (V. Brown)   De 8559
Note: Masters 93733, 93735 are solos by McShann.

JAY McSHANN AND HIS ORCHESTRA:
  Bob Merrill, Anderson, Mino (tpts). Bair, Lawrence, "Frog" Anderson (tmb).
Parker, Jackson (altos). Mabane, Freddy Culliver (tnrs). James Coe (bari).

McShann (pno). Leonard "Lucky" Enols (gtr). Ramey (bass). Johnson (drs). Brown (voc). New York City, November 18, 1941.

    93809 "One Woman's Man" (V. Brown)   De 8607
    93812 "New Confessin' the Blues" (V. Brown)   De 8595
    93813 "Red River Blues" (V. Brown)   De 8595
    93814 "Baby Heart Blues" (V. Brown)   De 8623
    93815 "Cryin' Won't Make Me Stay" (V. Brown)   De 8623
Note: Masters 93810, 93811, 93816 are solos by McShann.

JAY McSHANN AND HIS ORCHESTRA:
    Same personnel, plus Al Hibbler (voc). New York City, July 2, 1942.
    70993 "Lonely Boy Blues" (V. Brown)   De 4387
    70994 "Get Me on Your Mind (V. Hibbler)   De 4418, Coral 60024
    70995 "The Jumpin' Blues" (V. Brown)   De 4418, Coral 60034
    70996 "Sepian Bounce" (V. Brown)   De 4387

TINY GRIMES QUINTET:
    Parker (alto). Clyde Hart (pno). Tiny Grimes (gtr, voc). Jimmy Butts (bass). Harold "Doc" West (drs). New York City, September 15, 1944.
    S5710 "Tiny's Tempo"   Sav 526, 541, 915
    S5711 "I'll Always Love You Just the Same" (V. Grimes)   Sav 526, 613, 925
    S5712 "Romance Without Finance" (V. Grimes)   Sav 532, 613, 925
    S5713 "Red Cross"   Sav 532, 541, 915, MG 90000, Sav Fr 915
Note: 541 as by "Charlie Parker Alto Sax," 915 as by "Charlie Parker All Stars," 925 as by "Charlie Parker with Tiny Grimes Quintet."

DIZZY GILLESPIE AND HIS ALL STAR QUINTET:
    Dizzy Gillespie (tpt). Parker (alto). Hart (pno). Remo Palmieri (gtr). Slam Stewart (bass). Cozy Cole (drs). New York City, February 29, 1945.
    G554 "Groovin' High"   Guild 1001, Mu 485, Sw 299
    G556 "Dizzy Atmosphere"   Mu 488, Sw 299
    G557 "All the Things You Are"   Mu 488, Sw 317
Note: Master 554 is a remake of a tune cut at the earlier (555) session.

CLYDE HART'S ALL STARS:
    Gillespie (tpt). Trummy Young (tmb, voc). Parker (alto). Don Byas (tnr). Hart (pno). Mike Bryan (gtr). Al Hall (bass). Specs Powell (drs). Rubberlegs Williams (voc). New York City, March-April, 1945.
    W3301 "What's the Matter Now?" (V. Williams)   Con 6013, RJ 715
    W3302 "I Want Every Bit of It" (V. Williams)   Con 6020, RJ 746
    W3303 "That's the Blues" (V. Williams)   Con 6013, RJ 715
    W3304 "4-F Blues" (V. Williams)   Con 6020, RJ 746
    W3305 "Dream of You" (V. Young)   Con 6005, RJ 716
    W3306 "Seventh Avenue" (V. Young)   Con 6005, RJ 716
    W3307 "Sorta Kinda" (V. Young)   Con 6005, RJ 716
    W3308 "Ooh! Ooh! My! My! Oh! Oh!" (V. Young)   Con 6060

DIZZY GILLESPIE AND HIS ALL-STAR QUINTET:
Gillespie (tpt, voc). Parker (alto). Al Haig (pno). Curley Russell (bass).
Sidney Catlett (drs). Sarah Vaughan (voc). New York City, May 11, 1945.
  G565 "Salt Peanuts" (V. Gillespie)   Guild 1003, Mu 518, Sw 304
  G566 "Shaw 'Nuff"   Guild 1002, Mu 354, Sw 305, PaE R3077
  G567 "Lover Man" (V. Vaughan)   Guild 1002, Mu 354, Sw 317, PaE R3077
  G568 "Hot House"   Guild 1003, Mu 486, Sw 304

SARAH VAUGHAN (voc).:
  Acc. by Gillespie (tpt). Parker (alto). Flip Phillips (tnr). Nat Jaffe (1) and
Tad Dameron (2) (pnos). Bill De Arango (gtr). Russell (bass). Max Roach
(drs). New York City, May 25, 1945.
  W3325 "What More Can a Woman Do?" (1)   Con 6008, Len 500, Rem RLP
    1024
  W3326 "I'd Rather Have a Memory Than a Dream" (2)   Con 6008, Rem
    RLP 1024
  W3327 "Mean to Me" (1)   Con 6024, Len 500, Rem RLP 1024, RJ 729

A NITE AT CARNEGIE HALL:
  Gillespie (tpt). Parker (alto). with probably Al Haig (pno). Ray Brown (bass).
Stan Levy (drs). New York City, probably December, 1945.
  13000 Part 1 ("A Night in Tunisia")   "The Black Deuce" (1)
  13001 Part 2 ("A Night in Tunisia")   "The Black Deuce" (1)
  13002 Part 5 ("Dizzy Atmosphere)   "The Black Deuce" (3)
  13003 Part 3 ("Groovin' High")   "The Black Deuce" (2)
  13004 Part 4 ("Groovin' High")   "The Black Deuce" (2)
  13005 Part 6 ("Confirmation")   "The Black Deuce" (3)
Note: These were recorded at a concert. Only Gillespie's and Parker's names are
on the labels, not the titles. There are no catalogue numbers. Those in parentheses
are to indicate couplings.

SLIM GAILLARD AND HIS ORCHESTRA:
  Gillespie (tpt). Parker (alto). Jack McVea (tnr). Dodo Marmarosa (pno). Slim
Gaillard (gtr, vibs, voc). Tiny Brown (bass). Zutty Singleton (drs). Hollywood,
December, 1945.
  38 "Dizzy Boogie"   Bel Tone 753. Majestic 9002, 1001
  39 "Flat Foot Floogie"   Bel Tone 758. Majestic 9002, 1001
  40 "Popity Pop"   Bel Tone 753. Majestic 9001, 1000
  41 "Slim's Jam"   Bel Tone 761. Majestic 9001, 1000

JAZZ AT THE PHILHARMONIC:
  Gillespie, Al Killian (tpts). Parker, Willie Smith (altos). Charlie Ventura, Lester
Young (tnrs). Mel Powell (pno). Billy Hadnott (bass). Lee Young (drs). Los
Angeles, January 29, 1946.
  413 "Sweet Georgia Brown" (1), 12 in.   Disc 2004. Disc Fr 2004. Me 8010.
    Mercury MG 35004. Arco AL 2
  414 "Sweet Georgia Brown" (II), 12 in., as 413

DIZZY GILLESPIE JAZZMEN:

Gillespie (tpt). Parker (alto). Luck Thompson (tnr). Marmarosa (pno). Arv Garrison (gtr). Brown (bass). Levy (drs). Hollywood, February 7, 1946.

1000 "Diggin' Diz" Dial 1004, LP 207B

Note: Parker did not play on the other sides from this session. Rev. 1004: Gillespie Jazzmen.

SIR CHARLES AND HIS ALL STARS:

Buck Clayton (tpt). Parker (alto). Dexter Gordon (tnr). Charles Thompson (pno). Danny Barker (gtr). Butts (bass). Heard (drs). New York City, September 4, 1945.

R1030 "Takin' Off" Apollo 757
R1031 "If I Had You" Apollo 757
R1032 "20th Century Blues" Apollo 759
R1033 "The Street Beat" Apollo 759

CHARLIE PARKER'S REE BOPPERS:

Miles Davis (tpt on 5850, 5851, 5852). Parker (alto). Gillespie (pno and muted tpt on 5853). Curley Russell (bass). Max Roach (drs). New York City, October-November, 1945.

Sav 5849 "Warming Up a Riff" Sav 945. MG 9000. Sav Fr. 915. Met B510
Sav 5850 "Billie's Bounce" Sav 573, 918. MG 9001. Sav Fr and E 918
Sav 5851 "Now's the Time" Sav 573, 918. MG 9000. Sav Fr and E 918
Sav 5852 "Thriving from a Riff" Sav 903, 945. MG 9001. Sav Fr and E 945.
   Met B506
Sav 5853 "Ko Ko" Sav 597, 916. MG 9000. Sav Fr and E 916

Note: 903 and 945 as by "The Be Bop Boys." All the rest under Parker's name, if not exactly under the above label name. Rev. 597, 916, Sav E 916: Don Byas, 903: Stan Getz, "The Be Bop Boys," Sav Fr 916: Fats Navarro, Sav Fr and E 945: Leo Parker, Sav Fr and E 945 as "Thriving on a Riff."

CHARLIE PARKER SEPTET:

Davis (tpt). Parker (alto). Thompson (tnr). Marmarosa (pno). Garrison (gtr). Victor McMillan (bass). Roy Porter (drs). Hollywood, March 28, 1946.

1010-1 "Moose the Mooche" Dial LP 201A
1010-2 "Moose the Mooche" Dial 1004, 1003, BS 134, Esq 10-078
1011-1 "Yardbird Suite" Dial LP 201A
1011-4 "Yardbird Suite" Dial 1003, BS 134, Esq 10-078
1012-1 "Ornithology" Dial LP 208B
1012-3 "Bird Lore" Dial 1006
1012-4 "Ornithology" Dial 1002, LP 201A, BS 61, Esq 10-027
1013-4 "A Night in Tunisia" Dial LP 201A
1013-5 "A Night in Tunisia" Dial 1002, BS 61, Esq 10-027

Note: Rev. first issues of Dial 1004 and 1003: Tempo Jazz Men. Second issue of Dial 1003 has 1010-2 and 1011-4. Rev. Dial 1006: Sonny Berman Big Eight. 1013-5 as by "Miles Davis All Stars" on Esq.

JAZZ AT THE PHILHARMONIC:
Clayton (tpt). Parker, Smith (altos). Coleman Hawkins, Young (tnrs). Kenneth Kersey (pno). Irving Ahsby (gtr). Hadnott (bass). Buddy Rich (drs). Los Angeles, April 22, 1946.
 101 "JATP Blues" (I) Clef 101. Mercury 11003. MG 35007
 102 "JATP Blues" (II) Clef .01. Mercury 11004. MG 35007
 103 "JATP Blues" (III) Clef 102. Mercury 11005. MG 35007
 104 "JATP Blues" (IV) Clef 102. Mercury 11005. MG 35007

JAZZ AT THE PHILHARMONIC:
Killian, Howard McGhee (tpts). Parker, Smith (altos). Young (tnr). Arnold Ross (pno). Hadnott (bass). Young (drs). Los Angeles, spring, 1946.
 D241 "Blues for Norman" (I), 12 in. Disc 2001. Disc Fr 2001. Merc MG 35003. Arco AL1. Mel E 8803
 D242 "Blues for Norman" (II), 12 in. Disc 2001, Disc Fr 2001. Merc MG 35003. Arco AL1. Mel E 8803
 D243 "I Can't Get Started" (I), 12 in. Disc 2002. Disc Fr 2002. Merc MG 3503. Arco AL1. Mel E 8804.
 D244 "I Can't Get Started" (II), 12 in. Disc 2002. Disc Fr 2002. Merc MG 35003. Arco AL1. Mel E 8804
 D245 "Lady Be Good" (I), 12 in. Disc. 2005. Disc. Fr 2005. Mel. E 8007
 D246 "Lady Be Good" (II), 12 in. Disc 2005. Disc Fr 2005. Mel E 8007
 D800 "After You've Gone" (I) Disc 5100. Disc Fr 5100. Mel E 1014
 D801 "After You've Gone" (II) Disc 5100. Disc Fr 5100. Mel E 1014

CHARLIE PARKER QUINTET:
McGhee (tpt). Parker (alto). Jimmy Bunn (pno). Dingbod Kesterson (bass). Porter (drs). Hollywood, July 29, 1946.
 1021A "Max Making Wax" Dial LP 201B, BS 234
 1022A "Lover Man" Dial 1007, LP 201B. JS 514
 1023A "The Gypsy" Dial 1043, LP 201B. BS 234
 1024A "Be Bop" Dial 1007. LP 201B
 1024G "Be Bop" JS 514
Note: 1022 as by "Charlie Parker." 1024 as by "Howard McGhee Quintet."

RED NORVO AND HIS SELECTED SEXTET:
Gillespie (tpt). Parker (alto). Phillips (tnr). Teddy Wilson (pno). Red Norvo (vib). Stewart (bass). J. C. Heard (1) and Specs Powell (2) (drs). New York City, June 5, 1945.
 T8 "Hallelujah" (1) Dial LP 903B
 T8 "Sing Hallelujah" (1) Dial 1045
 T8 "Hallelujah" (1), 12 in. Comet T6, Dial LP 903A, BS 190
 T9 "Get Happy" (2) Dial 1035
 T9 "Get Happy" (2) Dial LP 903B
 T9 "Get Happy" (2), 12 in. Comet T7, Dial LP 903A, BS 187
 T10 "Slam Slam Blues" (1) Dial LP 903B

T10 "Bird's Blues" (1)   Dial 1045
T10 "Slam Slam Blues" (1), 12 in.   Comet T6, Dial LP 903A, BS 190
T11 "Congo Blues" (2)   Dial LP 903B
T11 "Congo Blues" (2)   Dial LP 903B
T11 "Congo Blues" (2)   Dial LP 903B
T11 "Congo Blues" (2), 12 in.   Comet T7, Dial LP 903A, BS 187

Note: These are listed in order of recording. Dial 1035 and 1045 are 10 in. mini-groove dubbings from original 12 in. masters. Some of these four sides, but certainly not all, may be identical to the ones on Dial LP 903B. First and second takes of T11 (on Dial LP 903B) started falsely and stop shortly after the start.

CHARLIE PARKER QUARTET:
Parker (alto). Erroll Garner (pno). Red Callender (bass). Harold "Doc" West (drs). Earl Coleman (voc). Hollywood, February 19, 1947.

D-1051-C   "This is Always" (V. Coleman)   Dial 1019
D-1051-D   "This Is Always" (V. Coleman)   Dial LP 202B
D-1052-A   "Dark Shadows" (V. Coleman)   Dial LP 901B, 202B
D-1052-A   "Dark Shadows" (V. Coleman)   Dial LP 901A
D-1052-A   "Dark Shadows" (V. Coleman)   Dial 1014
D-1053-A   "Bird's Nest"   Dial 1014
D-1053-B   "Bird's Nest"   Dial 1014
D-1053-C   "Bird's Nest"   Dial 1015, BS 62, Esq 10-017
D-1054-A   "Blow Top Blues"   Dial LP 901B
D-1054-CC   "Cool Blues"   Dial 1015, LP 901A, 202B
D-1054-D   "Cool Blues"   Dial LP 901B, BS 62, Esq 10-017

Note: D-1054-A as "Hot Blues" on LP 202B. Rev. 1015 (D-1054-CC): Charlie Parker Sextet.

CHARLIE PARKER ALL STARS:
McGhee (tpt). Parker (alto). Wardell Gray (tnr). Marmarosa (pno). Barney Kessel (gtr). Red Callender (bass). Don Lamond (drs). Hollywood, February 26, 1947.

D-1071-A   "Relaxin' at Camarillo"   Dial 1030, LP 901A
D-1071-C   "Relaxin' at Camarillo"   Dial 1012, BS 162, Esq 10-079
D-1071-D   "Relaxin' at Camarillo"   Dial LP 901B
D-1071-E   "Relaxin' at Camarillo"   Dial LP 901B, 202A
D-1072-A   "Cheers"   Dial LP 202A
D-1072-D   "Cheers"   Dial 1013, BS 109, Esq 10-031
D-1073-A   "Carvin' the Bird"   Dial LP 901B
D-1073-B   "Carvin' the Bird"   Dial 1013, LP 901A, 202A, BS 109, Esq 10-031
D-1074-A   "Stupendous"   Dial 1022, 1030, PaE R3142, Sw 305
D-1074-B   "Stupendous"   Dial LP 202A

Note: Rev. 1012: Chaloff-Burns Quintet; 1022: Dexter Gordon; PaE: Howard McGhee.

CHARLIE PARKER ALL STARS:
Davis (tpt). Parker (alto). Powell (pno). Tommy Potter (bass). Roach (drs).
New York City, June, 1947.
S3420 "Donna Lee" Sav 652, 928, MG 9000, Sav Fr and E 928
S3421 "Chasing the Bird" Sav 977, MG 9400, Sav Fr and E 977, Met B 512
S3422 "Cheryl" Sav 952, MG 9001, Sav Fr and E 952, Met B 510
S3423 "Buzzy" Sav 652, 928, MG 9001, Sav Fr and E 928

CHARLIE PARKER ALL STARS:
Personnel as for November 4. Detroit, late December, 1947.
D-830 "Another Hairdo" Sav 961, MG 9001
D-831 "Blue Bird" Sav 961
D-832 "Klaunstance" Sav 967, MG 9001
D-833 "Bird Gets the Worm" Sav 952, Sav Fr and E 952, Met B 511
Note: Rev. 967: Stan Getz: original title, "Klaunsen's Vansan's." Rev. Met B 511:
James Moody.

CHARLIE PARKER ALL STARS:
Same personnel. John Lewis (pno), and Curley Russell (bass) replace Jordan
and Potter. New York City, April, 1948.
B900 "Barbados" Sav 936, Sav Fr and E 936, Met B 508
B901 "Ah-Lou-Cha" Sav 939, Sav Fr and E 939
B902 "Constellation" Sav 939, Sav Fr and E 939
B903 "Parker's Mood" (no tpt) Sav 936, Sav Fr and E 936, Met B 509
B908 "Perhaps" Sav 938
B909 "Marmaduke" Sav 937
B910 "Steeple-chase" Sav 937, Sav Fr and E 937
B911 "Merry-go-round" Sav 937, Sav Fr and E 937
Note: These may not have been recorded in NYC.

MILES DAVIS' ALL STARS:
Davis (tpt). Parker (tnr). John Lewis (pno). Nelson Boyd (bass). Roach (drs).
New York City, July-August, 1947.
S3440 "Milestones" Sav 934, MG 9001, Met B 508
S3441 "Little Willie Leaps" Sav 977, MG 9001, Met B 506, Sav Fr and E 977
S3442 "Half-Nelson" Sav 951, MG 9000, Met B 512, Sav Fr and E 961
S3443 "Sipping at Bell's" Sav 934, MG 9000, Met B 509
Note: All of these have also been released under Parker's name. Rev. 951: Fats
Navarro.

DIZZY GILLESPIE'S BAND:
Gillespie (tpt). John La Porta (clt). Parker (alto). Lennie Tristano (pno).
Billy Bauer (gtr). Brown (bass). Roach (drs). New York City, September 29,
1947.
UP-49-B "Tiger Rag" Steinder-Davis 46
Note: Rev: Wild Bill Davison's Band. Taken from "battle" on Mutual Network.

CHARLIE PARKER QUINTET:

Davis (tpt). Parker (alto). Duke Jordan (pno). Tommy Potter (bass). Roach (drs). New York City, October 28, 1947.

D-1101-A "Dexterity"   Dial LP 203A
D-1101-B "Dexterity"   Dial 1032, BS 183, Esq 10-100
D-1102-A "Bongo Bop"   Dial 1024, LP 901A, BS 145, Esq 10-071
D-1102-B "Bongo Bop"   Dial LP 901B
D-1103-A "Prezology"   Dial LP 210B
D-1103-B "Dewey Square"   Dial LP 203B
D-1103-C "Dewey Square"   Dial 1019, BS 153, Esq 10-108
D-1104-A "The Hymn"   Dial LP 904B
D-1104-B "The Hymn"   Dial LP 212B
D-1105-A "Bird of Paradise"   Dial LP 904A
D-1105-B "Bird of Paradise"   Dial 1032, LP 904A
D-1105-C "Bird of Paradise"   Dial 1032, LP 904B, BS 183, Esq 10-109
D-1106-A "Embraceable You"   Dial 1024, LP 203B
D-1106-B "Embraceable You"   Dial 1024, LP 904A, BS 145, Esq 10-071
D-1106-C "Embraceable You"   Dial 1024

CHARLIE PARKER QUINTET:

Davis (tpt). Parker (alto). Duke Jordan (pno). Tommy Potter (bass). Roach (drs). New York City, November 4, 1947.

D-1111-C "Ferd Bethers"   Dial LP 207B
D-1112-A "Klactoveedsedstene"   Dial 1040, LP 207B, BS 216, Esq 10-129
D-1112-B "Klactoveedsedstene"   Dial LP 904B
D-1113-B "Scrapple from the Apple"   Dial LP 203B
D-1113-C "Scrapple from the Apple"   Dial 1021, LP 904B, JS 515
D-1114-A "My Old Flame"   Dial LP 207A
D-1115-A "Out of Nowhere"   Dial LP 207B
D-1115-B "Out of Nowhere"   Dial LP 904A
D-1115-C "Out of Nowhere"   Dial LP 904B
D-1116-A "Don't Blame Me"   Dial 1021, LP 203A, JS 515

CHARLIE PARKER SEXTET:

As above plus J. J. Johnson (tmb). New York City, December 17, 1947.

D-1151-B   "Giant Swing"   unissued
D-1151-D   "Drifting on a Reed"   Dial LP 904B
D-1151-E   "Drifting on a Reed"   Dial 1043, LP 207A
D-1152-A   "Quasimado"   Dial LP 203B
D-1152-B   "Quasimado" Dial 1015, LP 904A, BS 153, Esq 10-108
D-1153-D   "Bongobeep"   Dial LP 203A
D-1153-E   "Charlie's Wig"   Dial 1040, LP 904A, BS 216, Esq 10-139
D-1154-B   "Bird Feathers"   Dial LP 904B
D-1154-C   "Bird Feathers"   Dial LP 207A
D-1155-ABX   "Crazeology II"   Dial 1034, BS 162, Esq 10-079
D-1155-DDD   "Crazeology I"   Dial 1034, 104?, LP 207A

D-1156-A   "How Deep Is the Ocean?"   Dial 104?, LP 904A
D-1156-B   "How Deep Is the Ocean?"   Dial LP 211A

Note: On D-1155-ABX three masters were dubbed in on one side (takes probably are: -A, -B and -C). This was labelled Crazeology on BS and Esq as was D-1155-DDD on Dial 104? and LP 207A. Rev. 1015: Charlie Parker Quartet (D-1054-CC).

CHARLIE PARKER (alto) acc. by MACHITO'S ORCHESTRA:
  Mario Bauza, Davila Paquito, Bob Woodlen (tpts). Eugene Johnson, Freddy Skerritt (altos). Jose Madera (tnr). Leslie Johnikens (bari). Rene Hernandez (pno). Robert Rodriguez (bass). Machito (maraccas). Jose Manguel (bongos). Luis Miranda (conga drum). Uvaldo Nyeto (timbales). New York City, late December, 1948.
  2155-2 "No Noise" (II)   Mercury 11012
  2157-1 "Mango Mangue"   Mercury 11017
Note: 2154 ("No Noise," Part I) is by Flip Phillips with Machito as is, probably 2156.

METRONOME ALL STARS:
  Gillespie, Fats Navarro, Davis (tpts). Johnson, Kai Winding (tmbs). Buddy De Franco (clt). Parker (alto). Charlie Ventura (tnr). Ernie Caceres (bari). Tristano (pno). Bauer (gtr). Eddie Safranski (bass). Shelly Manne (drs). Pete Rugolo (arr. and dir). New York City, January 3, 1949.
  D9-VB-21-1 "Overtime"   Victor 20-3361, HMV B9818
  Gillespie, Winding, De Franco, Parker, Ventura, same rhythm. Tristano (arr). Same date.
  D9-VB-22-1 "Victory Ball"   Victor 20-3361, HMV B9818
Note: There were also cut 12 in. masters of the above two, but they remain unreleased.

CHARLIE PARKER (alto) acc. by MACHITO'S ORCHESTRA:
  Same personnel as December, 1948 session. New York City, January, 1949.
  2171-1 "Okidokie"   Mercury 11017
Note: Later copies of this side bear the title "Okiedoke Rhumba."

CHARLIE PARKER AND HIS ORCHESTRA:
  Kenny Dorham (tpt). Haig (pno). Potter (bass). Roach (drs). Vidal Bolado (bongos). Tommy Turk (tmb). Parker (alto). New York City, early April, 1949.
  2543-2 "Visa"   Mercury 11022
  Same personnel, minus Turk and Bolado. New York City, May 5, 1949.
  2756-2 "Passport"   Mercury 11022

CHARLIE PARKER (alto) acc. by NEAL HEFTI'S ORCHESTRA:
  Al Porcino, Ray Wetzel, Douglas "Doug" Mettome (tpts). Bill Harris, Bart Varsalona (tmbs). Vincent Jacobs (fr horn). LaPorta (clt). Murray Williams, Sonny Salad (altos). Phillips, Pete Mondello (tnrs). Manny Albam (bari). Sam

Caplan, Harry Catzman, Gene Orloff, Zelly Smirnoff, Sid Harris, Manny Fidler, Fred Ruzilia, Nat Hanson, Joe Benaventi (strings). Tony Aless (pno). Russell (bass). Manne (drs). Diego Iborra (bongos). Probably New York City, summer, 1949.

   2071 "Repetition," 12 in. The Jazz Scene (Mercury)

CHARLIE PARKER (alto) acc. by HANK JONES (pno):
   Brown (bass). Manne (drs). Probably New York City, summer, 1949.
   2081-5 "The Bird," 12 in. The Jazz Scene (Mercury)

JAZZ AT THE PHILHARMONIC:
   Roy Eldridge (tpt). Turk (tmb). Parker (alto). Phillips, Young (tnrs). Jones (pno). Brown (bass). Buddy Rich (drs). New York City, September, 1949.

   C382 "The Opener" (I)   Mercury 11054
   C383 "The Opener" (II)   Mercury 11055
   C384 "The Opener" (III)   Mercury 11056
   C385 "Lester Leaps In" (I)   Mercury 11056
   C386 "Lester Leaps In" (II)   Mercury 11055
   C387 "Lester Leaps In" (III)   Mercury 11054
      "Embraceable You" (I)   Mercury 110?, MG 350?
      "Embraceable You" (II)   Mercury 110?, MG 350?
      "Embraceable You" (III)   Mercury 110?, MG 350?
      "The Closer" (I)   Mercury 110?, MG 350?
      "The Closer" (II)   Mercury 110?, MG 350?
      "The Closer" (III)   Mercury 110?, MG 350?

CHARLIE PARKER WITH STRINGS:
   Parker (alto). Mitchell Miller (oboe and e. horn). Bronislaw Gimpel, Max Hollander, Milton Lomask (vlns). Frank Breiff (viola). Myor Rosen (harp). Stan Freeman (pno). Brown (bass). Rich (drs). Jimmy Carroll (arr. and dir). New York City, November 30, 1949.

   Clef 319-5 "Just Friends"   Mercury 11036, MG 35010
   Clef 320-3 "Everything Happens to Me"   Mercury 11036, MG 35010
   Clef 321-3 "April in Paris"   Mercury 11037, MG 35010
   Clef 322-2 "Summertime"   Mercury 11038, MG 35010
   Clef 333-3 "I Didn't Know What Time It Was"   Mercury 11030, MG 35010
   Clef 324-3 "If I Should Lose You"   Mercury 11037, MG 35010

CHARLIE PARKER AND HIS ORCHESTRA:
   Gillespie (tpt). Parker (alto). Thelonious Monk (pno). Russell (bass). Rich (drs). New York City, June 8, 1950.

   C-410-2 "Bloomdido"   Mercury 11058
   C-411   "An Oscar for Treadwell"   Mercury 11082
   C-412   "Mohawk"   Mercury 11082
   C-413-2 "Melancholy Baby"   Mercury 11058
   C-414-6 "Leap Frog"   Mercury 11076
   C-415-3 "Relaxin' with Lee"   Mercury 11076

CHARLIE PARKER WITH STRINGS:
Parker (alto). Sam Caplan, Howard Kay, Zelly Smirnoff, Harry Melnikoff, Samuel Rand (vlns). Isidore Zir (viola). Maurice Brown (cello). Edwin C. Brown (oboe). Joseph Singer (fr. horn). Verlye Mills (harp). Bernie Leighton (pno). Ray Brown (bass). Buddy Rich (drs). New York City, July-August, 1950.

C-442-5 "Dancing in the Dark" Mercury 11068
C-443-2 "Out of Nowhere" Mercury 11070, LP C-109
C-444-3 "Laura" Mercury 11068
C-445-4 "East of the Sun" Mercury 11070, LP C-109
C-446-2 "They Can't Take That Away From Me" Mercury 11071, LP C-109
C-447-4 "Easy to Love" Mercury 11072, LP C-109
C-448-2 "I'm in the Mood for Love" Mercury 11071, LP C-109
C-449-2 "I'll Remember April" Mercury 11072, LP C-109

MACHITO AND HIS AFRO-CUBANS
Parker (alto). Phillips (tnr). Rich (drs). acc. by same personnel as December, 1948 session, plus Al Stewart, Harry Edison (tpts). Sol Rabinowitz (tnr). Chino Pozo (conga drm). New York City, December 21, 1950.
AFRO-CUBAN SUITE:
"Cancion" Mercury MG 350?
"Mambo" Mercury MG 350?
"Jazz Rhythm Abrietta" Mercury MG 350?
Note: The listing of the titles should be taken with a grain of salt. This is a 10-inch LP.

CHARLIE PARKER'S BOPPERS:
Parker (alto). Walter Bishop, Jr. (pno). Ted Kotick (bass). Roy Haynes (drs). Jose Manguel (bongos). Luis Miranda (conga drm). New York City, March 12, 1951.
"Tico Tico" Mercury, unissued.
Note: There are three other unissued sides, too.

CHARLIE PARKER WITH STRINGS:
Chris Griffin, Bernie Privin, Al Porcino (tpts). Will Bradley, Bill Harris (tmbs). Parker (alto). Toots Mondello, Murray Williams, Hank Ross, Artie Drelinger, Stan Webb (saxes). Lou Stein (pno). Artie Ryerson (gtr). Bob Haggart (bass). Don Lamond (drs). Verlye Mills (harp). Plus strings. Joe Lipman (arr). New York City, January 23, 1952.

C-675-2 "Temptation" Mercury Clef 11088, EP 505, MG C-609, BS 507, GEP 12541, GLP 6964, Karusell KEP 210
C-676-3 "Lover" Mercury Clef 11089, EP 505, MG C-609, BS 612, GEP 12541, GLP 6964, Karussel KEP 210
C-677-4 "Autumn in New York" Mercury Clef 11088, EP 505, MG C-609, BS 507, GEP 12541, GLP 6964, Karusell KEP 210
C-678-4 "Stella by Starlight" Mercury Clef 11089, EP 505, MG C-609, BS 612, GEP 12541, GLP 6964, Karusell KEP 210

JAZZ AT THE PHILHARMONIC, VOL. 14:
From the concert on April 22, 1949, and with the same personnel as "JATP Blues": "I Got Rhythm" Mercury Clef MG vol. 14, BS GLP 6914, Karusell vol. 14.

CHARLIE PARKER QUINTET:
Kenny Dorham (tpt). Charlie Parker (alto). Al Haig (pno). Tommy Potter (bass). Max Roach (drs). Royal Roost, New York City, December 11, 1948.

F2504 "Groovin' High I"   Bop BP 3
F2505 "Groovin' High II"   Bop BP 3
G-1   "Big Feet I"   Bop
G-2   "Big Feet II"   Bop

Note: G-1 and G-2 were issued only with white labels.

CHARLIE PARKER QUINTET:
Dorham (tpt). Parker (alto). Haig (pno). Potter (bass). Roach (drs). Royal Roost, New York City, January 1, 1949.

F2506 "East of the Sun," 12 in.   Bop

CHARLIE PARKER ALL STARS:
Dorham (tpt). Parker (alto). Luck Thompson (tnr). Milt Jackson (vib). Haig (pno). Potter (bass). Roach (drs). Royal Roost, New York City, February 26, 1949.

F2507 "A Night in Tunisia," 12 in.   Bop

Note: F2506 and F2507 were issued only with white labels. Above six sides are "air shots."

CHARLIE PARKER AND HIS ALL STARS:
Red Rodney (tpt). Parker (alto). Haig (pno). Potter (bass). Roy Haynes (drs). Carnegie Hall, New York City, December 24, 1949.

"Ornithology"
"Cheryl"
"Ko Ko"
"Bird of Paradise"
"Now's the Time"

Note: These were pressed on a limited edition LP by "Hot Club de Lyon."

JAZZ CONCERT NO. 1. CHARLIE PARKER WITH STRINGS:
Parker (alto). Haig (pno). Potter (bass). Haynes (drs). Carnegie Hall, New York City, September 16, 1950.

"What Is This Thing Called Love" Norgran MG JC No. 1
"April in Paris" Norgran MG JC No. 1
"Repetition" Norgran MG JC No. 1
"Easy to Love" Norgran MG JC No. 1
"I'll Remember April" Norgran MG JC No. 1

CHARLIE PARKER AND SWEDISH ALL STARS:
Ericson (tpt). Parker (alto). Theselius (pno). Jederby (bass). Noren (drs).
November 24, 1950.
>"Anthropology" Oktav OKTLP164
>"Cheers" Oktav OKTLP164
>"Loverman" Oktav OKTLP164
>"Cool Blues" Oktav OKTLP164

CHARLIE PARKER AND SWEDISH ALL STARS:
November 24, 1950. Same personnel as above.
>"Anthropology" Sonet SLP27
>"Scrapple From the Apple" Sonet SLP27
>"Embraceable You" Sonet SLP27
>"Cool Blues" Sonet SLP27
>"Star Eyes" Sonet SLP27
>"All the Things You Are" Sonet SLP27
>"Strike Up the Band" Sonet SLP27

JAM SESSION:
Ericson, Greenberg (tpts). Parker (alto). Theselius (tnr). Nilsson (pno).
Noren (drs).
>"Body and Soul" Sonet SLP27
>"Fine and Dandy" Sonet SLP27
>"How High the Moon" Sonet SLP27

CHARLIE PARKER AND HIS ORCHESTRA:
Miles Davis (tpt). Parker (alto). Walter Bishop, Jr. (pno). Teddy Kotick
(bass). Roach (drs). New York City, February, 1951.
>C-489-3 "Au Privave" Mercury Clef 11087, MG C-646, BS 553, Aust 5192
>C-490-5 "She Rote" Clef 11101, MG C-646, BS 598, Karusell 5027
>C-491-1 "K. C. Blues" Clef 11101, MG C-646, BS 598, Karusell 5027
>C-492-3 "Star Eyes" Mercury Clef 11067, MG C-646, BS 553, Aust 5192

CHARLIE PARKER PLAYS SOUTH OF THE BORDER:
Parker (alto). Bishop (pno). Kotick (bass). Haynes (drs). Jose Manguel
(bongos). Luis Miranda (conga drm). New York City, March 12, 1951.
>C-540-6 "My Little Suede Shoes" Mercury Clef 11093, EP 507, MG C-513,
>BS 542, GLP 6938, Karusell KEP 235, GLP 108
>C-541-2 "Un Poquito de Tu Amor" Mercury Clef 11092, EP 506, MG C-513,
>BS 549, GLP 6938, Karusell KEP 234, GLP 108
>C-542-9 "Tico Tico" Mercury Clef 11091, EP 506, MG C-513, BS 634, GLP
>6938, Karusell KEP 234, GLP 108

CHARLIE PARKER AND HIS ORCHESTRA:
Rodney (tpt). Parker (alto). John Lewis (pno). Ray Brown (bass). Kenny
Clarke (drs). New York City, August, 1951.

C-612-2 "Back Home Blues"   Mercury Clef 11095, MG C-646, BS 503
C-613-2 "Lover Man"   Mercury Clef 11095, MG C-646, BS 503
   "Si Si"   Clef 11103, MG C-646
   "Swedish Schnapps"   Clef 11103, MG C-646

CHARLIE PARKER PLAYS SOUTH OF THE BORDER:
Benny Harris (tpt). Parker (alto). Bishop (pno). Kotick (bass). Roach (drs).
Miranda (conga drm). New York City, January 28, 1952.
   C-679-4 "Mama Inez"   Mercury Clef 11092, EP 506, MG C-513, BS 549,
      GLP 6938, Karusell KEP 234, GLP 108
   C-680-3 "La Cucuracha"   Mercury Clef 11093, EP 507, MG C-513, BS 542,
      GLP 6938, Karusell KEP 235, GLP 108
   C-682-3 "Begin the Beguine"   Mercury Clef 11094, EP 507, MG C-513, BS
      550, GLP 6938, Karusell KEP 235, GLP 108
   C-681-5 "Estrellita"   Mercury Clef 11094, EP 507, MG C-513, BS 550, GLP
      6938, Karusell KEP 235, GLP 108
   C-683-1 "La Paloma"   Mercury Clef 11091, EP 506, MG C-513, BS 634,
      GLP 6938, Karusell KEP 234, GLP 108

CHARLIE PARKER AND HIS ORCHESTRA:
Carl Poole, Jimmy Maxwell, Porcino, Privin (tpts). Harris, Lou McGarity, Bart
Varsalona (tmbs). Parker, Harry Terrill, Williams (altos). Flip Phillips, Ross
(tnrs). Danny Bank (bari). Oscar Peterson (pno). Freddy Green (gtr). Brown
(bass). Lamond (drs). Lipman (arr and cond).
   C-756-5 "Night and Day"   Mercury Clef 11096, MG C-609, BS GLP 6964,
      Karusell 5019
   C-757-4 "Almost Like Being in Love"   Clef 11102, MG C-609, BS 614, GLP
      6964
   C-758-1 "I Can't Get Started"   Mercury Clef 11096, MG C-609, BS GLP
      6964, Karusell 5019
   C-759-5 "What Is This Thing Called Love?"   Clef 11102, MG C-609, BS 614,
      GLP 6964

JAM SESSION VOL. 1 and 2:
Charlie Shavers (tpt). Parker, Johnny Hodges, Benny Carter (altos). Ben Web-
ster, Flip Phillips (tnrs). Peterson (pno). Barney Kessel (gtr). Brown (bass).
J. C. Heard (drs). Hollywood, June, 1952.
   C-802-2 "Jam Blues"   Mercury Clef MG C-601, C-4001, BS GLP 6966,
      Karusell LPX 507
   C-803-3 "What Is This Thing Called Love?"   Mercury Clef MG C-602,
      C-4002, BS GLP 6967, Karusell LPX 508
   C-804-2 "Ballad Medley"   Mercury Clef MG C-601, C-4001, BS GLP 6966,
      Karusell LPX 507
   C-805-2 "Funky Blues"   Mercury Clef MG C-602, C-4002, BS GLP 6967,
      Karusell LPX 508
Note: In "Ballad Medley" Parker plays the second solo: "Dearly Beloved."

THE QUINTET OF THE YEAR:
Dizzy Gillespie (tpt). Parker (alto). Bud Powell (pno). Charlie Mingus (bass).
Roach (drs). Massey Hall, Toronto, Canada, May 15, 1953.
"Perdido"   Debut DLP-2, Swing M 33.312, VogueE LDE 040, JS JSL 707
"Salt Peanuts"   Debut DLP-2, Swing M 33.312, VogueE LDE 040, JS JSL 707
"All the Things You Are"   Debut DLP-2, Swing M 33.312, VogueE LDE 040, JS JSL 707
"Wee"   Debut DLP-4, Swing M 33.318, VogueE LDE 087
"Hot House"   Debut DLP-4, Swing M 33.318, VogueE LDE 087
"A Night in Tunisia"   Debut DLP-4, Swing M 33.318, VogueE LDE 087
Note: Parker plays under the pseudonym "Charlie Chan." In "All the Things You Are" Billy Taylor is on the piano instead of Powell.

CHARLIE PARKER AND HIS ORCHESTRA:
Parker (alto). Al Black (flute). Tommy Mace (oboe). Manny Thaler (bassoon). Hal McKusick (clt). Junior Collins (fr. horn). Tony Aless (pno). Mingus (bass). Roach (drs). Gil Evans (arr). plus vocal group. New York City, May 25, 1953.
C-1238-7 "In the Still of the Night"   Mercury Clef 11100, MG C-646, BS 527
C-1239-9 "Old Folks"   Mercury Clef 11100, MG C-646, BS 527
"If I Love Again"   unissued

CHARLIE PARKER:
Parker (alto). Haig (pno). Percy Heath (bass). Roach (drs). New York City, probably August-September, 1953.
"I Hear Music"   Clef MG C-157, BS GEP 12574
"Laird Baird"   Clef MG C-157, BS GEP 12574
"Kim"   Clef 89129, MG C-157, BS GEP 12574
"Cosmic Rays"   Clef 89129, MG C-157, BS GEP 12574
Note: "I Hear Music" is actually "The Song Is You."

CHARLIE PARKER:
Parker (alto). Haig (pno). Percy Heath (bass). Roach (drs). New York City, probably August-September, 1953.
"Now's the Time"   Clef MG C-157, BS GEP 12575
"I Remember You"   Clef MG C-157, BS GEP 12575
"Confirmation"   Clef MG C-157, BS GEP 12575
"Chi Chi"   Clef MG C-157, BS GEP 12575

Most of the above-listed titles are now out-of-print collector's items. The following is a list of long playing records available when this book went to press.

ALL STAR	Roost 2210
APRIL IN PARIS	Verve 8004
BIRD & DIZ	Verve 8006
BIRD IS FREE	Carlton 401
BIRD LIVES	Continental
BIRD'S NIGHT	Savoy 12138
CHARLIE PARKER IN HISTORICAL RECORDINGS (3 vols.)	
	Le Jazz Cool 101, 102, 103
CHARLIE PARKER STORY (3 albums)	Verve 8100-3/8000/2
EARLY BIRD	Baronet 107
ESSENTIAL CHARLIE PARKER	Verve 8409
EVENING AT HOME	Savoy 12152
FIESTA (Genius #6)	Verve 8008
GENIUS OF CHARLIE PARKER (2 albums)	Savoy 12009, 12014
GREATEST RECORDING SESSION	Savoy 12079
HANDFUL OF MODERN JAZZ	Baronet 105
IMMORTAL	Savoy 12001
JAZZ AT MASSEY HALL	Debut 124
JAZZ PERENNIAL (Genius #7)	Verve 8009
MEMORIAL	Savoy 12000
NIGHT AND DAY (Genius #1)	Verve 8003
NOW'S THE TIME (Genius #3)	Verve 8005
PLAYS PORTER (Genius #5)	Verve 8007
SWEDISH SCHNAPPS (Genius #8)	Verve 8110

KEY TO LABELS

Aust	Austroton (German-Austrian)	Karusell	Karusell (Swedish)
		JS	Jazz Selection (Swedish)
Bop	Bop (French)	Merc	Mercury
Br	Brunswick	Met	Metronome (Swedish)
BS	Blue Star (French)	Mu	Musicraft
Con	Continental	PaE	Parlophone
De	Decca	Rem	Remington
DeE	English Decca	Sav	Savoy
Esq	Esquire	Sw	Swing (French)
HMV	His Master's Voice (English)	VogueE	Vogue (English)

CPSIA information can be obtained at www.ICGtesting.com
Printed in the USA
BVOW041837080112

279976BV00002B/12/A